HANS KELSEN'S POLITICAL REALISM

Robert Schu

EDINBURGH
University Press

Edinburgh University Press is one of the leading university presses in the UK. We publish academic books and journals in our selected subject areas across the humanities and social sciences, combining cutting-edge scholarship with high editorial and production values to produce academic works of lasting importance. For more information visit our website: edinburghuniversitypress.com

Edinburgh University Press Ltd
The Tun – Holyrood Road, 12(2f) Jackson's Entry, Edinburgh EH8 8PJ

First published in hardback by Edinburgh University Press 2021

Typeset in 10/12.5 Adobe Sabon by
IDSUK (DataConnection) Ltd, and
printed and bound by CPI Group (UK) Ltd, Croydon, CR0 4YY

A CIP record for this book is available from the British Library

ISBN 978 1 4744 8168 7 (hardback)
ISBN 978 1 4744 8169 4 (paperback)
ISBN 978 1 4744 8170 0 (webready PDF)
ISBN 978 1 4744 8171 7 (epub)

HANS KELSEN'S POLITICAL REALISM

CONTENTS

INTRODUCTION

'We are intellectual streetfighters'

Hans J. Morgenthau (1969)

One way to situate this book is to see two problems. The first is how we call the bluff of today's strongmen in a new era of nationalist populism and competition between the great powers. The second is how we reconcile foreign-policy realism with a progressive politics. Yet a third way to look at it is to judge *Hans Kelsen's Political Realism* on its ability to resuscitate this iconic man as a political thinker who helps us solve these challenges with new confidence.

To the specialist as much as to the general reader, Hans Kelsen ranks as one of the best twentieth-century jurists. In a beautiful piece written for *The New York Times* in 1999, former law professor and author of *The Reader*, Bernhard Schlink, suggested that this 'modest Old World gentleman' was the best of them all. He was a pleasant man – and sharp as a razor's edge. 'You not only kill your opponent, but you leave their bodies neatly dissected on the place of the battle,' as Hans Morgenthau (1948b) wrote in a letter to his mentor and friend of forty years. Little wonder that Carl Schmitt – 'the most evil man alive' (Morgenthau 1984a [1977]: 16) – hated Kelsen, and that today's decisionists still fear being unmasked by Pure positivists.

Make no mistake, Hans Kelsen is my favourite political philosopher, and for more than a decade I have explored Kelsenian themes and ideas (Schuett 2007, 2011, 2015, 2018). In the theory and practice of international politics,

I am a Kelsenian. What, then, is Hans Morgenthau, one of the last century's finest foreign-policy realists, doing at the head of an introductory chapter to a book ostensibly about a so-called idealistic jurist? The whole of this book must be the full explanation.

What matters at this point is to say where I am coming from, and in light of the book's method and tone, to sketch where I am headed with what really is my Kelsenian style of political thinking: that is to say, all errors are mine, not Kelsen's. Taking a fresh look at his life and thought from the point where I stand, I aim to set out a progressive vision of political realism, developed within a specific intellectual context: it is the ideal of the open society, made distinct by Karl Popper and his student George Soros, which allows me in this book to reach back, and to recruit Kelsen as a new and important ally in the battle against Schmittians old and new.

Loved or loathed – there was never much in between – the project of a Pure theory of law, state and international legal order was ground-breaking. No one in the West could ignore what was coming out of Vienna via Kelsen's pen and typewriter. And while, to this day, his political thinking is nowhere near as known as his writings on norms and international law, over the last ten years or so there has been a resurgence of interest in this iconic Austrian–American émigré on the part of political and international relations (IR) theorists who work in the twilight zone where philosophy, law and world politics meet. His *Pure Theory of Law* (1967 [1934a]) is still a go-to treatise of modern legal positivism. His wartime book, *Peace through Law* (1944a), contributing though it does to the many misperceptions of Kelsen as a naïve idealist, is a surgical take on the causes of war and the problems of a Kantian peace. Kelsen's *The Essence and Value of Democracy* (2013 [1929b]) is a classic in terms of what makes democracy.

And what is more, his 1952 Berkeley farewell lecture, 'What is Justice?', is one of the finest statements in the history of modern liberalism (Kelsen 1952a, 1957a).[1] To me, in this book, Hans Kelsen and his thought are calm and clear, gentle and bold, realistic and progressive.

Not only a man of Pure theory, he was also a man of pure action. He had seen it all. He dedicated his life to the pursuit of knowledge, but was not purely ivory-tower. There was drama too: lots of it, but nothing could really bring him down.[2] He survived the horror that befell Europe during the age of extremes. He experienced how fragile political systems are, and how international orders are contingent products of history, not any natural law. In his role as legal advisor to the de facto last *k. u. k.*[3] War Minister, he was there when imperial Austria–Hungary fell to pieces – and then, only a few days later, Kelsen's new task inside the State Chancellery was to work on a definitive Constitution for what was to become a new Austria. He had real access to the corridors of real power; and years later, once he was in the United States, he was to work for American foreign intelligence.

Hard to believe he was a reluctant jurist. He quickly climbed the academic ladder, becoming full Professor of Constitutional and Administrative Law in Vienna at the age of thirty-seven. In the early 1930s, Harvard Law Dean Roscoe Pound (1934: 532) called him 'the leading jurist of the time'. And Charles E. Merriam, one of America's most prominent political scientists, tried to lure Kelsen to Chicago (Boyer 2008). But his heart lay elsewhere. He loved philosophy and literature. He wrote the occasional poem and had three published in a Viennese newspaper, while realising, with a wink, that he was not as talented as he had hoped. His first book was on Dante. He was friends with Otto Weininger. A classmate of Ludwig von Mises. The best man at Joseph Schumpeter's second wedding. The uncle of Peter Drucker. He holidayed with Sigmund Freud. And being quite a networker, he helped an unknown Karl Popper meet F. A. Hayek in mid-1930s London, paving the way for the philosopher's later success.

One might say he was already living the open society ideal, soon to be made famous by Popper and Soros, which is not to say that Kelsen pre-empted these men and their ideas, but rather that he was an intellectual streetfighter for a set of ideas that make an open society: rule of law, human rights and individual freedom (see Soros 2019: 26–7). And even though it is early days in the book to explore this – and this goes out to the Schmittians – an open society does not shy away from using state power in domestic and foreign affairs; what it does do is 'broaden the understanding of self-interest in the use of power' (Breyfogle 2018: 565; Schuett 2015).

What did interest him from first to last – as I show in the book – is what has always interested the real realists in Western political and IR theory. It is the real You, the very intimate You (Schuett 2010b; Schuett and Hollingworth 2018). What is behind Kelsen's Pure positivism is the single Freudian story of how we as human beings are forced to battle the many frustrations in the many theatres of our social experience: the realm where pleasure clashes with pain; where the soft voice of the intellect competes with the crude drumbeats of mass emotions; where ideals of justice are outgunned by parochial power motives. It is the Kelsenian story of how, out of that battle within us, there emerges the reality of law, and the political moment. We are forced to make a moral choice. Are we, in Niebuhrian (1944) language, children of light? Or are we children of darkness? We miss the point if we go looking for whether Kelsen believed in a Kantian peace. It is not about believing. Politics is not the realm of Nature, God or any other natural law. A Kelsenian political realism focuses on how, only a tiny little fraction after the real You, there is always Your Interest; and on how, in some intimate place in between, there is the twilight zone where the battle over so-called national interests is raging. The rest is just invented drama, or modern mythology on social media steroids.

In other words – to Schmittians – he ranks as one of the West's most danger-ous men. Inching from the fringes to the centre, the champions of a mythical friend–foe politics are regrouping. Anti-establishment guns blazing, de-legiti-mising the Other in a 24/7 news cycle madness while exploiting the ruthlessly real and manufactured fears of the so-called little guys, the strongmen seem ever more willing to go for the political kill, and appear to get away with the big-gest of all frauds: that the Schmittian decider knows what is best for the flock, selling this or that policy as a self-evident necessity of an allegedly unideologi-cal political realism (see Stirk 2005a; Lind 2015; Drolet and Williams 2018; Scheuerman 2019; Krastev and Holmes 2019). If Kelsen were alive, he would call them out. There are no natural necessities. There are only positive interests. Chances are that whatever good or bad or ugly happens in political and inter-national life has been willed by someone for someone.

He was not destined to become one of the world's prime villains when he was born in 1881 in the reign of Franz Joseph, in the Prague of the Austrian–Hungarian Empire. His father, Adolf, was a hard-working man from Brody, which back then was a buzzing free-trade city in Galicia, or Austria–Poland, and today lies in Western Ukraine's Lviv Oblast. At the age of fourteen, and penniless, Adolf Kelsen had left for Vienna, where years later he would own a small business dealing in lamps and lighting fixtures in the Fourth District, at Goldeggasse 20, near the Upper Belvedere, a former Habsburg palace. His mother, Auguste, née Löwy, was from Neuhaus, a small city in Southern Bohemia, today's Czech Republic. She died at the ripe old age of ninety, in Bled, back then a small town in Yugoslavia, now north-western Slovenia. She bore Adolf four children, of whom Hans was the eldest. A child of the long nineteenth century, a star intellectual in the short twentieth, Hans Kelsen passed away in 1973 from a cardiac arrest, in President Nixon's Cold War America, in a nursing home in Orinda, California, just east of Berkeley, where in the mid-1940s he had bought a small house at 2126 Los Angeles Avenue. His ashes were scattered in the Pacific. With his wife, Margarete, née Bondi, from Vienna, who had been at his side for over six decades, he led a full life: the life of a true scholar.

His life journey was not of his own choosing. It was the age of extremes, and it was all real. He fled Vienna for Cologne in 1930. The ruling Christian Social Party, founded by the infamous anti-Semitic populist Karl Lueger, a former mayor of Vienna, had pursued a nasty campaign against him. He then left Cologne for Geneva in 1933. The Nazis, with Hitler as the new German Chancellor, were hell-bent on purifying the civil service of Jews. Kelsen was one of the first law profes-sors to be sacked. Even though almost the entire faculty at Cologne spoke out in favour of him, there was one man who did not. This man, of course, was Schmitt, which is particularly bitter because Schmitt owed his professorship at Cologne to Kelsen's positive intervention in the first place. Later, in 1938, Kelsen had to flee

Prague, where Völkische Nazi student groups were mounting malicious attacks on Jewish professors. And a couple of years later he had to quit Geneva, this time leaving Europe for good. On 21 June 1940, he arrived safely at the port of New York City, disembarking from the *S.S. Washington*, which he had boarded in Lisbon ten days earlier. At almost sixty years of age, with little money in his pockets as the Nazis had robbed him of his pension, he had to start all over again.

And of course, the battle rages on. It was on 22 September 2011, a Thursday, late in the afternoon, in the glass-domed *Reichstag* building in the middle of Chancellor Merkel's Berlin, that then-Pope Benedict XVI, a serious intellectual and former Prefect of the Congregation for the Doctrine of the Faith, lashed out against Kelsen. Addressing the German *Bundestag*, as part of a three-day state visit, Benedict (2011) spoke at length about the foundations of law. To him, it was crystal clear that the real *Kulturkampf*, or intellectual streetfight, in the West is between two foundational ideas: the Catholic doctrine of natural law versus the secular doctrine of a Kelsenian positivism (Dreier 2009; Brown 2011). Add to this (legitimate) intellectual war of ideas the constant (deplorable) anti-Semitic ploy against so-called 'Kelsen-Kohn' (see Robertson 2002: 247) and it is clear to me that Kelsen – and, for that matter, You and Me – need defending against Schmittians old and new.

Notes on Method, Style and Structure

I should add here, at this introductory stage in the book, what may be more than the allowed number of methodological disclaimers, but I believe they are necessary.

First, *Hans Kelsen's Political Realism* has two vantage points. I designed the book as a Critically inspired political and IR theorist, in the spring of 2010, when I was doing post-doctoral research at the University of California in San Diego. There and then I could already picture what I wanted to say about Kelsen's political thinking (Schuett 2011). But for a handful of reasons it took me until the summer of 2018 – in the years in between I had become a Civil Service foreign-policy professional – to sit down and start writing it all up, within walking distance of where Kelsen lived and worked in Vienna. What follows is a series of twenty-five dispatches written from the frontlines of the theory and practice of international politics.

I hope my balancing act of doing political and IR theory that is both analytical and accessible satisfies the scholarly expert as well as practitioners and general readers. Politics is where the rubber hits the road so there is no point in sugar-coating how rough it can get. Yet since all political action has its roots in political thinking, making sense of real-world problems requires clarity on concepts and ideas, which is a purely theoretical endeavour.

Second, my (over-)ambition has been to present the reader with a lively story about this iconic man's life and political thinking. As to Kelsen the man, I have been much inspired by the energetic and intimately interpretive style of Erica Benner (2017, 2018) and Miles Hollingworth (2013, 2018a, 2018b), both of them compulsively readable philosophers and writers, who, between them, have been treating – that is, bringing to life – Niccolò Machiavelli, St Augustine of Hippo and Ludwig Wittgenstein.[4] Note, though, that my picture of Hans Kelsen here is not even remotely a kind of intellectual biography; such a book remains to be written.

And as to Kelsen the political thinker – the progressive political realist – I would say that I stand squarely with those political and IR theorists who have argued that 'getting realism right' (Scheuerman 2019: 4) is important, politically and theoretically. For too long, the so-called Realist tradition and its so-called timeless realpolitik champions have been used and abused by theorists and practitioners to justify ideas and policies that are barely justifiable, at least not necessarily by the standard playbook of going back all the way to Thucydides and so on. In this sense, then, and without implicating any one of them in what I argue in this book, I must say that my own views of political and IR theory in general, and political realism in particular, have been shaped to a great extent by the work of John C. Williams (2015), Chris J. Brown (2002), Peter Stirk (2006), Richard Little (2007), Michael Williams (2005), William Scheuerman (2011) and Ken Booth (2008).[5]

All of this is to say, what I have done in this book is use techniques of intellectual biography and methods of conceptual analysis, and combine them to produce one account: Kelsen as a man of political realism for our time.

But then, third, as Kelsen's student John Herz (1951: 1) noted: 'In all selection there is a certain unavoidable element of subjective evaluation.' This book is no exception. Kelsen published the equivalent of 18,000 pages, not counting his unpublished material and letters. My focus was politics, *not* law; since I am not a trained jurist, whenever I had to enter jurisprudential territory I have relied, as clearly indicated, on the relevant law literature.[6] So *my* Kelsen, as presented in this book, is unavoidably subjective and partial: mine is *a* version of *the other Kelsen*. And my hope is that my reading helps someone at some point to synthesise the legal and political, as well as the biographical and theoretical, into one grand narrative.

Note also, fourth, that this book has been written in my personal capacity as a scholar: as a Critically inspired political and IR theorist, and as a Classical-style foreign-policy realist of a philosophical bent. All views expressed are my own. And unless indicated otherwise, all quotations from other languages are my own translation (Pils 2016 is helpful).

The book is organised to reflect the extent of the reinterpretation of Hans Kelsen's political thinking that I argue is necessary. Coverage of the subject is very much determined by the focus on him as a political thinker. By showing how he thought of man and the state, and of war and peace, what I really do in the following five chapters is portray Kelsen as a gentle liberal mind and a tough political realist.

Chapter 1 thus takes on his enemies and constructs a robust forward-defence. Chapter 2 explores his milieu, and presents him as a fearless scholar and practitioner who, throughout his life, was bitterly acquainted with what power is. Chapter 3 then zooms in on what I argue is his Freudian core, and reveals his shockingly realistic account of You and Me. Chapter 4 extends this analysis of the political to look at the realm of power politics, and brings to life Hans Kelsen the foreign-policy realist. Chapter 5 offers a broader assessment of Kelsen's style of political thinking, and directly challenges not only the Schmittians but also conventional notions of the so-called Realist tradition. Readers will hopefully find my analysis of Kelsen useful, but they may, or not, part company with me over how I will be using Kelsenian political thinking – and method – for my own purpose in normative political and IR theory.

Finally, I should add that, in writing this book, what Morgenthau (1969) wrote in a letter to Hannah Arendt has encouraged me: 'We are intellectual streetfighters. So if we don't make clear on which side of the barricades we stand, we have failed.' I leave it to the reader to decide whether Kelsenian ideas can help us solve some of today's political problems. What you get, either way, is my gloves-off defence of this open society prophet. I must say, I have experienced in his life and political thinking a powerful sense of a realistic yet progressive calm that I believe is necessary for keeping the Schmittians at bay, while guarding us against future strongmen.

Now, before the curtain goes up for Hans Kelsen, I would like to thank a number of people who provided me with help and support in the completion of this book.[7] Students in my Realism seminar at the University of Salzburg kept pressing me in lively class discussions on how foreign-policy realism needs updating. Miles Hollingworth gave me advice and encouragement at crucial stages: without him this book probably would not exist at this time. The Hans Kelsen-Institut, tucked away so beautiful and calm in Vienna's Nineteenth District, was always there for me. Anne Feder Lee (2011) allowed me to use unpublished letters and the cover image: her grandfather in Berkeley, 1968. Jenny Daly and her team at the Press have shared my enthusiasm from first to last, and Wendy Lee copy-edited the book with verve and great care.

As ever, I am endlessly grateful to Clemens Jabloner: without him, this book – and much else – would not exist. And as always, it was my wife, Susanne, who created the magically gentle atmosphere of Machiavellian GSD idealism in which hard work became easy.

CHAPTER I

KELSEN'S ENEMIES

'When you strike at a king, you must kill him'
Ralph Waldo Emerson (1843)

That the FBI was on to Kelsen is remarkable for a man of such impeccable character. But that they thought it possible that Kelsen could be a subversive Communist – a suspicion that led to a 190-page FBI file[1] on him, produced in the years between 1944 and 1955 – shows their astonishing lack of grasp of his philosophy and political thinking. Had only a few of all the FBI agents that were assigned to the case just skimmed his publication list, or at least speed-read one or two items on it, the FBI would have known, instantly, that, for Kelsen, there is no such thing as Utopia. In fact, he was a statist. A liberal etatist.

I THE FBI

Kelsen had run into trouble with the FBI on two occasions. The first was in the early 1950s, when the Second Red Scare was in full swing. By that time, an era driven by McCarthy-style politics, he had been in America for more than a decade and was a naturalised US citizen. And what is more, he was once again a Full Professor, running a successful international law programme out of Berkeley's Political Science department.

The second encounter with the FBI dates back to 1944. At that time he was working as a consultant for the Foreign Economic Administration (FEA), an intelligence agency run by the vibrant Leo Crowley, which, established by President Roosevelt's Executive Order 9380 in 1943, was created to unify all governmental activities relating to foreign economic affairs, including the multi-billion-dollar Lend-Lease programme designed to defeat Germany, Japan and Italy, the three Axis powers. It was wartime, and the American intelligence community was packed with European émigré scholars, some of them the very best in their respective fields (Katz 1989). Turf wars between government agencies were endemic. And so, one might say, Kelsen, like scores of other immigrants from all over Europe and the rest of the world, was fair game as a target on the FBI's security radar.

At no point in his life and career does Kelsen appear to have been a Communist (Potacs 2009, 2014; Gassner 2016). To be sure, he was what, today, we would call a progressive, or a left-liberal. But in essence, and inspired by Freudian insights (as we shall see later in more detail), he was way too realistic about human nature – which is to say, way too realistic about its many limits. We are, he thought, just not as good as some would have us believe. Or, to approach it another way and as he made clear on numerous occasions, the revolutionaries, the Marxists and the anarchists too, are naïve when they think they could do away with the state and government, or politics and its power struggles, or some basic level of repression and coercion.

And yet for a number of reasons the FBI took an early interest in Kelsen. For one, he appeared to be too close to Charles A. Gulick, a longstanding economist at Berkeley, who, as a child of the Progressive Era, held liberal views, and as a learned historian of inter-war Austria, acknowledged his ideological sympathy with the Austro-Marxists' so-called Linz programme of 1926. Second, the FBI questioned why Kelsen would sponsor the candidacy of Jack Howard for Assembly member for the 18th California District, running for the Independent Progressive Party, which they believed was a front organisation for the Communists. Third, the FBI wanted to probe the nature of the relationship between Kelsen and William Malisoff, a known biochemist and philosopher, who not only used to be editor of the University of Chicago Press's venerable *Philosophy of Science* journal, in which Kelsen published, but was also a Soviet spy.

And if all that were not enough, since the FBI had him in their files as 'eminent jurist, wrote Constitution of Austrian Republic' (quoted in Rathkolb 2009: 341), they probably also knew full well that Kelsen had links to the leading intellectuals of the centre-left bastion that Vienna, or so-called Red Vienna, was at the time. Thus he got on well with political heavyweight Karl Renner, Chancellor of German Austria in 1918/19, first Chancellor of the Republic of Austria in 1945, and eventually its first President until 1955; it was Renner who requested that Kelsen co-draft a definitive Austrian Constitution. Kelsen was also friendly with Otto Bauer, a leading Austro-Marxist and Foreign Minister in the first Renner Government, and he had a good relationship with Max Adler, yet another prominent left-wing intellectual (Leser 1966).

Yet, for a start, simply by subjecting his formative adolescent years in Vienna to close scrutiny, the FBI agents could have established from afar that Kelsen hardly fitted the bill of the Communist type of thinker. Kelsen was not at all brilliant in primary and junior school, but his parents, who were part of the 'Bildung-conscious Jewish bourgeoisie' (Jabloner 1998: 370), managed to steer Hans through the entry examinations for the Akademisches Gymnasium, a prestigious Viennese secondary school founded in 1553, and from which Hans graduated with the Matura, the Austrian university entrance certificate, in the summer of 1900. Incidentally, this was the year in which Freud, with whom Hans would later become friendly, published the ground-breaking Interpretation of Dreams (1900), working from the now world-famous apartment at Berggasse 19. Also a classmate and lifelong friend, it was no other than the young Ludwig van Mises, who would eventually become a leading figure of the Austrian School of Economics and one of the twentieth century's most notable economic and social philosophers. Like Kelsen and, for that matter, Freud, Mises was as strict a methodological individualist as you can possibly imagine. What these two young men received in their youth was a decidedly humanistic and liberal education, an ethics and a worldview that were taught to them at this very Gymnasium from an early age.

Perhaps understandably, though, the FBI had their eyes and ears focused on something other than what went on in Schorskean Vienna. Rather, they were alert to what was happening in post-war America, at the time a country dominated by a sustained fear of Communism. And thus eventually the FBI really did start a full investigation into Kelsen, at the point when, at the height of the Californian loyalty oath controversy, he had spoken out in favour of Harold D. Winkler, a young Harvard-educated Assistant Professor of Political Science at Berkeley, who was one of thirty-one faculty member non-signers to be sacked.

Up to that very point in what was his new life in the United States, Kelsen had kept rather a low profile, which, in many ways, was just how he had learned to operate in the Old World. In this case, however, Kelsen felt he had to make public his concerns about where the excesses of a McCarthyist style of politics might lead us. It all happened during the time of a Hoover-led FBI, in the wake of the 1947 Truman Doctrine, which had been instructing all elements of American power, at home and abroad, to counter any Soviet expansion. To Kelsen, though, his public protest was not so much directed at the details of any one current US grand strategy; rather, he was concerned about what he, as a true scholar, saw as potentially in great jeopardy – scholarly freedom.

And so he was quite unhappy about the 1950 Levering Act, which, enacted by the State of California, required all state employees to subscribe to a so-called loyalty oath. The University of California was no exception. Its Board of Regents had imposed a strict protocol that all university employees, both new and existing ones, were under an obligation to sign, effective from 1 July 1950:

an oath which, so ran the argument, reaffirmed that they were not members of the Communist Party or any other political organisation that sought to overthrow the US Government by violence or force (Gardner 1967).

Now, Kelsen himself did sign the loyalty oath. Why would he not? Everyone, save the FBI, knew that he was no Communist. And actually, he was acutely aware of the fact that he was not really in a position to risk another financial meltdown. Recall that the Nazis had robbed him of all earlier earnings and pension entitlements, and at the time, his American pension stood at a meagre US$102 per month. Understanding that living and operating low-key usually works best, as a former mandarin he also knew full well that one's battles must be chosen wisely.

This particular battle, though, he thought, was not one that was suited to silence. To see Winkler not only being fired but also publicly shamed by the university as a sort of academic rebel led Kelsen to make clear what he thought of the whole debate and the Winkler saga. A visiting lecturer in Government at Harvard at the time, Kelsen pointed out, in a series of statements in the university student daily *Harvard Crimson*, that Winkler not only was *not* a Communist but was, in fact, one of the most popular professors on campus; and he added that Harvard, which had offered Winkler academic refuge in the form of a visiting lectureship after he was kicked out of Berkeley, should feel 'lucky to get him' (quoted in Ottenheimer 1950). The smart young Winkler eventually joined Pacifica Radio, and as its President, eventually strengthened its progressive profile (Lasar 1999).

While, naturally, the FBI was not at all happy to see and hear Kelsen take Winkler's side so firmly, they none the less failed to grasp the whole picture, or at least where Kelsen was coming from. First and foremost, he was a scholar. He had a no-nonsense type of mind yearning for pretty much one thing in scholarly life – truth. So it should have been clear to the FBI that, almost by instinct, Kelsen could not but speak out against what he must have perceived as a political threat to the integrity of the sciences and humanities. It was not so much about Communism but rather about what he believed was an ill-attempted policy relating to a misconstrued loyalty oath that, *in extremis*, might in fact pave the way for what the bill's sponsors sought to avoid: ideologised research. According to his scholarly and democratic ethics, the scientific pursuit of knowledge must be free and must be critical, so as to avoid becoming itself a form of ideology. Quoting the then-President of Harvard, James Bryant Conant, in what is a timeless statement about the moral and cultural significance of free and critical scholarship, Kelsen (2006 [1937]: 247) made it unambiguously clear: 'The universities of a country are the sanctuaries of the inner life of a nation.'

Neither was he hyperbolic. Never. He fought hard, notably for open society ideals. But then he always sought not to lose perspective, to keep calm: which is to say, while idealistic in the sense of fighting for what is right, Kelsen was realistic in assessing what really matters in any given situation. And thus it is no wonder that, with regard to the loyalty oath controversy, his position was really this: the oath is superfluous and, according to him (1950a), not as dangerous as many seem to think. And yet, as Kelsen (1950b) said, he respected, if not admired, all those colleagues who, fighting for what are important principles, lost their positions.

From that perspective alone, then, the fact that the FBI had doubts over Kelsen's loyalty to the US Government and American Constitution seems awkward. At the time he was already in his early seventies. And from his previous life on the Continent, he knew the difference between being an academic and working in government, between theory and practice. He knew when to hold back and when to stand his ground. Moreover, his ethos was never to join any political party, as he thought it incommensurate to do research *and* politics. That is not to say, of course, that he was not a political man.

Colleagues and friends were entirely aware – and why not? – of which side of the barricades Kelsen was fighting on. Back in in his Viennese years, in Red Vienna, he was much in line with the reformist programme of what, today, is the Social Democratic Party of Austria, or SPÖ. And more generally, in his broader outlook and intellectual and political persuasion, Kelsen was all for a form of political liberalism revolving around three basic principles: democracy and rule of law; capitalism and private property; and progressivism and social and economic justice. To be sure, and quite contrary to what the FBI suspected, there was no room in Kelsen's philosophy and political thinking for any elements of Communism, Marxism or Anarchism.

What is perhaps the most striking aspect of this whole FBI investigation is that pretty much everyone with at least a little grasp of the work of Hans Kelsen had known of this man's anti-revolutionary posture, which nevertheless was a progressive one. When, in late February of 1953, the FBI asked him whether he had any interest in the Socialist programme, his answer was clear enough: 'I am very interested and as far as I am concerned I think it is absolutely necessary to adopt in our form of government some of the Socialist ideas.' Asks the interrogator: 'You are in sympathy with the Socialists?' Kelsen: 'Yes, I am.' Interrogator: 'With the Communists?' Kelsen: 'No, I am not. I published a book against them.' Another attempt by the FBI agent: 'Would you describe yourself as a Communist or a Socialist?' To which Kelsen replies: 'I would as a Liberal Socialist' (quoted in Rathkolb 2009: 347).

It is a bit of an irony perhaps that in 1944, the very same year in which the FBI started to investigate Kelsen, he published his first book on American soil. Kelsen was crystal clear about it all in *Peace through Law* (1944a), which Leo Gross (1945: 260), an Austrian–American student of Kelsen's,[2] who taught at Tufts University's Fletcher School of Law and Diplomacy for three decades, called an 'eminently interesting little book'. That Kelsen does not harbour any revolutionary ideas can be seen, literally, when reading the book's first two sentences. According to Kelsen (1944a: 3), 'Peace is a state characterized by the absence of force. Within an organized society, however, absolute absence of force – the idea of anarchism – is not possible.' It is just that human nature does not work that way, as we shall see. And thus to Kelsen, the very idea of the state withering away at some point in history is naïve.

In the end, then, it is fitting that after a decade's investigative work in 1955, the same year in which the FBI finally decided to drop the whole case against Kelsen as there was nothing really there (he was lecturing at the Naval War College), Kelsen published *The Communist Theory of Law* (1955a). The book was totally in line with his *Political Theory of Bolshevism* (1948a), which William Ebenstein (1952: 313), another Austrian–American student of Kelsen's teaching at Princeton and the University of California, Santa Barbara, called 'by all odds the best critical analysis of the political theory of Marx and Engels, and of its later development by Lenin and Stalin'. And again, in a book that was actually written at the height of McCarthyism, Kelsen (1955a: 51) left no one in any doubt as to where he stood:

> All these absurd contradictions are the inevitable consequence of the fact that the dictatorship of the proletariat is just what it calls itself: a dictatorship, not a democracy, and the fact that it must be interpreted to be a democracy, since it is called so by Marx and Engels, makes things even worse.

It was all so very clear to see. As early as in 1920, working in Vienna, Kelsen had written a concise and pointedly anti-Marxist book, *Socialism and the State*. And thirty years later, in the American 1950s, one FBI informant reported – frankly and fairly – that Kelsen was actually one of the 'best informed opponents of Communism in the world today' (quoted in Rathkolb 2009: 346). And, in fact, the FBI was also told that Kelsen was an 'outstanding democrat, of unquestionable loyalty, character, reputation and associations' (quoted in Rathkolb 2009: 343).

Even Hans Morgenthau (1948c), one of America's seminal figures in the study of politics and IR, and a close student of Kelsen's, acknowledged in one of his many letters that the hard-headed style of *The Political Theory of Bolshevism* 'will serve to improve my lectures in recent political theory'.[3] This really leads one historically to a theoretically interesting question: Why would Morgenthau and, for that matter, John Herz (and other realists) – in concert with the Schmittians – see in Kelsen a naïve idealist?

2 REALISTS VERSUS KELSEN

In today's terms, Kelsen was a global academic superstar. He certainly was one of the very best jurists of his own generation and subsequent ones. In his own time, Roscoe Pound (1942), Dean of Harvard Law, a passionate botanist and known philosopher of law, was certain that Kelsen is 'one of the outstanding figures in the science of law in the world'.

But then, in what was to become his second home, America, he led quite a reclusive life, even by his own standards. Funnily enough, as Richard Buxbaum, Emeritus Jackson H. Ralston Professor of International Law at Berkeley, recalled many years ago (in Olechowski 2011: 17), it took some nosy European and international diplomats, who were taking part in the legendary 1945 San Francisco Conference at which fifty Allied nations signed the United Nations Charter, to make Kelsen known at Berkeley. In fact, these men and women were so hellbent on finding out the whereabouts of Kelsen, and where he lived, that eventually the Dean had to become involved and was forced to make a rather embarrassing phone call. Knowing very little about Kelsen himself (which is strange enough), he had to telephone him almost entirely out of the blue, and enquire whether Kelsen really was this world-famous Austrian émigré jurist that the diplomats were looking for – to which Kelsen apparently responded drily with a short and sweet 'yes'.

More importantly, the course of Kelsen's life and political thinking is intimately intertwined with the story of two outstanding mid-twentieth-century so-called classical political realists, and how their own real and intellectual biographies relate to Kelsen, who was, in many ways, as Clemens Jabloner (2016: 331) put it, a true 'champion of modernity'. *Enter* Hans Morgenthau, as well as John Herz.[4] They both admired him, from the day they had met him as professor and mentor in the darkening Europe of the 1930s, until the very day Kelsen passed away in the liberal California of 1973. At one and the same time, though, while deploring Carl Schmitt for many reasons, Morgenthau and Herz joined the Schmittian chorus in suggesting that Kelsen was a formalistic idealist who had been too naïve about the dirty reality of national interests and international politics.

It is October 1971, two years before Kelsen's death, on the occasion of his ninetieth birthday. Morgenthau, in his late sixties, and Herz, sixty-three, are both now in New York City. Morgenthau has become one of America's leading foreign-policy realists. As Henry Kissinger said in the memorial remarks on Morgenthau's death in the summer of 1980: 'Hans remained always himself: clear in his perception, uncompromising in his insistence on getting to the essence of a problem.' Now, while Kissinger had a good teacher in Morgenthau, this fine foreign-policy realist in turn had an excellent one in a man who was widely known as a very fine Viennese jurist.

Both Morgenthau and Herz made Kelsen a proud professor. Morgenthau had retired from the University of Chicago and was now teaching at the City University of New York, as well as at the New School for Social Research, from where he continued to launch his scathing criticism of Vietnam. Herz was known, notably, for his early conceptualisation of the now-standard concept of the security dilemma, and had taught at City College since the early 1950s. Up until his death in 2005, he would defend the realist position, especially fierce in the run-up to the 2003 Iraq War. And it was clear enough to Herz (2005) that if Morgenthau had been alive at the time of the George W. Bush White House, his realist companion and friend with the fairly heavy German accent would not have seen the neoconservative-inspired invasion of a far-away country as being even remotely in any US national interest.

Yet back then it was not at all about realism, or Vietnam, or Iraq or anything like that. Instead, it was about Kelsen and the upcoming big birthday. In fact, one way to honour the scientific legacy of this major Western intellectual was for the Austrian Government to set up the Hans Kelsen-Institut in Vienna, a public endowment chaired, *ex officio*, by the Federal Chancellor.[5] And to be sure, countless scholars and intellectuals from around the world sent their best wishes to the West Coast. Naturally, Morgenthau and Herz were among them – each for a particular, though similar, reason. And what is more, for this special day, Morgenthau travelled out from the East Coast to California to see him. As Virginia McClam (1971a, 1971b), one of Kelsen's closest disciples and friends, recalled a little later, Kelsen 'was looking splendid and was in good spirits', while adding: 'He and Morgenthau conversed in German and Kelsen even sang an old Austrian song in his native tongue.'[6]

Like Morgenthau, Herz also held Kelsen in the highest esteem. Their relationship was a bit different – meeting one another in a slightly different context – but as was the case with Morgenthau, Kelsen's impact on Herz's life and career was profound, as was Herz's admiration of Kelsen. As Herz wrote to his former teacher and mentor in his birthday letter, dated 4 October 1971: 'The very day I had reported to you in Cologne as a doctoral candidate, my intellectual formation took a turn that has affected me to this day.' The historical background to this, in short, dates back to the early 1930s. Forced out of Vienna by a toxic combination of anti-Semitic harassment at the university and a smear campaign against him run by Catholic-conservative circles, he took up a professorship at Cologne. In fact, it was only a few days after his arrival, in 1931, that Herz sought him out. Kelsen did not even have his own apartment yet, and hence it happened that Herz knocked at the door of Kelsen's room in Cologne's famous Dom Hotel and asked him, almost entirely out of the blue, whether he would accept him as his doctoral student. Kelsen said he would be glad to, and thus was formed an interesting relationship, biographical and intellectual, between this consequential senior jurist and a man who was to become a very fine political realist.

It was in the Berlin of the 1920s, while an undergraduate, that Herz really became drawn to Kelsen's Pure theory of law and state. He was fascinated by the positivist's account of what the law is, and by Kelsen's clarity about what the law is not. And so when he heard that Kelsen was slated to become Chair of Cologne's Faculty of Law, he did not think twice; he took this chance and headed south-west. His initiative paid off, for quite soon afterwards, Herz, with Kelsen as his *Doktorvater*, was working on his dissertation. Given the intellectual dynamics in German-speaking legal and political theory, or *Staatslehre* – at a time that Kelsen was reacting primarily against Georg Jellinek's dualistic theory of law and the state (see Stirk 2006, 2015a, 2015b) – it was perhaps little wonder that Herz was interested in the question of the identity of the state. And following Kelsen's overall intellectual lead, he fervently rejected the notion of a two-sided theory of the state. For Herz (1931: 70–1), as he wrote in his dissertation, 'only the juristic state should be the object of the legal consideration'.

In many ways, one might say, Herz was a Kelsenian, and yet at the same time he was not. In his autobiography, *Vom Überleben* (1984), a fascinating tale of a very original man, Herz discussed how the Pure theory provided him with what he was looking for as a curious young academic – that is, a 'scientific–philosophical basis of jurisprudence' (p. 88) – and said that he deeply respected Kelsen as a charismatic man and scholar. And so he fled with him to Geneva, and then finally to America, where they parted company. Herz remained on the East Coast, while Kelsen eventually found a new home at Berkeley.

Pretty much all European émigrés struggled to find their place in the United States, at least initially, but Herz was particularly pessimistic about his prospects; it was Kelsen who helped him as best as he could. Capitalising on his transatlantic network, he helped secure for Herz a place in the US delegation to the Nuremberg trials (Feichtinger 2009; Ehs 2010; Ehs and Gassner 2014). Moreover, it was Kelsen who, in 1951, promoted Herz's (1951) new book for the Woodrow Wilson Foundation Award of the American Political Science Association: that is to say, he helped to make possible the ground-breaking *Political Realism and Political Idealism*.

The background story to Morgenthau's lifelong admiration of Kelsen is even more serious. To be sure, perhaps like most of the world's great intellectuals, Morgenthau was a complex man and a complex thinker. As Kissinger (1980) once remarked: 'Not everybody agreed with Hans Morgenthau; nobody could ignore him.' And in light of Morgenthau's sustained criticism of what he called either idealism, moralism or legalism, it is remarkable that he seemed to have been influenced by two different men who represented what are two altogether different intellectual positions.[7] One such strand of influence stemmed, of course, from the neo-Freudian Protestant theologian Reinhold Niebuhr, of whom Mr X, the great American diplomat George F. Kennan, famously said that he was the 'father of us all' (quoted in Craig 1992: 696). And another intellectual influence – quite surprisingly, to be sure – was Kelsen. After all, as the Critically inspired American political theorist William E. Scheuerman (2014: 81) put it, Kelsen was 'perhaps the mid-twentieth century's most significant continental

European liberal political and legal thinker'. How do we square the Niebuhrian with the Kelsenian?

Three years after Herz's stunt at Kelsen's hotel room door in Cologne, it was the turn of the young, ambitious Morgenthau to meet Kelsen, in Geneva. The bond they formed back then was strong enough to survive into old age. Four decades later, in America, from his Upper East Side apartment on 4 October 1971, Morgenthau sent an intimate birthday letter to Kelsen, and in it could not have been clearer:

> Your life has meant one thing for me: the consistent fearless pursuit of truth, regardless of where it may lead to. Your example has taught me what it means to be a scholar. For that lesson I owe you a debt of gratitude which can only be discharged by following your example.

Unlike in the case of Herz, theirs was pretty much a chance encounter. Neither of them had planned to be in Switzerland. Leaving Cologne – that is, escaping the Nazis and Schmitt, Kelsen taught at Geneva's Institut Universitaire des Hautes Études Internationales, until finally fleeing Europe for good in 1940. And in fact Morgenthau, born in the Bavarian city of Coburg into a German–Jewish family, had come to Geneva from Frankfurt, on the exact day he turned twenty-eight. It was quite an unstable period in this young man's life, but at least he was able to obtain a teaching position at Geneva, hoping he could now kick-start what he so longed for: becoming a serious academic.

Yet, he struggled in Geneva. The situation was quite bad, and back then he could not possibly have known that it was to be the so-called formalist Kelsen who was to rescue him at what really was the eleventh hour. He had little money. His French was poor. But the real problem was the *Habilitation*: that is, his scholarly attempt, typical of the German-speaking world at the time, to pave the way to a full professorship or faculty appointment by writing a sort of grand thesis. And so it was a real shock for him to realise how pretty much the entire senior academic staff in Geneva doubted his academic abilities. Yes, Morgenthau botched his first inaugural lecture, and also the second. It was at this seemingly hopeless point that he wrote to Kelsen, asking for his help and backing. And what he then did, rather impressively, was to fight his way through two major revisions of his *Habilitation* thesis.

Interestingly enough, Morgenthau was not, strictly speaking, a Kelsenian, or as inclined towards the Pure theory as Herz was at the time. Quite the contrary: what he was arguing, with a Freudian twist, was that to understand the reality of the state and its laws or norms properly is to understand the political, which in turn, in terms of first principles, is to understand human nature, including individual and social psychology (Morgenthau 2012 [1930b]; Schuett 2007; Solomon 2012). And, as a matter of fact, it was none other than Kelsen himself, the Pure jurist, who saw the worth of Morgenthau's intellectual project, and who was much taken by his boldness and courage in dealing with what was one of the thorniest questions: what is the state? This is another way of saying that, from Morgenthau's standpoint, it was pure luck that Kelsen was there when he so desperately needed someone big and fair, for in the end, it really came down to this: Kelsen sat on the examination board, and it was Kelsen who sanctioned what was in fact a *Habilitation* thesis that was critical of Kelsen (Morgenthau 1934; see Jütersonke 2010). Morgenthau then received the *Habilitation*. Decades later, interviewed in America, Morgenthau (1984c: 354) publicly acknowledged Kelsen's very important intervention: 'If it had not been for Kelsen, my academic career would probably have come to a very premature end.'

And it got even better, for who could possibly have known that Morgenthau might one day be given a professorship, in the University of Chicago's Political Science department, that in some ways had been earmarked for Kelsen? As early as 1938, the early champion of behaviouralism, Charles Merriam, wanted Kelsen to leave Europe for Chicago. They had met in Geneva, in August 1934, when Merriam was on one of his many European travels, reporting back to his Chicago colleagues that Kelsen was not only a great scholar but also much in sync with contemporary American politics, notably Roosevelt's New Deal (Boyer 2008: 13). And so Merriam offered him a total of $7,000 for the academic year 1938/9 – to which Kelsen replied in the summer of 1938, 'I could find no other place in the United States better suited for my work of an ideology-critical analysis of the idea of justice on which I have been working since many years.' It did not work out, though. Kelsen just could not leave Geneva, while indicating his interest for the following year.

Only after arriving in New York City in the summer of 1940 did he let Merriam and Quincy Wright know that he had left Europe for good and was now looking for a position in the United States. Since Kelsen had already accepted Harvard Law's prestigious Oliver Wendell Holmes Lectures 1940–1, published in 1942 as *Law and Peace in International Relations*, efforts were made to bring him to Chicago the next year. At exactly this point, unfortunately, along came the Schmittian political theorist Waldemar Gurian, a Russian-born German–Jewish émigré, Catholic convert, longstanding professor at Notre Dame and founder in 1939 of the *Review of Politics*.

The problem was that Gurian did not like Kelsen's style of legal and political thought, and through John U. Nef, a longstanding historian at Chicago, he had access to Robert Maynard Hutchins, the famed Chicago President. Here is what Gurian (1940) wrote in one of his negative interventions:

> I would not understand if President Hutchins invited Kelsen to lecture on political science . . . Kelsen is a positivist . . . he is in his most important

works opposed to natural law, metaphysical concepts, etc. I think he represents a mentality which is completely out of date and which is responsible for the threatening breakdown of European civilization by the victory of primitive political religions. These religions rose partially in opposition to the empty logicism and relativism of an attitude à la Kelsen.

Among the German Catholic intelligentsia Gurian was one of the closest disciples of Schmitt. Though he broke with him, bitterly disappointed over his Nazi role, what stayed with Gurian was the sustained Schmittian criticism of the modern secular state (Benersky 1983: 51–2, 223–5).

The fact that Kelsen was not accepted at Chicago created, in fact, an important space for Morgenthau, who, in 1943, had started teaching international law and politics there. The competition over permanent positions was tough but he could produce a powerful reference: it was, of course, Hans Kelsen (1934c) who, in his letter of recommendation to Chicago, wrote that Morgenthau was 'an excellent young man with a special and extraordinary talent in political theory'. Eventually, Morgenthau out-performed all other candidates, thereby turning his visiting appointment into a tenure track position. And thus, in the end, Morgenthau held the very professorial position that Merriam, years earlier, had originally intended for Kelsen (Boyer 2008: 13–15).

Now, all three had to start afresh in what was a new country, and only a few years after setting foot on American soil, they went their different ways, accepting new positions. Kelsen left the East Coast for Berkeley. Herz joined the City College of New York. And aided by Kelsen, Morgenthau settled in Chicago. What is more, over time, both Morgenthau and Herz, the former more so than the latter, established themselves as serious political and IR theorists in general, and American post-war realists in particular. They fought their battles with intellectual integrity and boldness, just as they had learned from their teacher. Yet still, their battle was one that pitted so-called realists against so-called idealists, and in many ways they put Kelsen in the latter camp, thereby echoing the sentiment voiced by the formidable British diplomat and historian E. H. Carr (1939: 259), who, in *The Twenty Years' Crisis, 1919–1939*, mocked Kelsen's legal philosophy and political thinking as just 'another distinguished international lawyer's dream'.[8]

Unlike some Schmittians, Herz and Morgenthau were never below the belt in their critique of Kelsen. They remained loyal, and since they knew how much they owed him, sought to give back to him as much as they possibly could. A lucid example is the making of Kelsen's (1955b) colossal 100-page essay 'Foundations of Democracy', published in *Ethics*. It is not only a massive defence of liberal democracy, and as sharp and good an anti-authoritarian handbook or arsenal of pro-democracy arguments today as it was in early Cold War America, but also, in important ways, the product of Morgenthau's co-making.

The essay has its roots, by and large, in Kelsen's April 1954 Chicago lectures under the auspices of the Charles R. Walgreen Foundation. At the time, Morgenthau was already quite a settled scholar at Chicago, and the fact that Kelsen was doing the Walgreen Lectures was, in effect, thanks to his initiative and early lead. Two years earlier, Morgenthau (1952) had written to Kelsen:

> Do you plan to return to the United States this coming academic year? If so I should like to try to get the Walgreen Lectures for you. They pay well, about $1000 for six lectures plus travel expenses within the United States. If you drop me a line at your convenience I shall be glad to see what I can do.

Receiving Morgenthau's letter in Europe, where he was guest lecturing in Geneva at the all-too-familiar Institut Universitaire des Hautes Études Internationales, and after completing a year at Rhode Island's Naval War College, Kelsen finally had good news for Morgenthau. Formally invited by the Walgreen Foundation, Kelsen (1954) dropped him a line: 'I know that I owe this invitation to your initiative and I wish to thank you very warmly for your kind interest.'

Nor was Morgenthau or Herz at any time against Kelsen's anti-ideological impetus. That is to say, they were not at all against their mentor's progressive inclination for more international law, and less anarchy and war. At a time when nuclear annihilation was a real possibility and a frightening prospect, the two foreign-policy realists in effect shared Kelsen's goal of a largely pacified world order – but then, they were not convinced by the Kelsenian way or method. They argued that the Pure theory of law, state and international legal order carries within itself all the many flaws that they believed are so common in the so-called idealist position of politics and IR. To be sure, Morgenthau and Herz, as William E. Scheuerman (2014: 98) aptly puts it, were really 'preoccupied with exposing the flaws of Kelsen's one-sidedly "idealistic" views'.

Needless to say, and as we shall see throughout the rest of this book, these two realists built their critique on what is surely a questionable characterisation of what makes an idealist (and, for that matter, what makes a realist); but then, it is what it is. As Herz says, for example (1951: 31):

> Some unconscious or conscious feeling that it 'should not be so' drives him to devise an outline of human relations built, not on the 'egoistic' instincts and the ensuing 'power policies' of individuals and groups, but on considerations beyond mere self-preservation and self-interest.

While we are still at an early point in this book, to me anyway it is pretty evident that if we take Herz's definition of idealism for what it is, then Kelsen does not appear to be a naïve idealist at all, as I will discuss at length with respect to his intellectual milieu (Chapter 2), to what seems to me to be his Freudian moment (Chapter 3), and in terms of what I suggest is Kelsen's astute foreign-policy realism (Chapter 4).

Yet – save a few exceptions (see Kennedy 1994; von Bernstorff 2010; Schuett 2011; García-Salmones Rovira 2013, 2020; Ingram 2014; Schuett 2015, 2018) – the standard view in political and IR theory situates Kelsen firmly in the idealist camp: this is not only problematic in terms of any theoretical and conceptual analysis, but also unfortunate, to say the least, because it paints a distorted picture of a man who undoubtedly happens to be an iconic philosopher and twentieth-century intellectual. What is even worse, though, is that by continuing uncritically to adopt the views of, let us say, Morgenthau and Herz – and, for that matter, English School political and IR theorist Hedley Bull, a former Montague Burton Professor of International Relations at Oxford (see Bull 1977, 1986) – we might not fully grasp Kelsen's significance for our times: which is that he helps us understand the limits of politics and IR, while at the same time reminding us, day in, day out, that progress is really possible when it is *willed* (see my discussion, at times my polemic, in Chapter 5).

What political realists, and self-styled realists, really said was that Kelsen's legal and political thinking, well, is *not* realistic. Vis-à-vis Morgenthau, Carr or Bull, Herz was the one foreign-policy realist who seemed to be most in sync with Kelsen's Pure theory of law and its vision of a universal legal order. But even he disagreed with the Viennese jurist on many accounts, most notably with regard to the most challenging question of all: how do we move from the daily dramas of international anarchy to a viable form of a reasonably stable and just global society? And so Herz (1964) believed that Kelsen, a really harsh critic of conservative-style state sovereignty, underestimated or misjudged the real significance, strategic and psychological, of traditional notions of state sovereignty. From early on, he also questioned Kelsen's strict interpretation of the Humean is–ought separation in matters of law and the state, and politics and world politics, recalling decades later that 'I was never in his view a 100% member of the Vienna School' (quoted in Sylvest 2010: 424).

In many important ways, Morgenthau styled himself as the most realist of them all, so to speak. Challenging the neo-Kantian Kelsen on the grounds that the positivist jurist's focus on the normativity of law understood as a system of norms was a fairy tale about a political condition that was really the realm of power and sovereign states ruthlessly pursuing national interests, Morgenthau was not per se against the idea and politics of a rule-based order and international order. Morgenthau (1940: 269, 283) just thought that Kelsen failed to comprehend the political, the psychological and the economics in all of this. That is, as early as 1932, around the time of his botched inaugural lecture at Geneva, from Morgenthau's Freudian–Nietzschean standpoint of a sustained psychological, social and political realism, he thought that Kelsen was way too naïve for failing to grasp the ferocity of a reality driven by the *animus dominandi*, individual and collective (Scheuerman 2009: 20–31; 2013: 810).

Likewise, E. H. Carr was not at all as pessimistic, deterministic or uncompromising about global reform as some neorealists would have us believe (Mearsheimer 2005). What he was arguing in his 1942 quasi-Socialist book *Conditions of Peace*, though, was that the decisive factor for achieving European and international peace is a situation where we have successfully managed to change the dynamics and justice of Western economics. According to E. H. Carr, peace really is about (to paraphrase the 1992 Clintonian campaign slogan) the economy, stupid. It is not, he argued contra Kelsen, a product of international law. And even though Bull (1986: 336) explored at some length the Kelsenian project of legal positivism with respect to the English School pluralism's concern with international society and power politics, he concluded that 'Kelsen's understanding was confined by the idealist or progressivist assumption so common in that period.'

Now, that is all fair enough, but then I still wonder: what if we were all so one-sidedly preoccupied with exploring the so-called naïve idealism in Kelsen's philosophy and political thinking that we overlooked Kelsen the political realist?

3 Imaginary Foe

One might say that – in the eyes of his many enemies – Kelsen was the monster of Vienna. At the same time, it is also true that his friends and allies were shaking their heads in disbelief over how some Schmittians on the left and the right were reacting to Kelsen's scientific and intellectual project. Am I overreacting? Am I over-protective of a man who, ever since his mighty 1911 *Habilitation* thesis, *Main Problems in the Theory of Public Law*, has been stirring up jurisprudence?

Kelsen polarised, and he still does. It is not too much of a stretch to suggest that his fate was similar to that of the so-called 'monster of Malmesbury' that Hobbes was in the eyes of his contemporaries (see Mintz 1962: vii). Over time, like Hobbes, Kelsen became one of the most vilified philosophers, not only in the German-speaking arena but in the wider Western world too. Both as a man and as a Pure positivist – recall then-Pope Benedict XVI lashing out at Kelsen in the *Bundestag* – Kelsen has had to battle it out on the frontlines of an increasingly fierce *Kulturkampf* over the meaning of politics and law, and the roots of democracy and justice. From almost the very start of his intellectual project he has been hitting a wall of opposition in many different intellectual, ideological and political circles. There was Schmitt. There were the many, overt and covert, ideologues (as he would call them) coming out of the natural law tradition. There were the political realists and foreign-policy realists. There were many more. What they shared was a sustained opposition to what they thought was Kelsen's naïve or dangerous formalism of political and international life.

Later in this section, we will see that, of course, past and present, Kelsen has had a great many friends and allies too. Yet, to this day, the problem has been that both the core Kelsenians and the fair-minded interpreters of the Kelsenian project are being silenced by the loud drumbeats of the Schmittians, and by other important and powerful voices in Western philosophy and political thinking.

As for the voices criticising Kelsen, William E. Scheuerman (2014: 86) is totally right when he writes that 'the list of critics reads like a *Who's Who?* of famous refugees from Nazism'. If we single out three such cases, perhaps the most important is Eric Voegelin. Starting out as a student of Kelsen in Vienna, he had turned into quite a reactionary thinker and became a fierce Popper critic who, eventually admiring America's non-positivist intellectual environment, was really one of the first to despise Kelsen's vision of liberalism (see Voegelin 1945).

The second critic is Franz L. Neumann. A Frankfurt School-associated Marxist at Columbia, he found the Pure theory of scientific terms useful but rejected what he saw as Kelsen's in-built politics. As Neumann (1944: 46) criticised:

> By throwing out of account all relative problems of political and social power, it paves the way for decisionism, for the acceptance of political decisions no matter where they originate or what their content, so long as sufficient power stands behind them.

I will certainly come back to this particular line of attack, not least because, if Neumann is right with his critical emphasis on the role of power in Kelsen's Pure theory, would that not make Kelsen a sort of arch-Realist?

The third man is Leo Strauss. A most influential conservative and one of the finest interpreters of classical political philosophy, he criticised Kelsen in a way that has been very typical ever since: Kelsen is a political softie, and as a positivist he is dangerously neutral on the question of legitimacy, the problem of Nazism, and the meaning of God in Western life. As Strauss (1953: 5) put it: 'The contemporary rejection of natural right leads to nihilism – nay, it is identical with nihilism.' In short, criticism is plentiful and powerful – though not necessarily justified.

Kelsen did suffer – but not as man. He was way too bold, and calm, to allow someone else to bully him, or to take too personally any possible criticism or critique of what was literally his Pure theory. But of course he suffered at the hands of his commentators. To his friends and allies, he was the man who, importantly enough, successfully purified the study of law, or jurisprudence, of such alien elements as psychology, sociology and ethics. To his critics and enemies, he was a card-carrying member of an intellectual, political and progressively inspired conspiracy that was allegedly seeking to indoctrinate a new generation of intellectuals with a dangerously false method of formalistic legal philosophy in which the law has no basis whatsoever in any timeless notion of morality revealed to us through either Nature or God, or both. All of this is to say that, to me at least, Kelsen was an imagined foe; and he still is.

You do not necessarily have to be a committed Kelsenian to see that the Schmittians and other critics – including, in some ways, the FBI – have relentlessly targeted Kelsen for committing all sorts of crimes. Here is a selection. It is almost commonplace in the West, and particularly in the circles of the Schmittians and the political realists, to maintain that Kelsenian legal and political philosophy is idealistic, naïve, sterile, utopian, or all of these things at one and the same time (see Llewellyn 1962: 356; Laski 1938: vi). The intellectual and political right keeps saying that Kelsenian formalism reduces the very concept and idea of the state to a mere system of norms, thereby sucking out all Hegelian grandeur associated with conservative notions of political community. What is more, they say, the Kelsenian focus on positive legality reveals a morally and politically charged unwillingness to accept political reality as it is. By contrast, the left keeps arguing that the Pure theory was, from the very start and in its essence, not at all a critical, or Critical, intellectual–scientific project, and that the very idea of the so-called neutral state allows everyone to see, or so they claim, that Kelsen's legal and political philosophy is, in the end, a conservative ideology, firmly rooted in the idea of a liberal capitalist order. Some other commentators have claimed – rather bizarrely – that the Pure theory is a Jewish invention, which plainly and simply 'is wrong' (Jabloner 2016: 336). And to be sure, pretty much all of the mighty heirs of natural law philosophy have sought to indict Kelsen for sponsoring either nihilism or culturelessness, or both.

Now, Kelsen was never one for hyperbolism or the like. But even if you are not a Kelsenian, or if you are keeping a critical distance in the case of Kelsen and these matters (which I do not), you may be hard pressed not to acknowledge that there is something quite awkward about how he has been treated in his time, and in ours. I do not use the word 'treated' lightly in this respect. Kelsen (2008 [1934b]: 5) is right, and is certainly not overdoing it, when he writes, in the Preface to the first edition of the *Pure Theory of Law*, that much of the opposition to it 'borders on hatred'. Let me put it this way: what must he have thought of himself, and of his critics, when he read, pretty much the entire West over, that his Pure theory is a politics of 'crass Bolshevism' or 'hidden Anarchism' or – equally seriously – that he was a 'pacemaker for fascism' (Kelsen 2008 [1934b]: 6)? That must have been tough to swallow for a man who was one of the last century's most passionate defenders of liberal democracy.

He did fight back, of course. But even though, in the raging Weimar-ish battles old and new, the Schmittians have tended to voice their side of the story much more loudly in style and tone, there have been fair-minded attempts ever since to rescue Kelsen and Kelsenian themes, at least from the worst excesses. One can see how bad the situation is when even arch-pragmatist Judge Richard Posner, an extraordinary thinker whose pragmatic view of judicial decision-making is almost unrivalled, has been jumping to Kelsen's defence.

First, was Kelsen a nihilist? No, says Judge Posner, for a very simply reason: to have a purposeful, scientific Pure theory of law that is, for epistemological reasons, content-neutral is one thing; but it is quite another to look at Kelsen's legal and political thinking, which is anything but neutral and rooted firmly in the liberal camp. Second, what about the question, or allegation, of whether Kelsen or Kelsenian legal positivism was one element in weakening Weimar and paving the way for Nazism? On this point, in *Law, Pragmatism, and Democracy*, a strong defence of the American political system and the rule of law, Judge Posner (2005: 290) is equally clear:

> It is fanciful to suppose that a theory of law propounded by a Jewish professor would have done anything to stop Hitler. Anyway, if as I believe Kelsen's was a genuinely positivist theory of law, criticism based on its social consequence is misplaced. It is like criticizing atomic theory for having led to the destruction of Hiroshima and Nagasaki.

You may, or may not, agree with Judge Posner's defence of Kelsen (note that I agree with him on both counts here). The point, for the time being, is simply this: when it comes to Kelsen, there are other important voices out there, not only the Schmittian ones seeking constantly to manufacture a foe.

Perhaps equally drowned out by today's Schmittians, yet equally important, is the realistic take on Kelsen of David Kennedy, Manley O. Hudson Professor of Law and Director of the Institute for Global Law and Policy at Harvard Law. In contradistinction to much of the popular wisdom in the study of law and politics, according to Kennedy (1994: 22), Kelsen is 'no bean-counting formalist'. On the surface, Kelsen may appear to be dry and formalist, but as soon as one digs deeper into the vast and rich Pure theory of international legal order, it is hard to understand why, in the field of international law, Kelsen has been pushed somewhat to the sidelines on the argument that his public international law theory was idealistic, rendering it pretty much useless. To be sure, the marginalised Kelsenians in the United States, of which Leo Gross was one of the most outspoken, saw it totally the other way round: it was not Kelsen who was the idealist, but it was American post-war international law that was infected by a painful naïvety as to how the world works. The intellectual, if not methodological, challenge has, of course, always been how to be realistic about power politics among nations and yet stick to Kelsen's core scientific principle, *not* to mix the study of law with the study of other subjects. Law is one thing, while the political is another. But being a Kelsenian jurist does not make you by default a political idealist. Kelsen was both Pure and well versed in real politics, a major Western figure somewhere in between political realism and political idealism (see also Kennedy 1994; Ingram 2014).

That a commitment to positivism in international law and a hard-nosed realistic view of the struggle for power in international politics are not strange bedfellows, and especially not in the case of Kelsen, has been recently argued by European-based theorist of law Mónica García-Salmones Rovira. In important ways, she has shown, frankly and fairly, what the inner circle of early Kelsenians have known all along: that Kelsen was in some manner both an idealist and a realist. Kelsen the idealist had a vision of a cosmopolitan world order that is firmly based on the principle of universally applicable international law; and Kelsen the realist was pretty clear about the core political problem in all this, which is the pervasiveness of a sustained Weberian striving for a share of power, or the influencing of the distribution of power, in any given society and international order (García-Salmones Rovira 2013, 2020). And of course, as I would put it (a point to which I will repeatedly come back in the rest of this book): unless you are a crude Bismarckian realpolitik type of political thinker and actor, there is always an element of idealism and optimism, if not at least a moral hope for progress, in any realist logic of politics. Or seen the other way round: why would Kelsen, or any other Kantian-inspired political and IR theorist, be so focused on questions of justice and peace, if it were not for the realism that, sadly, we are hewn out of such timber that makes conflict and war, violence and blood, very possible at any time and in any place.

And then, interestingly enough, there is the case of Kelsen versus Schmitt, or let us say, the peculiar case of Kelsen *and* Schmitt. It is all too well known how, and why, they were on totally opposite sides of the intellectual and political scene in inter-war Continental Europe: Kelsen the normativist was firmly rooted on the liberal left, and Schmitt the decisionist was on his way to becoming the Crown Jurist of the Third Reich. The major rift between the two men has been clearly established. But then, as Jochen von Bernstorff, German law Professor at Tübingen and former diplomat, points out with clarity and care, both Kelsen and Schmitt were sceptical about the real possibility of any comprehensive moral basis of international law. What they did share was a fundamentally antagonistic understanding of politics as a struggle for power. According to both men, the realm of world politics is the ugly sphere of power politics, where the conflicting interests of nations are pretty much irreconcilable. And what is even worse, Kelsen and Schmitt are (obviously) agreed, all political and international life is driven by the seemingly impermeable cultural sensibilities of nationalism, if not also prestige and status (von Bernstorff 2010: 255–8; Koskenniemi 2000: 17–35). All of this begs the questions: who is the Realist now? Where is Kelsen the idealist?

In many ways, there is nothing worse in the realm of government and international politics – whether in the lecture halls of the ivory towers or in the briefing rooms of the many Western capitals – than to be called a softie or a naïve quixotic idealist, which, in terms of everyday mob psychology, amounts to the same thing. As Carl Gustav Jung (1963: ch. 12), founder of analytical psychology, once quipped: 'Every form of addiction is bad, no matter whether the narcotic be alcohol or morphine or idealism.' That Kelsen and Kelsenians are a bunch of such Jungean addicts, fleeing this world while escaping into another one, has been a Schmittian-style mantra since Weimar. And at one point in the heated debate between Kelsen and Schmitt on the most fundamental question of who should be the very guardian of the constitution, Schmitt infamously castigated Kelsen as one of the 'zealots of a blind normativism' (quoted in Vinx 2015: 99).

Although repeating such charges over and over again might be appealing to hold the Schmittian base together in turbulent times, it makes them not a bit more accurate: that is, much of what has been thrown at Kelsen is either misleading or false. As Matthias Jestaedt, German law Professor at Freiburg and head of the Hans-Kelsen-Forschungsstelle (Hans Kelsen Research Centre), also editor of the collected works of Hans Kelsen,[9] puts it so nicely: much of the criticism levelled at Kelsen has proved to be based more on 'legend than reading'. A central narrative of this legend for decades has been that Kelsen was a sort of naïve ivory-tower recluse (Jestaedt and Lepsius 2006). That, from a purely biographical standpoint alone, Kelsen is more of a realist than anything else, was noted long ago by legal theorist Clemens Jabloner (1998), former Vice-Chancellor and Justice Minister of the Republic of Austria and longstanding co-director of the Viennese Hans Kelsen-Institut. Kelsen the professor had a considerable amount of experience of how the real world of the state, government and politics works. He was hired to co-draft the Austrian Constitution of 1920, and served between 1919 and 1930 as a judge at the Constitutional Court. To sum it up in the words of Iain Stewart (1990: 273), an Australian-based law Professor at Macquarie, Kelsen has been 'of all major legal theorists the most bitterly acquainted with political realities', and thus he 'is an implausible perpetrator of "formalism"'.

And to be sure, there is so much more to explore in his life and political thinking that shows us quite *a different Kelsen*. But for now it suffices to throw it all back at the Schmittians: can you not see, or do you not want to see for whatever ideological reason, that you have been creating for yourself an imaginary foe?

4 There Is No Utopia

Now, the gloves are off. From whatever angle we look at his life and political thinking, what we come to see is a Freudian stoic who offers us little consolation other than the call for political action by You and Me. To Kelsen, then, there is no such thing as utopia. Essential goodness of human nature? Laughable! Infinite malleability? No! A peaceful living together of Us all without any coercive centralised order or without any legal Leviathan? Dream on!

To be clear as to where we are in my re-reading of Kelsen as a political realist, I suggest that we bushwhack our way through the Kelsenian jungle by combining methods employed by the idealist John Rawls and the realist Samuel P. Huntington. That is certainly a rather odd pairing, but none the less I find it a helpful one when it comes to the question of human nature in the core Realist logic of politics and international relations. From the tweedy American political philosopher Rawls (1971), whose innovation in social-contract theory gave us new meanings of liberalism, justice and happiness, I take the thought experiment of the original position under the veil of ignorance, though adapted to our present purpose here, of course. And from Huntington, a former Albert J. Weatherhead III University Professor at Harvard, founder of the John M. Olin Institute for Strategic Studies, and a former Democratic foreign policy adviser in Hubert H. Humphrey's 1968 presidential bid, I take the following advice: 'If you tell people the world is complicated, you're not doing your job . . . They already know it's complicated. Your job is to distill it, simplify it' (quoted in Zakaria 2011; Friedman 1953 was similar in spirit).

So let us imagine that we know very little about Kelsen the man and his philosophy, but also that the very part to which we do have access is something very fundamental in all styles of political thinking. This is exactly what Kelsen says about You and Me, or human nature. It is not about criticising what he said, or about interpreting what he should or could have said; rather, it is about Kelsen's anthropological premises or assumptions as they *are*, or as he penned them in black and white. The Huntingtonean element is my focus here on the concept of human nature. It has always proved to be a very controversial concept, but has always been at the very heart of Realist logic since its very inception more than 2,000 years ago. My methodological point is that I want to juxtapose Kelsenian 'man' with the man of political realism, and I will do the testing against the backdrop of distilling and simplifying it. Here is my formula: *if* political realism equals human nature pessimism, *then* Kelsen is a political realist. Naturally enough, the burden of proof is on me; I suggest that I say something first about the concept of human nature in realism, focusing on Morgenthau and Herz, and then bring in their teacher and mentor Kelsen, who may, after all, not be as idealistic as some would have us believe.

To be fair to Morgenthau, the notion of a fundamental analytical and normative divide in Western political thought, between the so-called political realists on the one hand and the so-called political idealists on the other, was not his invention. This divide pre-dates him, of course, by many centuries. But then it is in *Politics among Nations*, probably the most influential textbook on diplomacy and international affairs during the Cold War, that he could not have been clearer – as he obviously saw it – that realists and idealists are in almost absolute theoretical, intellectual and political opposition to one another. Likewise, and even though I appreciate why some of us in the field no longer want to talk about what he, and other Freudians and Nietzscheans before and after him, have aptly called *the will to power*, it was Morgenthau who was rather absolute in his claim that what separates these realists and idealists from one another is their totally different image of human nature (Morgenthau 1967 [1948a]; see also Niebuhr 1940).

Call it realism versus idealism, or call it reality versus utopia (Carr 1939, 1961), it amounts to the very same thing: one of the most fundamental yardsticks to determine who is standing on which side of the barricades is intimately tied to what you know, or believe, or assume about human nature.

According to Morgenthau (1967 [1948a]: 3–4), you are firmly in the idealist camp if you trust in 'the essential goodness and infinite malleability of human nature'. And inversely, you are one of the political realists if you have a more pessimistic assessment of the situation: which is to say, you are a realist if you believe that 'the world, imperfect as it is from the rational point of view, is the result of forces inherent in human nature'. The whole body of philosophy of political realism old and new, Morgenthau says, has its roots in the 'theoretical concern with human nature as it actually is'.

And surely, as we learn in what is perhaps his boldest work on the virtues of realism and the defects of idealism, *Scientific Man vs. Power Politics* (1946), Morgenthau's conception of human nature not only portrays You and Me as fundamentally selfish, but – what is even worse – states that, as individuals and collectives, We are possessed by a limitless lust for power, the infamous *animus dominandi*. The political in all social and international life, universal in time and space, has its roots in a very complicated human nature: at least that is how it is for Morgenthau (2012 [1930b]).

And thus it is with the majority of political realists – including Herz! While a most important forerunner of the neorealist–structuralist concept of the security dilemma, sketched out in *Political Realism and Political Idealism* (1951), it is not that Herz wanted nothing to do with the concept of human nature. He certainly was not as intransigent as Morgenthau (he was a different character too), but it has always been centre-stage. Let me have Herz speak for himself at some length here so that there can be no misunderstanding. Following the lead of earlier realists, to him it 'is clear that political thought starts from some quite definite notion of the nature of man'. It is equally clear to him that the history of Western political thought is, in essence, the battleground where realists and idealists meet, each of them armed with different concepts and ideas, notably when it comes to the question of human nature. The political idealists, according to Herz (1951: 33), assume 'that man, or at least the majority of men, is basically "good", "considerate", "peaceful", or that he is at least morally colourless so that education, right environment, or the right structure of society can render him good'. And it is in this sense, Herz (1951: 33) writes, that they part company with the political realists, for the idealists '[do] not believe in the premise of Political Realism – the irreconcilability of interests and policies, and the inevitability of the struggle for security and power'.

One might say, then, that political idealists are human nature optimists and that political realists are human nature pessimists. The undertone in the realism/idealism battle in general, and as regards the fact of human nature in particular, is of course that the idealists are a naïve bunch, while the realists – paraphrasing here Michael C. Williams (2005: ix), Professor of International Security and Political Theory at Ottawa – style themselves as the ones with 'a clear-sighted ability to understand the world the way it is, a willingness to confront the dynamics of power and interest that are held to govern world politics'. For now I will leave it at that, for the point was to let Morgenthau and Herz speak.

Against this background – note, this human nature background – it is premature, misleading and false to say that Kelsen was a starry-eyed political idealist, someone out there on a quixotic quest to find the one easy formula for bringing us all perpetual peace. And to begin with, who would have thought that Kelsen would be turning the tables on the realists? In pretty plain language he made it clear to Reinhard Niebuhr, perhaps last century's most important philosopher and public intellectual to emerge from the Christian Realist tradition (see Lovin 1995), that Niebuhr is the one who seems to be naïve.

In the mid-1950s, when Kelsen was already well into his seventies, he was as no-nonsense as he ever was. He was certain, at least as certain as a scholar can be, about the virtues of legal positivism and political relativism – and for that matter, just as unrelenting about the problems of natural law and the idea of an absolute justice – and in 1955, on the basis of his 1954 Walgreen Lectures at Chicago, he published 'Foundations of Democracy'. In fact, as G. O. Mazur, a Russian-trained scholar of international law and editor of two insightful Morgenthau memorials, points out, this massive essay 'was the product of Kelsen's and Morgenthau's correspondence of over 25 years since they first met in Europe, and was finally penned by Kelsen himself' (quoted in Rice 2016: 135). This is interesting, for it speaks to the fact that there is every sign, as William Scheuerman (2014: 99) put it, that the 'relationship between Kelsen and IR realism is a rich and complicated one'. Anyway, in his 'Foundations of Democracy', Kelsen (1955b) critically discusses the major ways to vindicate democracy. He explored the procedural, the Rousseauian and the Soviet doctrine, the capitalist, the Lockean, the Hegelian and the Marxist vision. And he also tackled Niebuhr's position on how religion might relate to democracy, or democracy to Christian theology (see also Rice 2016).

Kelsen was in some ways very gentle with Niebuhr, devoting almost 10 per cent of his essay to this thoughtful yet pugnacious Protestant theologian, of whom President Barack Obama (quoted in Brooks 2007) was very fond: 'I love him. He's one of my favorite philosophers.' At one and the same time, though, Kelsen grabbed him directly by the horns. He accused Niebuhr of distorting liberalism and the liberal view of human nature, thereby seeking to expose Niebuhr and the Christian image of democracy, human nature and justice as fundamentally pre-modern and anti-democratic. He really sought to expose the Niebuhrian position as naïve.

From Kelsen's standpoint, the question was this: in light of the many attacks accusing a Kelsenian positivism of being a pacemaker for radical movements, in that these movements are filling a cultural void created by technocratic relativists, does democracy require a religious vindication so as to be a safeguard against such movements? Certainly, Niebuhr (1944: 82) thinks so, arguing that the 'most effective opponents of tyrannical government are today, as they have been in the past, men who can say, "We must obey God rather than man."' And naturally enough, Kelsen (1955b: 54) responds by saying that this is not only dangerous, but also historically inaccurate:

> For the source from which Christian theology takes the argument that 'we must obey God rather than man' furnishes also the argument: all governments are given their powers from God; this argument has been formulated by St. Paul for the very purpose of being used in favor of a demonic Caesar, and since then has been again and again used to support tyrannical rulers such as Ivan the Terrible of Russia, Louis XIV of France, or Frederick II of Prussia. Also Mussolini and even Hitler found Christian theologians who justified their governments.

This gets him going, for the Niebuhrian idea that we ought to rely on God rather than on Us when it comes to the ultimate questions of life, including how we can most effectively defend democracy against its enemies, is absurd to him.

The whole point of democracy, Kelsen (1955b: 40) says, is that it 'leaves the decision about the social value to be realized to the individual acting in political reality'. Or, as one might say, a Kelsenian democracy leaves these important decisions to the day-to-day relativism of – or the day-to-day political realism in – Western parliaments and the rule of positive law. Now, the problem, as he sees it, is that the positive idea of democracy and, for that matter, the positive idea of justice are not as widely accepted as Kelsenian-inspired legal and political theorists would perhaps wish. Sounding somewhat elitist, though realist, if one takes a hard look at the question of a Kelsenian democracy in practice, he (1955b: 40) says that one very soon sees that

> many people are not able, and not willing, to accept the responsibility for the decision about the social value to be realized, especially in a situation in which their decisions may have fatal consequences for their personal welfare. Therefore they try to shift it from their own conscience

to an outside authority competent to tell them what is right and wrong, to answer their question, what is justice? – seeking for an unconditional justification in terms of which they long to appease their conscience. Such an authority they find in religion.

While both the Schmittians and the strongmen, appealing to the so-called little guys, might respond that this is just confirming the bourgeois–elitist bias that is inbuilt in what is a Kelsenian pseudo-liberalism, this is not what Kelsen says, means or implies. Writing in the Kantian spirit of the Enlightenment ideal, Kelsen wants, or hopes, that people will no longer lack the courage to use their own reason or, I dare say, use their own interests. In this sense, Kelsen is *for* the little guys, not against them.

But then, of course, Kelsen the realist knows full well where the resistance to a Pure vindication of democracy has its real and powerful roots: in Freudian psychology. In the sweet scent of natural law, too. And so Kelsen knows he must go on the attack. In *The Children of Light and the Children of Darkness*, perhaps the most detailed statement of Niebuhr's political philosophy, the very starting point is, at least to Niebuhr (1944: xii), that to save Western democratic society from peril is to have a 'more realistic vindication than is given it by the liberal culture [and its] excessively optimistic estimates of human nature and of human history'. Naturally, then, Kelsen must confront Niebuhr: *what* optimism? He knew of no serious liberal thinker, neither political nor social or economic, who did not factor into all social and international life both the element of self-interest and the element of egotism. It is exactly because of their profound human nature realism, Kelsen (1955b: 55) writes, that 'none of the leading liberal philosophers . . . considers a coercive order as superfluous'. Why would they? Why would Kelsen?

He is as committed a human nature realist, or for that matter political realist, as any other realist in the history of Western political philosophy. He takes it as the very basic assumption of social life that, unless you want to see the chaos and violence of the Hobbesian *bellum omnium contra omnes*, all social orders require at their core a centralised monopolisation of the use of force. Taking a hardnosed look at You and Me through a Freudian prism (as we shall explore later in detail), Kelsen (1941: 83) says that to believe in the power of natural law – that is to say, in any coercive power of a 'higher' law – is 'an illusion, the product of wishful thinking'.

It is totally naïve to believe, he says, that, given human nature is what it *is*, any existing social order on this planet could regulate human behaviour without the establishment of a coercive order. In fact, it is Kelsen who almost mocks those he calls 'political dreamers' and 'optimists' when he (1941: 83) writes:

> If it were possible for the human mind to establish the content of a social
> order that could count on the voluntary obedience of all its subjects – because

it corresponded to the nature of man and his mutual relations requiring of
human beings only what they themselves wished – an order that would
make everyone happy and was therefore a just order, then it would be hard
to understand why such an order had not yet been realized.

So, make no mistake, rooted in what is quite a seriously realistic account of
human nature, to him there is *no withering away of the state*, nor of law, nor of
coercion, nor of politics, nor of the struggle for power. He would, then, totally
agree with E. H. Carr (1939: 222) that only utopians put their faith in natural
law. And so he would also totally agree with Kennan (2002 [1956]) that Soviet
Communism not only was almost purely a natural-law philosophy, but also
was fundamentally flawed because it was at heart wrong about human nature.

Do not, then, expect too much from Kelsen. That social relations are pow-
ered by an indestructible drive to dominate one another completely is a fact
of human nature, proven time and again in human history. Nor, though – as
discussed in Chapter 5 – should we expect too little, for, as he says (1955b:
26), 'the attitude of the individual toward the problem of government is essentially determined by the intensity of *the will to power* within the individual'.
While there is hope, we cannot do without being constantly guarded by a
political realism rooted in human nature. However we sugar-coat our deeds,
or present ourselves on the social, political and international scene, the fact is,
says Kelsen (1957a: 8), that our 'behaviour is not very different from that of
animals. The big fish swallow the small ones, in the kingdom of animals as in
that of men.'

Now, I do not think you can be more much more realistic about human
nature and social life than Kelsen – and on the basis of how Morgenthau and
Herz conceptualised what makes political realism and political idealism in
terms of their respective human nature assumptions, I do not see in Kelsen a
political idealist. So, let us again have Kelsen speak for himself. Let him warn
us (1941: 84) that the whole idea of a natural law is dangerous and naïve, for it

> proceeds from the notion that man is 'by nature' good. It ignores the
> innate urge to aggression in men. It ignores the fact that the happiness of
> one man is often incompatible with the happiness of another, and that
> therefore a natural just order that guarantees happiness to all, and so
> does not have to react against the disturbances with measures of coer-
> cion, is not compatible with the 'nature' of men as far as our knowledge
> goes. The 'nature' of natural law is not the nature of our scientific expe-
> rience, it is a moral postulate.

This is to say, because I want to be really clear about the basic conceptual starting point for the rest of this book, that Kelsen was no political idealist: he was

a human nature realist. Or as he (1941: 84) put it, actually trying to warn us: 'To count on a human nature different from that known to us is Utopia.'

5 A Most Misunderstood Man

Striking at a king is one thing (the Schmittians have tried), but it is quite another to kill him (thus far they have missed Kelsen). And if Ralph Waldo Emerson (1979 [1841]: 34) is also right that 'to be great is to be misunderstood', by this standard alone Kelsen ranks as one of the greatest in Western thought. To mention a Transcendentalist co-leader in one and the same sentence as the creator of Pure positivism might perhaps seem bizarre. It is really hard not to be more idealistic than the Fruitlanders, and much harder still to be less utopian than Kelsen. I repeat: you cannot be less utopian than Kelsen!

But then, there is something quite practical in Emerson's statement, for it serves as an aphoristic forward-bridge to the next chapter, 'Kelsen's Milieu'. It would have been possible for the Schmittians to see that Kelsen is anything but a naïve, quixotic idealist, had they bothered to look at Kelsen's work in the *k. u. k.* War Ministry; or at his consulting role efforts for American foreign intelligence two decades later; or at why he was so interested in Dante, the 'supreme realist' (Dirda 2007); or in Freud, 'the most thoroughgoing realist in western thought' (Kaplan 1957: 224); or in the arch-individualistic liberalism of the Austrian School of Economics, co-led by his schoolmate and lifelong friend, Ludwig van Mises. A great many important additional bits and pieces of what one day may form a coherent intellectual biography of Kelsen will be explored in the next chapter.

In this chapter we have learned what was already out there for us, and for the Schmittians and Kelsen's many other critics, to see: the FBI was on to Kelsen, but had to drop the case that he was a Communist. Some of the most illustrious mid-twentieth-century realists, including his former students Morgenthau and Herz, called him an idealist, but merely on fabricated charges. More generally, some of the most consequential Western philosophers of quite different intellectual convictions relentlessly attacked Kelsen, but did not succeed in manufacturing a wholesale imaginary foe. And what is more, they have all tried very hard to create an idealist bogeyman out of him, but failed. Kelsen not only was quite clever at saying out loud what he meant but also made it clear on numerous occasions what his fundamental assumptions or core political principles were. One of these, of course, was a sustained human nature realism – a Freudian-inspired one, as we shall see soon enough.

So the next task is the same as the one before: to continue to rescue Kelsen from the ideological battles into which his foes have sought to trap him, by saving him from the confusion into which he has sunk at the hands of his commentators, notably the Schmittians and the pseudo-realists. Surely we have been here before, and chances are that we will have to cope with a similar situation in the future: that is, to make the very idea of liberal democracy and a cosmopolitan-inspired peace as resilient as possible against external attacks. One way of doing that is to take us out of our intellectual comfort zone, and to talk about the political and the struggle for power and peace in Morgenthauian terms, while not giving up open society ideals of justice and the rule of law. That is to say: why not talk about these ideas and principles in the style of Kelsen's political thinking?

He has been hated by the Schmittians in the same way that Hobbes's coldly analytical geometry of government and the state had been hated by the Hegelians. Likewise, Kelsen appears to have been as misunderstood and misjudged as a very Jean-Jacques Rousseau, who, not unlike Kelsen, was called a 'utopian' and also the 'deepest of the Realists' (Hoffmann and Fidler 1991: lxxvii). And surely, it is the fate of all genuine philosophers, old and new, and for very different reasons, to defy an all-too-easy compartmentalisation into neat boxes, conceptual or political. Kelsen is no exception. If you want to find the naïve and idealistic liberal in him, you will. If you want to see a cold and positivistic monster, no problem. And for a long time, and for obvious reasons, the Schmittians have done just that and almost perfected this kind of all-too-easy pigeonholing of Kelsen. Surely they are going after him as relentlessly as they possibly can, for as Emerson's (1843) aphorism, confirmed by history, has it: 'When you strike at a king, you must kill him.' And to be sure, why would the Schmittians not do just that?

Now, in the perennial battle between political realism and political idealism, the Schmittians will keep on trying to place Kelsen firmly where they want him: in the idealist corner. Nothing seems to be more powerful than to de-legitimise a political idea or vision completely from the very start by making it seem totally naïve or idealistic, or even utopian. Since I am not content with throwing white sand at their incoming battle cruisers, what comes next is another layer of what I hope is a robust forward-defence of Kelsen as a political realist.

CHAPTER 2

KELSEN'S MILIEU

'Kelsen values intellectual honesty above all virtues'
Helen Silving-Ryu (1964)

The telephone at his apartment rings in the middle of the night. It is autumn 1918, the final weeks of the Austrian–Hungarian Empire. The final days, really. And it is Schorskean (1979) Vienna. The majestic Ringstraße, the grand boulevard of a glorious capital, encircling as it does the winding, cobbled streets and alleys of the First District. It all unfolds near its north-eastern end: at Stubenring 1, to be most precise, which is sandwiched in between what was the Imperial Royal Arts and Crafts School, now the University of Applied Arts, known as *die Angewandte*, and the Urania, a popular adult education centre, one of Red Vienna's *Volkshochschulen*.

In the Imperial Royal War Ministry, a colossal building that today houses several federal ministries of the Republic of Austria, Kelsen is summoned to see the *k. u. k.* War Minister. Colonel General Rudolf Stöger-Steiner Freiherr von Steinstätten, a Styrian, wants to hear Kelsen's opinion of the latest cable from Washington. And he wants his assessment of the current situation. As was so often the case in Kelsen's life, he was widely recognised as a top scholar and Pure theorist of law, but was quite a practical man too, keeping a foot in two camps: a little in theory and a little in reality.

6 THE *K. U. K.* WAR MINISTRY

He was called in to talk strategy, and about how he saw the whole situation on the ground. It was, after all, war. The monarchy was, to put it mildly, in anything but good shape; and, realistically, the only really relevant question at the time was how to save what was left of it. What was required, and what Kelsen brought to the table, was both a healthy dose of political realism and, in situations like these, the intellectual courage to give his most honest assessment and the best possible advice. And to be sure, raw facts rarely lead to rosy pictures: not for the Minister, nor the Emperor.

Kelsen could not have foreseen, as a young man, that eventually, and in many different ways, he was to become involved in what were the high politics of the fate of the Empire, Austria and thereby the European order, or that he would take part in many such dramas of reality: not only on one occasion, but rather at several points in his long life on two continents. And the very fact that the War Minister came to trust and respect him, and wanted Kelsen as his legal advisor in the first place, was, as Kelsen (1947a: 47) aptly puts it, due to a rather 'curious concurrence of circumstances'.

War had broken out. The Great War, a war that was supposed to end all wars (Wells 1914). How naïve. Or, as Walter Lippmann, an early Freudian and one of last century's towering figures in American journalism and political analysis, had put it: how delusional (see Steel 1980). If there is only one element of certainty in the fog of war, it is that war is hell – and one might add here (of which more later), war is rarely ever over. But even a stoic thinker such as Freud, with whom Kelsen was in close touch by this time, was quite patriotic. In the beginning, at least, Freud proved to be as excited as scores of other people and soldiers across Europe, when, following the assassination of Archduke Franz Ferdinand, the Austrian–Hungarian Empire declared war on Serbia, which saw Europe and much of the world spiralling into a world war, pitting the Allies against the Central Powers. It did not take Freud long to realise the madness and bloodshed that came with modern trench warfare (Jones 1955: 192). There is nothing heroic in what were hellish conditions for the soldiers: gas attacks, shell-shock (now known as post-traumatic stress disorder), pain and disease, and mass death. Only six months after a rather cheerful start to the killing in that fatal summer of 1914, Freud would write in his essay of early 1915, 'Thoughts for the Times on War and Death', that the only sensation that the Great War had really brought upon us all was 'disillusionment'.

Now, Kelsen, a reserve officer with the rank of second lieutenant since 1902, having completed the so-called One-Year-Voluntary military training programme in 1900/1, was told to report for active duty: to present himself, by 4 August 1914, at *Traindivision 14*, a logistics and supply unit in Innsbruck, situated in the midst of the stunning scenery of the Austrian Alps.[1] But not even two months later, due to his suffering from a serious bout of pneumonia, he was declared unfit for active service. Thus it came about that Kelsen was enlisted to work in the Ministry's Justice division. It was quite a logical move. By this time, in his mid-thirties and newly married to Margarete, he had the

Habilitation in the bag, along with lots of research and teaching experience in public and administrative law.

It all started normally, then, if not to say innocently. He was assigned to prepare imperial pardons, which, Kelsen (2007 [1947a]: 47) recalls, was a 'most satisfactory task'. And at some later point the division's jurists were asked to submit articles for a new in-house journal of military law. At the time he was sitting on a lengthy draft article that analysed the tricky question of post-war constitutional reform, and had intended to submit the piece to another law journal. But since this draft paper included a suitable section on the issue of breaking up the Common Army (a policy the Hungarians pursued), what Kelsen literally did was cut out the relevant pages from the draft manuscript and submit them as a stand-alone piece to the new Ministry journal. And over time, he had all forgotten about it.

The War Minister did not take Kelsen's article lightly; it had not even been published yet. He fumed at its author, and eventually Kelsen had to come to see him. The Minister, visibly annoyed, lambasted him for publishing an article without prior ministerial permission to do so. But then, Kelsen was accused of something he had no part in, at least not on the two counts that the Minister insinuated. And Kelsen told him so: he had submitted the article through the chain of command, and therefore could not have guessed that anyone would find such a written piece of legal scholarship objectionable. Moreover, as Kelsen was soon able to make clear, he was loyal – loyal beyond any doubt – to the War Minister.

Unbeknownst to Kelsen, the real reason why Stöger-Steiner summoned him was because he suspected that he was working as a sort of agent for the Army High Command, which constantly challenged the Ministry's authority, and was the de facto editor of this new in-house journal in which Kelsen's article was to appear quite prominently at the head of its inaugural issue. From the Minister's perspective, then, in terms of internal power politics, it must have seemed as if one of his own legal officers wrote – read: worked – for the not so friendly side. To all of this, Kelsen (2007 [1947a]: 48) said, truthfully, that he simply had not known the internal context, and that he had 'no greater ambition' than to make available his juristic expertise to the Minister, and 'only' to him, which reassured Stöger-Steiner. Thus, in next to no time, in the autumn of 1917, Kelsen had his own office near the War Minister, working for him as a trusted legal and political advisor. This also meant that, over time, Kelsen had to report, directly, to the Kaiser, Karl I, Supreme Commander of the Imperial and Royal Armed Forces of the Austrian–Hungarian Empire.

Unlike Freud, who, as we shall see, inspired Kelsen's philosophy and political thinking in significant ways (and vice versa), to the best of my knowledge Kelsen said very little, or nothing, about the Great War: not a word about the politics and the foreign policy, nor anything about what surely was the only aspect of the war that deserves to be called 'great': the sheer horror, and the number of atrocities. But then, he was part of it all: serving in various Ministry functions and, in the end, in the highest echelons of imperial and royal power. As a government official, he knew that his role was to serve, rather than to comment; in his case, he was to serve the War Minister, and only the War Minister. He understood the need to keep a low public or political profile, and knew the difference that it makes to work inside the strategic machinery, rather than to look at it clinically from the outside. He knew what all this meant: to be loyal and to be low-key. At this stage, I do not want to make too much of it, but it appears that throughout his life and career, Kelsen – altogether a political realist – had mastered quite successfully what is a distinct art: knowing the political difference in time and space between when to speak up and when to work one's way silently, while always pursuing one overarching moral goal – speaking truth to power!

Now, the hour is late on this autumn night. The War Minister is in his nightgown when he receives Kelsen and hands him the cable itself. This latest US communication is yet again frank and firm about American war aims and Washington's terms of peace. More than half a year had passed since President Wilson, on 8 January 1918, had given, to a joint session of the US Congress, his historic Fourteen Points speech, outlining a set of principles and his vision for a post-war world order. Of the fourteen points, all in some ways both challenging and fascinating, the tenth was particularly important for Vienna: 'The peoples of Austria–Hungary, whose place among the nations we wish to see safeguarded and assured, should be accorded the freest opportunity to autonomous development' (Wilson 2006 [1918]: 405). The message was loud and clear. But then, that was America's position of more than six months ago; it might very well be that it was obsolete, outdated because of changing public dynamics, or at least drowned out by a mixture of domestic and international politics.

Kelsen takes the cable from the War Minister. We do not know exactly which one it was, but the strategic context, and Kelsen's autobiographical recollection of these events, point to the US telegram that President Wilson sent on 18 October 1918 and which, through Swedish intermediation, reached Vienna on the 20th. While Kelsen studies its content, going through point by point what Washington wants, Stöger-Steiner, still in his nightgown, is putting on his uniform jacket, and together they head from the Minister's private residence inside the *Kriegsministerium* toward his office. Walking along the corridors, they pass the Ministry's private ballroom, which, typically Viennese, was grand and glamorous. At this point the Minister slows down, turns to Kelsen, and mumbles that he actually feels quite embarrassed that, in terrible times of war like these, he resides in chambers as splendid as his in the Ministry, in the very heart of what is beautiful Ringstraße Vienna. A fair comment to be sure, to which Kelsen (2007 [1947a]: 50) responds drily: 'Especially, your Excellency, if one knows that one is the last Minister of War of the Monarchy.'

He was right, of course. Yet, as all senior government officials – or, for that matter, political appointees and staff – know only all too well, operating as they do, day in, day out, in the twilight zone of bureaucratic versus political loyalty, as well as political philosophy versus personal ethics, it is one thing to speak truth to power behind one's writing desk. It is quite another to confront senior public figures realistically with any ongoing or future dynamics of the balance of power – or explain, and report, in no uncertain analytical terms, what is likely to happen next if things unfold the way they currently look as if they will evolve. In the rather brutish business of national security and international politics, this means: do not be afraid to deliver bad news to the King, or the Kaiser, or the Minister; and do not be afraid that, although you are merely the messenger, you might even be killed.

Kelsen was, one might say, too good at what he did, and too clever in terms of *how* he did it, thereby avoiding serious trouble. Not so one of his most prominent students, Morgenthau, who was in many ways of different character, and who, unlike Kelsen, never worked inside government. That is, Morgenthau appeared to have underestimated domestic power politics, and perhaps overestimated, from the comfort of his professorial chair, his political abilities. Surely one of the earliest and most reasonable, yet also most forceful and vehement, critics of the Vietnam War, Morgenthau was to pay for voicing his strategic and moral concerns about this war so publicly. The State Department cut him off, ending his advisory role. His colleagues soon called him a Communist. The White House and the FBI collected dirt on him, known as 'Operation Morgenthau' (see Rösch 2015: 126). All the usual stuff of politics – nothing more, nothing less, really.

Much of Morgenthau's critical, or perhaps even Critical, inspiration was of Kelsenian origin: relating not so much to Vietnam, but to a scholar's fundamental role to speak truth to power. Morgenthau and many other Vietnam critics were totally right, in my view, to protest in the strongest terms against what they thought to be a war that either was not in the American national interest (Morgenthau) or, from a more pacifistic point of view, could not be justified in terms of any interest at all (anti-war movement). Morgenthau felt strongly about Vietnam; he wanted to speak up. And, no less intensely, he wanted to speak up about all problems – social, cultural and political – that deserved public intellectual criticism. It was a deep-seated conviction, scholarly and morally – as was impressed upon him by none other than his former teacher in Geneva. And at the time of the Guam Doctrine and the strategic turn towards the Vietnamisation of the Vietnam War, with Henry Kissinger as President Nixon's National Security Advisor, Morgenthau wanted to make known to his contemporaries his philosophical roots as a Kelsenian-inspired public intellectual.

Thus it happened, in the year in which Morgenthau was in the process of publishing *Truth and Power* (1970a), a collection of essays written during the 1960s and judged 'a major historical document of a troubled decade' (Hanrieder 1971: 879), that he reached out to his ageing teacher on the West Coast. Writes Morgenthau to Kelsen, in a letter dated 28 April 1970 (1970b): 'I can think of nobody worthier of the dedication of such a book than you. For if I understand the work of your life correctly, it has been its leitmotif to speak truth to power.'

Morgenthau meant exactly what he said, and he was right. If there is one all-encompassing theme in Kelsen's Pure theory of law and state, in Kelsen's philosophy and political thinking, it really is: to be *critical*. It did not take Kelsen even a week to have his words of appreciation typewritten and his letter of reply of 4 May 1970 back at Morgenthau's Manhattan apartment at 19 East 80th Street. In the end, Morgenthau was in a position to come up with what he wanted the whole world to see, which was a heartfelt yet most serious book dedication that in one clear sentence sums up everything that Kelsen and, for that matter, Morgenthau (1970a) stood and fought: 'To Hans Kelsen, who has taught us through his example how to speak Truth to Power.'

Now, imagine the situation in the War Ministry: there is the jurist and the War Minister. There is a reserve officer promoted rather quickly to Captain and a long-serving General. There is a thirty-seven-year-old and another who is two decades his senior. And then the underling says to his superior, in what is quite an intimate moment, that the very end is near, strategically, and also that *his* end is near. Naturally, as Kelsen (2007 [1947a]: 50) recalls the event, Stöger-Steiner's immediate reaction came quick as a shot: 'Are you crazy? How dare you say something that awful!' Who can blame him, really? Surely the 'old officer' had no illusions about the magnitude of the forthcoming military defeat. It was obviously, though, too much for the War Minister to admit to such a defeat: and what is more, it was clearly too much for him even to conceive of something so unthinkable as a truly European great power of several hundred years being in the process of being wiped off the map of world history.

But then, what else was there for Kelsen to say? The situation was not good, not even close to being at least a bit hopeful that things might eventually turn around. And, of course, Kelsen (2007 [1947a]: 50) kept on telling the War Minister how he saw and assessed it: 'Considering President Wilson's answer to our peace proposal, I see no prospect of preserving the monarchy.' He saw it all clearly. It really was over. Political realism! The strategic situation of Austria–Hungary had actually, and fundamentally, deteriorated since President Wilson's Fourteen Points speech. The nationalists had been pressing relentlessly for ever greater and even, in the final analysis, full independence; and what had changed too, keeping up with recent developments on the ground, was the strategic calculus of the Wilson government.

Kelsen, in that very moment, took the American telegram for what it was: a real exercise in the political realism of power politics. That is, he took it as a practical exercise in what matters most in international politics: either to have sufficient power and prevail, or *not* to have it and face the consequences. It is not that this particular cable had been a sort of epiphany for him about the workings of power politics (by all accounts, a pleonasm anyway). As we shall see, Kelsen had grasped well before the War Ministry episode what the political really meant, but it was with Stöger-Steiner that he, the hardnosed political realist, needed to be as clinical and analytical as he was as a Pure positivist, exactly because the situation required him to speak truth to power. So he was very quick to point out what the cable really said: that mere autonomy for Vienna and Budapest was no longer enough! It was crystal clear and even comprehensible why President Wilson (2006 [1918]) was

> obliged to insist that [the peoples of Austria–Hungary], and not he, shall be the judges of what action on the part of the Austrian–Hungarian Government will satisfy their aspirations and their conception of their rights and destiny as members of the family of nations.[2]

America was now fully committed to the cause of what were back then the Czechoslovaks and the Yugoslavs. Thus it really was the end of the Austrian–Hungarian Empire.

Only a few days later, on 31 October, Kelsen's work in the War Ministry formally ended. It was the date of his so-called demobilisation, and naturally enough under the circumstances, there was a farewell occasion. As it happened, it was the very day when, outside the Ministry, an angry mob had thrown stones at the Minister's car, and as a result, pieces of broken glass had cut Stöger-Steiner's cheek. It was, in many ways, tragic for the Minister, and on what was a Thursday, in Kelsen's (2007 [1947a]: 50) vivid memory, a deathly pale old man shook the young jurist's hand, saying to him rather emotionally: 'You were right. I am the last Minister of War of the Monarchy.'

By 11 November, his last day as *k. u. k.* War Minister, Stöger-Steiner was history. But Kelsen the jurist, political realist and widely recognised expert in constitutional and administrative law, moved on. And rather swiftly: As early as 7 November, only one week after he had left what was then the Imperial Royal War Ministry, he was re-hired by the new government of the Empire's successor state, the Republic of German-Austria. His new task, in the State Chancellery at the Ballhausplatz under Karl Renner, was to prepare the new and definitive Constitution for Austria – all the more remarkable for a man who only reluctantly studied law in the first place.

7 DANTE AND PHILOSOPHY

When, on 7 July in the summer of 1900, at the Akademisches Gymnasium, he had safely bagged the *Matura*, what Kelsen really wanted to do was to study, but *not* law. Instead, he needed to get the compulsory military service out of the way, which he did through entering the One-Year-Voluntary programme. And according to his plan, he then wanted to go on to the University of Vienna's School of Philosophy and enrol in philosophy, mathematics and physics. Things turned out differently. That he eventually chose a different academic path, that he did not follow through where his intellectual heart lay, was a consequential decision – and also one that Kelsen (2007 [1947a]: 33) said, even decades later, 'I have regretted all my life'.

What he in fact did, of course, was study at Vienna's School of Law, the Juridicum, founded in 1365 and one of the first law schools in Europe. But he did so reluctantly, and his choice was made mainly for practical reasons. It was the gap year in the *k. u. k.* Army, as Kelsen (2007 [1947a]: 33–4) recalls it, that made him change his mind: the military training, naturally more physical than cognitive, cost him or robbed him of his intellectual life, and over time, he had become more and more convinced that a degree in philosophy would merely allow him to become a schoolteacher. This was a prospect he abhorred, not least because of his own not-so-positive experience of early school life.

And so the making of Kelsen as one of last century's star jurists and timeless philosophers of law and the state – and fascinating progressive political realist – is really a tale of circumstances and chance. Sketching the bigger picture of where he was coming from is key, though, to understanding his personal and political philosophy, and the uniquely realistic style of his political thinking. He did become a law student; and he did become one of the best legal theorists of his generation, a timeless one to be sure. But then the curriculum at university was tedious, he thought, and many of the lectures were a waste of time – so much so that, in order to escape his total frustration, he decided, pretty much on his own, to do some serious work on Dante Alighieri – the so-called 'supreme realist' (Dirda 2007).

When he decided to go for a law degree, rather than doing philosophy, he knew that the chances were quite high that he would become a lawyer, though he hoped he might accomplish a career as a judge. Back then, he could not have foreseen that, not even two decades after he first set foot in one of the Juridicum's lecture halls, he would be a law professor, and a Constitutional judge at a court that he was about to help establish as part of his working out of Austria's definitive Constitution under Renner. It began bleakly, and pretty much stayed that way for many years, until the point when, on 18 May 1906, he held in his hands the degree of *Doctor iuris*. To Kelsen (2007 [1947a]: 34), even the first lectures that he had attended were a 'bitter disappointment'. Most professors were poor either in style or in content, or both. It was so bad, in his view, that after just a very short while, he simply stopped going to most lectures altogether – and instead, as Kelsen (2007 [1947a]: 35) says, began to immerse himself in 'reading philosophical works'.

Thus it happened that, in one of the lectures on the history of the philosophy of law, given by the widely recognised international law professor Leo Strisower, of Brody (like Kelsen's father), whom he held in high esteem, Kelsen came to know Dante, the famed Italian diplomat-turned-poet, who had authored a genuine work of political philosophy, *De Monarchia*. He read it at once, and he was so very hooked that he formed the desire to flesh out Dante's view on politics, law and the state in the historical context of life and ideas in the late Middle Ages, in the Republic of Florence and beyond. Motivated to pursue this intellectual endeavour seriously, he consulted Strisower for advice, but the Professor's message was loud and clear: do not do it; focus on finishing your law degree! Undeterred, Kelsen did it anyway, of course, which is in itself remarkable, given the rigid or quasi-authoritarian university culture at the time. And so eventually, Kelsen came to write what would turn out to be *The Political Philosophy of Dante Alighieri*. This monograph is *not* his doctoral dissertation. It was published in 1905, one year before he had even finished his law degree. It is a relatively major intellectual piece, given that it was written at the age of only twenty-four. And last not least, it is not so much a study in law as one in politics.

In other words, what we have in front of us here is a reluctant jurist, a man whose desire was to study philosophy, whose very first publication was a serious work in political philosophy – and as we shall see, this was all part of a formative experience, one that stayed with him literally for the rest of his life. Now, I do not want to start, or become embroiled in, a debate over whether Kelsen was more of a jurist or more of a political philosopher; my own view is that he surely was both. Building upon what I have argued in the introductory and previous chapters, my point is to emphasise that there really is *another Kelsen*, by which I mean: there is Kelsen the jurist, to be sure, yet there is also Kelsen the social and political philosopher, and what is more, at least to me, there is Kelsen the progressive political realist.

Put differently, there is a reason why Kelsen, once on American soil, eventually did *not* join Berkeley's Law School, but the Political Science department instead. One important element, to be sure, was that Kelsen's positivist Pure theory of Law was not at all in line with the American jurisprudential zeitgeist of natural law, legal realism, and the case method in American legal education. Thomas Reed Powell, then, Professor at Harvard Law, was neither wrong nor unfair when he wrote, in his 1942 letter of reference, that Kelsen 'is not at all a lawyer from our American standpoint'; or, to put it the other way round, Powell was probably right under the circumstances to say that Kelsen 'is a philosopher and sociologist [and] that in either political theory or in international law, or both, he would be a most acceptable classroom teacher in a Department of Government'.

One might add here that Kelsen would have also been a most acceptable addition to any Philosophy department, notably in questions of moral, political and social philosophy. His 1957 essay collection, *What is Justice? Justice, Law, and Politics in the Mirror of Science*, is really a most powerful statement and re-statement of what was his lifelong and firm moral conviction: that for justice, conceptual and political, there can be neither a rational nor an absolute definition. For now, it suffices that we take note of his self-image: when asked, in 1963, about his area of expertise, he wrote down, interestingly enough, two academic disciplines – Legal Theory and Social Philosophy – a critical admission that says a lot about his concept of a fundamental division of intellectual labour into essentially two camps. Kelsen the positivist jurist was to study the law as it *is*; and in some ways, Kelsen the normative philosopher was to study what the laws of a good society *ought* to be. And I want add here, coming back to this theme particularly in Chapters 3 and 4, that Kelsen the political realist was to study what the laws of a society and international *can* be.

What he did with Dante says quite a lot about his style of thinking. As Mónica García-Salmones Rovira (2013: 296) put it so well in her *Project of Positivism in International Law*: 'Kelsen's reading of Dante is very original, and . . . offers the reader the opportunity to taste what his international political and legal theory would become.' What Kelsen and Dante shared with much conviction, or what fascinated Kelsen in Dante's early lead, was the normative political idea of a universal legal order, a cosmopolitan project. Where Dante sought a world monarchy with a supreme judge settling disputes over a worldwide jurisdiction, Kelsen was to argue that the only ordering principle of international society that has a realistic chance of securing a stable peace would be the establishment of some kind of a positivist world state.

He was interested in how Dante handles the big questions: the timeless problems and everyday dilemmas of man, society and life that any genuine political philosopher would seek to solve. And, surely, among these questions are what makes the state, and what really justifies the wielding of power by the ruler over the ruled. As a political philosopher, mindful of the brute reality of history and its power struggles, Kelsen did not grapple with the politics of Dante from the safe standpoint of ivory-tower normativity, but instead sought to take political life as it really is, or as it really was in the thirteenth century: a world of awakened national consciousness, an Italy on the verge of a new post-Middle Ages era, and a wealthy city-state of Florence marked by a sustained battle between the reactionary forces of the nobility and the progressivism of the rising middle class, not to mention the legitimate demands of the proletariat, or the have-nots. Exploring Dante from such an angle, taking into account 'the whole of his great Weltanschauung and philosophy' (Kelsen 2007 [1905]: 138), he came to view Dante as quite a realistic philosopher of politics who clearly was ahead of his times.

Most notably, what Kelsen treasured in Dante's political philosophy was how the Florentine put You and Me at the centre of all things political, and how, out of this concern for individual liberty and happiness, grew what is the firmest of all Dante's convictions: the need for Us all to secure a kind of cosmopolitan peace – which is to be realised in Dante through a form of single world authority, the *universal monarch*, who is restrained by a global law with teeth, and separated from the Church. What is more, Kelsen could really relate to what he recognised as Dante's political realism in general, shining through in *De Monarchia* in particular: there always is history that we must reckon with; class struggles are relentless; and power is a much sought-after commodity. As Erich Auerbach (2007 [1929]: 174–5), still an authority on Dante, had put it so well: what makes Dante so powerful is that he confronts 'man, not as a remote legendary hero, not as an abstract or anecdotal representative of an ethical type, but as man as we know him in his living historical reality'. And, in fact, Kelsen does pretty much the same, using both Freudian insights and what the classical liberal economists had to say about human self-interest.

But then, as much as he could relate to the basic tenets of Dante's political thinking, favouring the triptych of strong government, individual liberty and a universal legal order, Kelsen proved, yet again, to be quite a political realist when the time came for him really to assess Dante's political project. Or per- haps we should say, to judge the merits of Dante's political *utopia*, because this is exactly how he thought of it in the final analysis. Again, he was, so to speak, wearing two hats. As a positivist legal theorist, arguing from the point of view of pure legal technique, he was happy to see universal law as centralised, and as enforceable, as it was in Dante's idea of the *universal monarch*. By stark con- trast, though, as a realist political philosopher rooted in first principles, notably a dim view of human nature, Kelsen (2007 [1905]) was unhappy with what he could not help but criticise scathingly as an 'ingenious utopia' (273) or a 'dreamt culture of humanity' (210) at work in *De Monarchia*. Ever heard about nationalism? About everyday cultural parochialism? And what about the brut- ish power struggles, even in the smallest of communities? In other words, as Oliver Lepsius (2017: 1164), law Professor at Münster, put it recently: Kelsen is one who 'sticks to the facts with a passion for reality'.

My point here was not to compare Kelsen with Dante, or to explore every nook and cranny of their political thinking. Rather, what I wanted to do is take the biographical fact of Kelsen writing his very first book on Dante's political philosophy, and then use this fact to get on with what is the main purpose of this book: to focus on Kelsen as a political thinker, and to re-balance him away from the idealistic camp, while portraying him for who he really was – a more-than-timely political philosopher who justifies open society ideals not in any naïve opposition to a realistic account of man, society and politics but instead *through* it.

What this Dante episode from Kelsen's formative university years tells us, then, is this: he was so frustrated with reading law that he took refuge in doing political philosophy. And at one and the same time, it tells us that this imaginative yet bold Dantean moment in this man's young life, with his thought only just beginning to emerge, was not at all episodic. In fact, what he took with him from this early Dante book (about which he once said that it was the only work for which he had not been criticised) were three core themes, all of which, over the years, would shimmer through more and more strongly in pretty much his entire philosophy and political thinking. The first was seeing humanity through the political and moral prism of a universal cosmopolitan order. Second was recognising the need for a stable and just peace through a world authority that has the ultimate enforcement mechanisms of law. Third was confronting realistically all things political, social or cultural that stand in the way of progress and peace. In terms of a chronological intellectual biography, Kelsen's 1905 Dante book gives us the first glimpse of what I argue is Kelsen the political realist: he applauds Dante's progressive political philosophy of a universal peace, individual liberty and human happiness, while judging this very progressivism against the not so rosy reality of what we can realistically expect from You and Me. This is not to say that Kelsen is a pessimistic fatalist, only that utopias are one thing, and a piecemeal progress through politics – through a careful balancing of interests – is quite another.

There is much, then, to suggest that Dante inspired Kelsen's own ideas of an international society as a unitary legal order, with coercive power sitting at the top, to a great extent. And what we know for sure is that Kelsen kept Dante very close to his heart for literally his whole life. On publication of Kelsen's Dante book, two years after the suicide of the notorious Otto Weininger, a self-hating thinker with whom Kelsen was friends, it was Leopold Weininger, a well-known Viennese goldsmith and Otto's father, who presented Kelsen with a 6-inch bust of Dante decorated with gold. It was a thoughtful gesture, and for the rest of his life Kelsen would have it standing, together with a picture of his father, Adolf, in clear sight on his writing desk. Surviving all the turbulent times between the Vienna of 1905 and the California of 1973, the bust is now in the possession of Kelsen's granddaughter, Anne Feder Lee (see Kelsen 2007 [1905]: Jestaedt's commentary on p. 150).

Now, it looks as though Dante was just the tip of the iceberg, precisely because Kelsen had always been a fan of literature and philosophy – and, in fact, it was Weininger, author of the influential 1903 shocker *Geschlecht und Character*, a 600-page philosophy of sexuality that Freud scorned as 'rotten' (quoted in Abrahamsen 1946: 55), who encouraged him to do philosophical work. At times they were closer, and at other times less so, personally and intellectually. But even half a century after Weininger's tragic premature death, Kelsen spoke very highly of his friend: he was a 'genius' to the world and an intellectual mentor. Says Kelsen (2007 [1947a]: 35): 'Weininger's personality and the posthumous success of his works have greatly influenced my decision to do scientific work.' It would be an exaggeration to say that the early intellectual life of Kelsen, notably the literary and philosophical part, was the product of his friendship with Weininger; but then, the influence is there. It was Otto's sister, Rosa Weininger, who gave Kelsen a copy of the 1892 novel *Mysteries*, a major work in psychological realism penned by the notorious Norwegian novelist Knut Hamsun, the Nobel Laureate in Literature of 1920, who would later turn into a lackey of Hitler (Gibbs 2009). As Rudolf Aladár Métall (1969: 3–6) put it so clearly, it was Rosa's gift that 'furthered his love for the Norwegian writer' and it was this early literary exposure to Hamsun's novels that 'presumably laid the basis for Kelsen's pessimistic Weltanschauung'.

Speaking of pessimism, this was a trait, both personal and cultural, that defined Kelsen's intellectual milieu. This was Schorske's fin-de-siècle Vienna, a zeitgeist that looked out upon a world of pleasure and pain, optimism and pessimism, science and irrationality, highs and lows. To borrow a phrase from Miles Hollingworth (2013: ix), philosopher and writer, it was a zeitgeist marked by some Augustinian battles, and the recognition that when 'we battle the indignities of flesh and death . . . we keep a foot in either camp, a little in heaven, a little in hell'. The young Kelsen was soon to become a leading figure of what we call Viennese Modernism, embodying the good, the bad and the ugly coming out of this progressive age. Yet, what needs emphasising is that, through his friendship with Weininger, what he came in touch with in his formative years was, actually, a strongly realist reading of social and political life, including a heavy dose of human nature realism through reading, *inter alia*, David Hume, Arthur Schopenhauer, Charles Darwin and, not least, Friedrich Nietzsche.

For the young Kelsen, to be sure, from Dante's political philosophy; from the cultural pessimism and the human nature realism of Weininger and Hamsun; from Hume's political realism; from Schopenhauer's realistic fable of the porcupines; from Darwin's earth-shattering biological theory of natural selection; from Nietzsche's obsession with the will to power – that is, from all these realisms – it was not a long walk to Freud's Berggasse apartment.

8 FREUD AND ECONOMICS

Who would have thought that the Pure positivist saw in the creator of psychoanalysis a true example? What are Ludwig van Mises and Joseph Schumpeter doing here? And why was Peter Drucker, a pioneer of twentieth-century management theory, *not* really fond of Uncle Hans?[3]

And yet – at least in my opinion, in this book anyway – of all the men in Kelsen's fascinatingly rich and diverse intellectual milieu, perhaps the most important was really the Viennese doctor, whom Abraham Kaplan (1957: 224), the Odessa-born American philosopher, called 'the most thoroughgoing realist in western thought'. Now, make no mistake, the task in this section, to which I return at some length in Chapter 3, of exploring what I call Kelsen's Freudian moment, is driven less by an über-interest in intellectual history but rather, instead, by my analytical ambition to see Kelsen for who he was – a realistic political thinker – and by my normative (over-)ambition to flesh out a Kelsenian vision of a progressive political realism. One important element in my re-reading of Kelsen is therefore to identify in his intellectual milieu the role of Freud.[4] Indeed, psychoanalysis continues to provoke, most notably because one really can use Freudian insights for many different purposes, cultural and political, thereby challenging the real limits of You and Me, and Us; and ever since Freud's 1930 *Civilization and Its Discontents*, there has been a great deal of debate about Freud's politics and their place in the history of Western political thinking (see Roazen 1969; Schuett 2010b; Zaretsky 2017). That said, there is much truth in what the late American political philosopher and intellectual Jean Bethke Elshtain (1989: 54), former Laura Spelman Rockefeller Professor of Social and Political Ethics at Chicago's Divinity School, stated with astute clarity: 'As between the "realists" and "idealists" of international relations discourse, Freud would be one of the leading realists – tough and no-nonsense.'

From first to last, Kelsen's interest in psychoanalysis was huge. And in fact, his interest went way beyond a mere reading of this or that, or of what Freud set out to tell Vienna and Western civilisation. To be sure, in the heyday of Viennese Modernism, who among the cultural and intellectual intelligentsia would *not* have read at least a bit of Freud? My point here, though, is that Kelsen really engaged with psychoanalysis. He knew what he was doing with it, and he knew how to use Freudian ideas for his own purposes, intellectual and methodological.

He had all the personal links to Freud and the inner circle of orthodox psychoanalysis: both to the 15–20-cigars-a-day neurologist at the very centre of this new psychology, and to some of his most important followers. His father, Adolf Kelsen, knew Freud through B'nai B'rith, as both were of a similar generation, born in the 1850s. Hans's wife, Margarete, was friendly with Freud's daughter, Anna, an eminent psychoanalyst in her own right. One of Hans's close friends was the Viennese lawyer and core Freud intimate, Hanns Sachs, a practising member of Freud's ultra-loyal Secret Committee that was tasked with keeping psychoanalysis pure. He had links to Eduard Hitschmann and Paul Federn, two first-generation Viennese analysts who were very loyal to Freud throughout their lives; and also to Paul's son, Ernst Federn, a Marxian émigré and analyst, who would return to Vienna in 1972, thanks to then-Chancellor Bruno Kreisky's initiative. He was also impressed by Wilhelm Stekel, a former close disciple of Freud, who would later break away from the orthodoxy and turn into one of Freud's most outspoken critics.

It all started in Vienna, while certainly not ending there. As early as around the age of twenty, Kelsen discussed psychoanalysis with his friend Otto Weininger. Most likely at the invitation of Hanns Sachs, he went to Freud's Wednesday evening meetings at Berggasse 19, where a select group of doctors, intellectuals and laypersons talked neuropathology. He joined the Vienna Psychoanalytic Society in 1911, the year he passed the *Habilitation*. In the *Sommerfrische* (an extended summer break in the countryside) of 1921, in Seefeld, Kelsen and Freud went for walks in the sun of Austrian Tyrol. And three decades later – on 19 December 1953, to be precise – Kelsen, already in America, volunteered to do a psychoanalytic interview with the Viennese émigré Kurt Eissler (n.d.), a Manhattan-based analyst and founder of the Sigmund Freud Archives. In the 1950s and 1960s, Eissler sought out intellectuals, and colleagues, relatives and patients of Freud, and had them talk about their thoughts on the man (see Rathkolb 2000: 85; García-Salmones Rovira 2013: 161); Edith Kurzweil (2008), the late American writer with Viennese roots and last editor of *Partisan Review*, aptly called him the 'conquistador of the unconscious'.

Kelsen's attraction to Freud was driven by two elements. One was that he was interested in this new philosophy of human nature, and in all that it really meant: we are not as good as some would have us believe, not least because we cannot just wish away our hellish desires and earthly interests. The other point that fascinated Kelsen was the new method of *doing* psychoanalysis. Kelsen and Freud – and, for that matter, all political realists – are agreed that whatever we wish or hope to see out there, the bottom line is what Rousseau (1997b [1762]: book I, paragraph 2) advised us of in the *Contrat social*: there is no point in *not* 'taking men as they are'. This amounts to the same thing as the quip from the first Chancellor of West Germany, Konrad Adenauer, *der Alte* from the Rhineland: 'Take people as they are, there are no other ones' (quoted in Köhler 2005: 205). Yet, to think and act like a human nature realist in a Freudian mould is one thing; it is quite another to use psychoanalysis as the intellectual sub-structure with which to confront the old, but venerable, question of the nature of political communities. What Freud was able to do, then, was to help Kelsen conquer, or demystify, the concept of the state: a revolutionary act, and one that had been long overdue in Western jurisprudence, and the analytical and normative study of politics. His critical unmasking of natural law through psychoanalysis is perhaps nowhere clearer than in the 1924 English version of a talk that Kelsen had given, three years earlier, on 30 November 1921, at one of Freud's Wednesday evening meetings. It was published in what, back then, was Freud's flagship journal, *The International Journal of Psychoanalysis*, under a rather tedious title: 'The Conception of the State and

Social Psychology: With Special Reference to Freud's Group Theory' (Kelsen 1924; see also Kelsen 1922a). But what lies in this dense article of almost forty pages is a powerful attempt to do away with organicist theories of the state, the ideological gibberish of a *raison d'État*, and the lofty notion of a timeless set of self-evident national interests.

At the time, in 1921, Kelsen was particularly impressed with Freud's core logic, or Freud's core methodological logic, of *Group Psychology and the Analysis of the Ego* (1921), which sprang fresh from the neurologist's mind and typewriter, and was important in two ways. First, Freud set out to explain the inner and behavioural dynamics of the masses on the basis of changes in the psychology of the individual mind. It meant, according to Freud, that all facts of social psychology are necessarily facts of individual psychology. Second, Freud sought to hasten his investigation into the anatomical structure of the mind. Almost instantly, Kelsen the Pure positivist realised that Freud was a major ally in the scientific attempt to free the study of law, and concept of the state, from the ancient myth of Nature, or God, or causality. It is the analytical task of the next chapter, called 'Kelsen's Freudian Moment', to explore in greater depth how Freud's psychoanalysis relates to Kelsen's neo-Kantian theory of law, state and international legal order. For the present purposes, it suffices to say that the one core revolutionary moment in Kelsen's philosophy was to show that from a Pure perspective there is no psychological concept of the state, nor a sociological one. If one seeks to establish a scientific jurisprudence, one that is based on a specific autonomy of law, there is only a juristic concept of the state: the state as a centralised legal order – the state as a normative order, *not* a natural one.

He must have thought that Freud was almost too good to be true. When you come to think of it, at a time when Kelsen was hellbent on ridding Western philosophy and legal and political thinking of the mythical notion of the Hegelian state, here was Freud: a man, living within walking distance, with the latest innovation of human nature in the bag, who could provide a scientific psychology lambasting the concept of a *Massenseele*, or group mind, which the likes of Gustave Le Bon had sought to popularise. Using the latest Freudian psychology – that is, using psychoanalytical methodology and applying it to the question of the concept of the state – Kelsen was able to resolve reified social wholes such as the Hegelian state into the only reality there is: You, and Me, and all the good, bad and ugly that will come from our vicious intra-psychic battles between the id, ego and super-ego.

And, there is so much more. Perhaps one might be tempted to think of Kelsen as a sort of committed methodological individualist who, pretty much in line with the zeitgeist of Viennese Modernism, was merely toying with Freud, perhaps quite similarly to many others at the time. Who did not? And yes, as we have already seen and will be seeing time and again, he was exactly of that kind of intellectual persuasion that takes a solid conception of human nature as the core starting point of pretty much all philosophy and political thinking. But then, reducing the Kelsen/Freud relationship to a zeitgeist phenomenon would not do justice to how rich the exchange between these two men actually was. For one thing, Kelsen talked to Freud at a time when his colleagues at Vienna's Law faculty either had little clue about psychoanalysis, found it obscure for the study of law or waved it off with anti-Semitic undertones (Rathkolb 2000: 88–90). What is more important, though, is to acknowledge that Kelsen and Freud shared a fearless and bold willingness to confront all forms of animistic or mythical styles of thought. And so let us say it out loud here: it is primitive to think of the state as a real thing, or as an organism, or as a person endowed with a will. It is pre-modern. It is anti-democratic. And as the Kelsenian-inspired political realist (in Chapter 5) says, there is no such thing as a *national* interest.

He was such a staunch methodological individualist that, in the end, Kelsen even accused Freud of having hypostatised the state. He feared Freud would think that what makes a political community, or a state, could be explained by the fact of mass cohesion or a sort of collective libidinal structure; he was therefore inclined to think that the Freudian concept of the state was a sociological one, treating the state as a mass reality. On this point, though, Kelsen really may have over-interpreted what Freud was actually saying. As Freud (1921: 87, note 2) pointed out in a footnote added to the 1921 edition of *Group Psychology and the Analysis of the Ego*:

> I differ from what is in other respects an understanding and shrewd criti-cism by Hans Kelsen . . . when he says that to provide the 'group mind' with an organization of this kind signifies a hypostasis of it – that is to say, implies an attribution to it of independence of the mental processes in the individual.

I must say I will not be a judge in this, but I can see why Kelsen – who really has proved to be quite super-anxious about never, ever reifying the state – argued the way he was arguing. Let us leave it at that here. And so, most of the time they were agreed, and on this point they just were not.

The fact, biographical and intellectual, remains the same anyway: Kelsen was very close to Freud, and he admired how Freud attempted to resolve *Our* many myths, hiding as they are behind the fig leaf of ideology, into the real deeds of real people. And between the two men there was this fascinating back-and-forth about the use, and abuse, of psychoanalysis for the human sciences. What is more, as Étienne Balibar (2017: 228), the Marxist philosopher and one of the French Communist Party's eminent intellectuals, hypothesises, it may have been Kelsen's astute critique of Freud that 'must have pushed Freud toward a theoretical inflection if not an outright turning point'. The question is whether Kelsen's critique of 1921 that posited the state as a normative coercive order, *not* a libidinal one, led Freud to develop the concept of the super-ego. It may be a mere coincidence that Freud, in *The Ego and the Id*, published in April 1923 – not even two years after Kelsen's Wednesday evening lecture – stated there is a threefold division of the mind, with the powerful super-ego functioning as a coercive agent that keeps the id at bay. If that were so, this would be Freud's answer to Kelsen's question: why do we obey the law? Do we do so, to paraphrase Balibar (2017: 240), because we have the state inside the head?

Now, in many ways, Kelsen was a methodical Freudian human nature realist. However, as much as he saw the real living-together of You and Me as a rather messy affair, driven by instincts and desires, there was no way he would allow his Pure theory of law, and political thinking, to become dominated by any sort of a determinist essentialism. Throughout his life, he fought hard against all forms of anti-democratic ideologies, notably natural law theories. And to him, and for us to understand, there were three core concepts that formed a powerfully progressive yet realist triad: individuals, interests and imputation.

And so, of course, it is not really that implausible that there were also links between the Pure theorist and Austrian School economists such as Mises, Schumpeter or Hayek. For a start, Kelsen and Mises were school-friends, not only enjoying the same liberal education taught at the Akademisches Gymnasium, but sitting together in the same classroom. Out of that shared experience, they had developed a lifelong friendship that survived their time in Vienna, Geneva and the United States. In fact, when Hitler's Nazis sacked Kelsen and pushed him out of Cologne in 1933, it was Mises who at once sought to initiate a *Kaffeehaus* meeting in Vienna with Lord Beveridge, then-director of the London School of Economics and Political Science (LSE); as a result of their deliberations, the three of them jointly lobbied the Rockefeller Foundation until a new position was secured for Kelsen at the Institut Universitaire des Hautes Études Internationales. As it happened, Mises would also come to Geneva roughly a year later and stay there until they both fled to America in 1940.

What is more, in the autumn of 1925, Kelsen was best man for Joseph Schumpeter at what was his friend's second wedding, to Annie Reisinger, who tragically died in childbirth a year later, an event that triggered Schumpeter's manic-depressive episodes. And in the early 1920s, the left-liberal Kelsen co-examined, with Othmar Spann, a notorious figure in the Conservative Revolution, Hayek's dissertation on the theory of imputation, a work that had been supervised by the Austrian School's first-generation giant Friedrich von Wieser.

Kelsen was impressed by Wieser, who was a *Doctor iuris* stemming from an old and distinguished Viennese family. At the same time as Kelsen was the *k. u. k.* War Minister's legal advisor in the *Kriegsministerium*, Wieser in fact was *k. u. k.* Minister of Commerce. As a young law student, and bored by just about all of the law professors, Kelsen regularly attended Wieser's lectures in political economy, and was soon taken by the latter's clear focus on what has proved to be very systematic analysis. More specifically, Kelsen was impressed by Wieser's argument that there is actually little causation in the realm of economics, but that much of what is going on in markets is better understood as imputation. Contra Socialist economic theory, it really means this, as Wieser put it: 'if one wants to set forth a rule about the value of the products in relation to the productive goods, then it does not read "it is" but rather "it ought to be"' (quoted in Silverman 1984: 387). The value of any given good, then, is not at all directly related to the labour that goes into its production, as the Marxists would have it. Rather, the value of this or that good actually depends on how much value You and Me attribute, or impute, to exactly this or that good. There is nothing natural, or causal, or inherent, or objective in all of this; instead, the value of any given good is, to the very core, quite a subjective matter. In turn, this depends on the marginal utility that You and Me attribute, or impute, to any one of these given goods. In turn, this depends on one very simple thing: what is it that we want to have? Or, put differently: what is it that is in our interest?

To be sure, I am not interested here in the question of whether Kelsen's Pure theory of law and state has its roots, in any meaningful way, in the core theoretical basis of the Austrian School of Economics (see Silverman 1984; García-Salmones Rovira 2013). What I want to show is where Kelsen was coming from, who his friends were and in what circles he was moving. I am interested in all the bits and pieces that help us sketch out the intellectual biography of a man who, it would seem, had been socialised in ways that would not allow for a utopian or idealist to develop, let alone flourish. You know where this is going: like pretty much all of the classical realists, particularly Morgenthau, Kelsen too was an arch-methodological individualist. Surely, as a Freudian-inspired thinker, he would subscribe to the very position – voiced, for example, by Morgenthau (1930a: 4) – that we have 'no other access to the knowledge of . . . social facts or social structures than through individual beings'.

So, yes, there is Kelsen's strong insistence on methodological individualism as a fundamental analytical and normative principle in philosophy and the human sciences. We can see how convinced he was that, although we are all haunted by our drives and desires, we none the less tend to think and act in terms of what we express as our interests, be it at the ballot box or in the markets. And, contra Marxists and structuralists of any other kind, to him it makes little sense to speak, or complain, about impersonal forces at work in the realm of politics and economics, or, for that matter, international politics. There are none: it is all about You, and Your Interest. In other words, there is much Freud in Kelsen, but then, as Judge Posner (2001: 2) pointed out almost two decades ago, if we explore the intellectual sub-structure and methodology of Kelsen's Pure positivism, we can see that there is a great deal of 'congeniality to the economic approach'.

One might say that Kelsen lived and breathed economics. Certainly, he was never a banker or the like, and as much as he had his feet quite firmly in both Theory and Practice, he never worked in the realm of business. But then, through his father, Adolf, a small-business owner, he would know the reality of business cycles: the freedom, the risks, supply and demand. Through Wieser, he would know that markets do not really exist, but are abstractions mirroring merely human interests and actions in an aggregated form. And through Adolf Drucker, a very senior bureaucrat in the *k. u. k. Handelsministerium* or Trade Ministry, father of management guru Peter Drucker and a Grand Master in Austria's Freemasonry, he was positioned as close to the epicentre of Vienna's economic intelligentsia as you could possibly be at the time. He met his future wife through Adolf Drucker, who was married to Karoline Bondi, the sister of Margarete, meaning that Kelsen was part of the Drucker family. And now guess who the regular guests in the Drucker villa in Döbling, Vienna's affluent Nineteenth District, really were? Naturally, the likes of Mises, Schumpeter, Hayek and many more.

Kelsen's links and access to what were Vienna's most vibrant circles and spearheads of economics were intellectual, methodological and personal. These links were so close, and Kelsen around the dinner table so often, that Peter Drucker, who had the luxury of soaking up at an early age the latest gossip and hottest news emerging from Vienna's many different circles through the eyes and ears of those who were at the centre of the many storms, once revealed: 'I couldn't stand the ultra-rationality of my Uncle Hans' (quoted in Drucker Society, n.d.). And, yes, by all means he was an almost hyper-rational man. That was so because, as a Freudian, he was acutely aware that the only real safeguard against the worst excesses of a Schmittian-style mass politics rests with how each one of us handles our worst impulses. Also, he was convinced (rightly so) that to be reasonable and rational is extra-important not only in the realm of science, but also in the realm of real power – the state.

9 GENERALS AND GOVERNMENTS

Kelsen was a man steeped in the culture of a city hanging in the balance, rocked by old forces and new minds. As Carl Schorske (1979) put it, at the time Vienna was a hotbed fuelled both by 'acutely felt tremors of social and political disintegration' (xviii) and by 'great intellectual innovators' (viii). Kelsen was part of this mix, and himself a mix: a pessimist and an optimist. A man of theory and action. Of war and peace. A positivist jurist and a normative philosopher. A liberal and a realist. Very rational and passionate. Calm and candid. He is not easy to grasp. Like many other towering figures in Western thought, we cannot press him squarely into our neatly confined boxes. Let us take, for example, E. H. Carr (1939: 19–26), who distinguishes political idealists from political realists: while the former are typically theory-loving intellectuals, the latter tend to go for the real world, confronting statecraft as it is, and surviving it as bureaucrats do. If that were so, what then would we make of, let us say, Morgenthau or Herz? And, likewise, what of Kelsen?

In many ways, it is almost impossible to be more theoretical than Kelsen. He presented us with what really is a Pure theory of law, state and international legal order. And even if one were in total disagreement with him over his positivist project, any fair-minded observer would none the less recognise that his work is a work of genuine theory at a most profound level. This is not to say, however, that Pure positivism is built on lofty ideas or assumptions, nor that Kelsenian methodology is impractical or of no use in the real world (ask the Schmittians why they are so afraid of him). Kelsen hits the nail on the head when he argues (1932: 144; quoted in García-Salmones Rovira 2013: 266) that the Pure theory's mix of methodological individualism with Kantian imputation makes it a 'realist theory' (see also García-Salmones Rovira 2013). And similarly, Martti Koskenniemi (2001: 245), in *The Gentle Civilizer of Nations*, is right that Kelsen's Pure theory

> was by no means a Lebensfremd abstraction. On the contrary, as Kelsen himself stressed, it intervened in politics in the way a critique of ideology did: by revealing the political content of theories that had been thought of as neutral.

Kelsenian legal *theory*, in short, has proved to be a pretty *practical* tool, helping us unmask pre-modern ideas and anti-democratic visions of statecraft. Why else would Kelsen have many foes on the left and right? What is more, though – and I say that with respect to many of today's self-styled foreign-policy realists who appear to be quite armchair (more on this in Chapter 5) – Kelsen's track record of real work in the real world of politics and power, in turbulent times of Fascism and war, is, in fact, quite impressive. That is, on E. H. Carr's take, Kelsen shows himself to have been both an idealist and a realist.

He was by no means some kind of naïve ivory-tower idealist who lived as a recluse in a distant fairy-tale land. Even if he had wanted to escape reality, Kelsen could not have escaped history, or the politics of his time. In Vienna, during the *Dispensehen* crisis, at a time when he was a life-tenured judge at Austria's Constitutional Court, powerful Catholic-conservative circles and their press organs agitated against him, practically forcing him out of Austria (Neschwara 2009). In Cologne, the Nazis dismissed him from his chair, more or less overnight (Lepsius 2009). In Prague, at the German University on 22 October 1936, a violent anti-Semitic demonstration took place at Kelsen's first lecture, marking the beginning of the end of his time in Europe (Ladavac 2009; Osterkamp 2009). And in America, he had to fight yet another battle – the war against Nazi Germany. Now, this was the stuff of which his life was made. This was the kind of political reality he faced. Kelsen's life is really a 'tragic story' (von Bernstorff 2010: 273) of what Eric Hobsbawm (1995 [1994]), the pre-eminent English Marxist historian with Viennese roots, called the age of extremes.

War was raging once again. And once again Europe was in the middle of it all. We are not in the autumn of 1918, though. Kelsen was not in Vienna, once the grand capital of a European great power, where he had grown up and, for a half a century, had had a good life. Neither was he operating out of the corridors of power at Stubenring 1, or out of what used to be the *k. u. k.* War Ministry, now under the flag of Nazi Germany and staffed by the generals, officers and soldiers of the *Wehrmacht*. This time, it was all different. It was late spring in the United States. Rather than the grand chambers of a dying monarchy's government, he found himself in one of the many office buildings of a soon-to-be superpower. It was a Friday – 5 May 1944, to be most precise – one month short of D-Day, when Kelsen, as the delegate of the Foreign Economic Administration (FEA), was sent to Washington for an inter-agency meeting at the State Department. The strategic topic to be discussed was clear enough: what to do with Austria after the Nazis?[5]

It was not his first assignment in government. And he had seen it all before. States come and go, are born and die. If history proves anything at all with any degree of certainty, it is that states are locked in some kind of perennial struggle for power and peace, for security and prosperity, fighting the occasional battles over ideas and interests too. Some presidents and prime ministers are better statesmen/stateswomen or diplomats than others, and some political communities, mainly for reasons of great power politics or geography or both, just have to live under some kind of permanent and real threat of conquest, occupation and annexation. And so, born as he was in what Hobsbawm (1988a [1962]; 1988b [1975]; 1989 [1987]) and also I. G. Ehrenburg (1972 [1962]), a Soviet cosmopolitan writer, called the 'long' nineteenth century, at the beginning of the 'age of empire', though blessed with a long life, Kelsen witnessed pretty much all of the real-life dramas and political upheavals that the peoples of his native Austria had to endure: Austria–Hungary under a Kaiser. The Great War and the mass slaughter. The provisional Republic of German-Austria, a rump state. The democratic Republic of Austria, or the so-called *Erste Republik*. Next the quasi-fascist Federal State of Austria, or *Ständestaat*. Then, of course, Nazi Germany, the *Anschluss*. There followed World War II and the fight against the gas chambers. After that, the democratic Republic of Austria, the *Zweite Republik*, under Allied control until 1955. And thereafter, a fully independent, democratic Austria – whose Constitution to this day is that of 1920, re-enacted as it was in April 1945, so as to ensure a modicum of constitutional continuity. One might say it is Kelsen's Constitution, and it is the one still in place, even after Austria joined the European Union in 1995.

He had the opportunity to co-draft a Constitution from scratch, and knew of course that positive law equals *ought*: that is to say, he knew that positive law equals political *ought*, which, in turn, equals politics, reflecting the distribution of power and ideas in any given society at any given time. In a televised address to the Austrian public in 1960 on the occasion of the fortieth anniversary of the Austrian Constitution of 1920, aired by the Österreichischer Rundfunk (ORF), the national public radio and television broadcaster established in 1955, Kelsen (1960b) recalls how it all came about:

> It was then-Chancellor Dr Karl Renner, who had drafted the provisional constitution of the German–Austrian Republic, who tasked me to work out the draft for the definitive constitution. In doing so, he stipulated two political principles as guidelines: the principle of a parliamentary democracy, and the principle of a decentralisation that corresponded to the fact that the Austrian Republic consisted of autonomous states, but with the qualification that this decentralization should not overly constrict the authority of the central government. I believed that in terms of legal technique I could perform this task most successfully through the drafting of a Federal State Constitution.

There was very little time. In October of 1918, from the *k. u. k.* War Ministry, he had to watch the failed eleventh-hour rescue mission by Kaiser Karl: the so-called *Völkermanifest* to the peoples of Cisleithania, in the monarchy's north-western region, which would have granted all factions represented in the Imperial Council their own national assemblies. And since that failed, only a few days later, in early November, at the Palais Modena at Herrengasse 7, today the seat of Austria's Ministry of the Interior, Kelsen found himself working for Renner, Chancellor of a new state.[6]

The popular image of Kelsen is that he was a Kantian-inspired professor of a Pure law, a Pure positivistic formalist to the core. Certainly, this is not false if one looks at what the Pure theory of law was meant to do: put the study of law and international law on a new methodological footing. Yet, in many important ways, such descriptions of, or pigeon-holes for, Kelsen are not entirely correct either. What they tend to leave out is the fact that he was, at one and the same time, a frontline man.

And thus it was that in 1967, three decades after he fled Europe and half a century after the fateful autumn events of 1918, an eighty-six-year-old Kelsen asked a visiting law professor from Baden, the old-world *Kaiserstadt* situated in the southern foothills of the Vienna Woods, if the electric tram-train service between the Kärtnerring, opposite the Vienna State Opera, and Baden was still running. The answer was (and is): yes, operating as smoothly as it always has (Schambeck 2015). The more serious background to this story is that, in fact, Kelsen used the so-called Badner Bahn whenever he had to go to Baden: not only did the Emperor have a private residence there, but also, since 1917, the picturesque spa town housed the headquarters of the High Command of the Austrian–Hungarian Army. The truth is that, even though Kaiser Karl had signed off on the *Völkermanifest*, as soon as it became clear, within days, that this rescue attempt would fail badly, the Emperor re-considered a strategic course of action that Kelsen had suggested all along – which was to set up a committee of trusted delegates of the various peoples, tasked with preparing for, and carrying out, the orderly liquidation of the monarchy, and the creation of nation-states on the basis of a nation's right to self-determination, so as to avoid economic and political catastrophe for all.

Eventually, Karl gave the nod, and together with Heinrich Lammasch, a retired *Hofrat* and Emeritus Professor of Law, Kelsen went to see him in Baden, where Lammasch was officially tasked with being lead negotiator between the various groups and peoples. The negotiations failed, but rather than resigning the Kaiser's mandate, Lammasch proposed that Prime Minister Max Hussarek be dismissed, and that Lammasch would lead a new government. Kelsen was sceptical, not least because the political situation on the ground was pretty hopeless; and so, when Lammasch tried to lure Kelsen by offering him an elevated position in his *Ministerratspräsidium*, the Prime Minister's Office, he declined. History was to prove him right once again: the Lammasch Cabinet, widely referred to as the *Liquiditätsministerium*, or liquidation cabinet, was finished within just a few days, and Kaiser Karl gave up his throne on 11 November 1918. In many ways, and more than once, Kelsen the political realist could obviously grasp or tell, better than others, from which direction the wind was blowing in concrete political circumstances. Recall too that he accepted Renner's invitation to co-draft the new Constitution *prior* to Karl's abdication.

These were tumultuous times, to say the least; it is not that often that world history, or world politics, chews up an empire, spitting out a rump state and other new nation-states. But then Kelsen the political realist was never one for idealistic romanticism about the great powers. He saw things *not* how many of his colleagues in the War Ministry and wider bureaucracy wished them to be, but how they really *were*: that is, how power and interests are distributed among the most relevant political actors on the ground. From first to last in his life and career, he operated on the basis of what was quite a methodical approach to government and political and international life, and did so when co-drafting the 1920 Constitution (Busch 2009: 75).

Thanks to his longstanding work in legal theory, he was very good by this time at matters of legal technique – not only at the drawing board in the lecture hall, but also when he had to apply the Pure logic of law to the political reality of government: the sort of 24/7 feeding frenzy in which the heavy demands of high-level politics, partisan power play and bureaucratic shadow jealousies relentlessly prey on the one civil servant who has a strategic task at hand. Kelsen, then, had to balance the demands coming from three directions. First, there were Renner's priorities. Second, there was a tri-partite government manned by the Social Democratic Party, Christian Social Party and Greater German People's Party to be handled, surely an ideological stretch. And third, there were two heavyweight departments in the Chancellery: one for constitutional matters, and the other for administrative reform, each of them trying to feed in their own ideas. Kelsen managed it all quite well, however, securing for himself considerable room for manœuvre. When Renner had to leave Vienna for the Château de Saint-Germain-en-Laye on 12 May 1919, in order to negotiate with the Allied powers the terms of the formal dissolution of Cisleithania and the future of Austria, he gave Kelsen a fair bit of leeway. And it worked well. The first draft reached Renner in July. Just a year later, with minor changes only, the work was all done. On 1 October 1920, the Constituent National Assembly passed what was (and still is) the Austrian Federal Constitution.

Forever the legal positivist, as well as the political realist, Kelsen of course knew all along that what really matters for a constitution to work is, in the final analysis, the political will to make it work; it is trivial, but in politics surely nothing is fixed (see Chapter 5). He had seen the 1920 Constitution abolished by the Nazis and then saw it brought back on 1 May 1945 – with Karl Renner yet again as head of government, this time as the Federal Chancellor of the Republic of Austria, the so-called *Zweite Republik*. Recalls Kelsen in the 1960 ORF address:

> The question as to the efficiency and usefulness of the Austrian Constitution is, for someone like me, who has not lived in Austria for more than thirty years, difficult to answer. As far as I am able to tell from afar, the Austrian Constitution has proved itself excellently. Proof is the fact that after the liberation of Austria from Nazi rule, this Constitution got re-enacted. So, we shall hope that this Constitution will remain for a long time the legal foundation of a free and independent Austria and be of use and profit for Her citizens.

Certainly, except for the regular attacks by the Schmittian Right, Kelsen is seen to this day as a most important figure in Austria's cultural and political history. And as I want to emphasise here (call me biased), I would be hard pressed to name many public figures at the intersection of academia and government who were as cool and rational in their strategic and political assessments as Kelsen.

Now, he had been away from Europe for not even five years when he found himself working for the American foreign intelligence community. Unlike his friend Mises, who continued his Viennese lifestyle in New York, running private seminars similar to those he held in his office at the Stubenring in the 1920s (see Hülsmann 2007: part vi), Kelsen did not feel entirely comfortable in what was to become his new home for another thirty years. Truthfully, one reason was that the English language was not at all easy for him. In fact, after the Nazis had sacked him from his chair at Cologne, when was sitting down with Mises and Beveridge in a Viennese *Kaffeehaus* to discuss future options, he actually declined to go to the LSE, the real reason being that he feared that his English was not good enough. This was true: as James G. Lowenstein (1994: 14), a former Ambassador to Luxembourg and assistant to Kelsen at the Naval War College, recalled, he really 'couldn't write English too well'.

Over sixty at the time, he ranked as a kind of Old World legal superstar. He had written tons of books and journal articles. He had seen pretty much everything that was to be seen in academia and in practice: that is to say, he worked in both the executive branch and the judicial branch of the Austrian government, at very critical stages and handling enormous tasks. Of course the Americans wanted to have him as a strategic expert on what was, for both American and Allied policy-makers, a very imminent challenge: what to do with a new Austria soon to be freed from Nazi rule? What would make Vienna a good future citizen of international society? Or, what amounts to the same pressing question: what could possibly be done to avoid yet another major war in Europe?

The FEA sent him to the inter-agency meeting at the State Department. The terms of his one-year contract, starting February 1944, stated that he could stay at Berkeley, and while having no teaching commitments, fly in and out of Washington every three weeks. A pretty impressive group of bureaucrat-scholars was assembled. One was David Harris, Associate Chief of the Central European Division at State, who after the war would become a Full Professor of History at Stanford, teaching international diplomacy and European intellectual history. He was flanked by three colleagues: Harry N. Howard, an expert in diplomatic history and Eastern European affairs, who after a post-war posting in Beirut would return to academia, taking up a professorship at the American University in Washington; Howard M. Smyth, who would become a distinguished State Department historian; and Phillip E. Mosley, a Kremlinologist and known authority on Russia inside and outside the Beltway, who would later become the Adlai E. Stevenson Professor of International Politics at Columbia. And then there was Kelsen, who argued that the best way forward for us all was to restore Austria fully – and he was as sharp, methodologically and politically, as he ever was.

What he was really arguing, while not saying it too loud, was that we had perhaps better not take the Moscow Declaration at its word (Kelsen 1944b). And he was right. If the annexation (*Anschluss*) of Austria by Nazi Germany really were to be treated as 'null and void', which was what the foreign secretaries of the United States, Britain, the Soviet Union and China had signed off in the October of 1943, what this would actually mean is that, under international law, Austria would need to revert exactly to the legal pre-*Anschluss* state of play. The problem with that pre-*Anschluss* legal framework, however, as Kelsen pointed out, was that in 1938 the Austrian Constitution was 'a fascist constitution'; and of course, as he went on, it 'is evident that the three Powers do not intend to establish a fascist State' (Kelsen 1944b: 6). To avoid this legal–political conundrum, he therefore recommended that the Allies organise, and properly back, a referendum in which the Austrians had a chance to call for full independence. This political approach would, in legal terms, be qualified as a revolutionary act: doing it like this would mean not breaking free from Nazi Germany by ending up at 1938 again, but rather starting *anew*, opening a new chapter for a post-Fascist/Nazi Austria.

Altogether a clinical and consequential political realist, he would actually argue *not* to re-enact the 1920 Constitution (the one co-drafted by him). He was sceptical about whether it would work this time. Whether or not, back then, it was the strategic rationale to prevent the total break-up of what was left of the Austrian–Hungarian Empire, Kelsen feared that the structural federalism or Renner's principle of decentralisation built into the 1920 Constitution was not realistically or economically sustainable for what was going to be a new – and much smaller – post-1945 Austria (Olechowski and Wedrac 2015: 284–5). And what is more, even though he himself was surely one of the most astute of Viennese émigrés, with a good grasp or insider's view of Austrian culture, politics and bureaucracy, Kelsen the political realist did not believe that exiles could or should be leading the efforts to construct a new Austria, what is known today as the *Zweite Republik*.

But perhaps even more importantly in terms of contemporary world politics and international law – or the globalisation of justice – Kelsen did significant consulting work for the Judge Advocate General of the United States Army (TJAG) – that is, he worked for the War Crimes Office (WCO), a major TJAG sub-unit tasked with collecting and processing evidence of war crimes during World War II.

It was on 4 June 1945 that Kelsen, still under financial pressure, received a telegram from Major General Myron C. Cramer, a Harvard-trained lawyer then head of the Army's legal branch, urging him to come to Washington as soon as possible (García-Salmones Rovira 2020). The General was looking for highly skilled jurists with a proven track record in military and international law, as well as knowledge of the Axis powers, and so of course Kelsen was a perfect candidate for the task. They seem to have settled on a fee of roughly $25 per day.

As a result, he then travelled to Washington, on at least two occasions in the summer of 1945, to take part in relevant meetings and discussions about what were thorny issues in international law in general and international humanitarian law in particular, all of which led to eight Kelsen memoranda.[7] And in fact, much of his work reached the desk of Justice Robert H. Jackson, then Chief of Counsel for the prosecution of Nazi war criminals and President Harry Truman's appointed Chief Prosecutor at the Nuremberg Trials. In this way, Kelsen's thoughts, memoranda and lines of arguments have contributed a great deal to the concept of individual criminal responsibility and the punishment of war criminals in international society and way beyond (see Olechowski 2016b: 106–10; Hathaway and Shapiro 2018: 268–72; Kropsky 2019; García-Salmones Rovira 2020).

And thus it looks as though the Schmittians are trying to perpetuate what is actually a myth – for not only in Europe but also in America, his new home, Kelsen the Pure theorist, perhaps the Purest of all jurists, had proven to be quite an applied or real-world scholar and man, to say the least.

10 A Most Realistic Man

'You are a fool. You like this, it is interesting, why don't you take a year and go to law school before you submit yourself to this crazy government?' (Lowenstein 1994: 16) – this is exactly what Kelsen said to his research assistant at the Naval War College in Newport, Rhode Island. The situation, in short, was that James G. Lowenstein, a Yale graduate, who back then was a lieutenant, was undecided as to whether it might be better to go into the Foreign Service or do some serious work in the law. Certainly, the young research assistant enjoyed studying the law and working with Kelsen: as Lowenstein later recalled, 'the experience of working with Kelsen was absolutely marvelous' (Lowenstein 1994: 23).

Kelsen was a charismatic person, with the gift of inspiring students and colleagues as both a man and a scholar. Years earlier, he had snatched from the Navy a young man named Robert W. Tucker, the distinguished Professor Emeritus of American Diplomacy at the Johns Hopkins Paul H. Nitze School of Advanced International Studies and a founding editor of the foreign-policy quarterly *National Interest*. Just out of the Naval Academy in the mid-1940s, Tucker, a political realist, had audited a few of Kelsen's classes at Berkeley, and became so fascinated by him and by Kelsenian international legal theory that he decided to try for a PhD on the problem of individual responsibility in international law.[8] It was, in fact, Harold Winkler (1947) himself who, in his function as Graduate Adviser, recommended Tucker to Kelsen. Tucker eventually resigned from the Navy, actively pursuing what turned out to be a long academic career. And of course, Tucker too sent his warmest regards in 1971: 'My students often ask of my student days at Berkeley and I tell them about you and the lasting influence you had,' and so 'I salute you on your 90th birthday.'

Kelsen was a real scholar, a fine legal theorist. And he was a master networker who supported and always looked after his *Schüler*, aiding them as best he could to achieve good positions. Back in the Vienna of the 1920s, his circle of jurists, young and senior, overlapped with the circle of excellent economists who orbited around Mises. Like Kelsen, Mises was exceptionally gifted and a man with first-rate contacts. Together they were able, mostly through the Rockefeller Foundation, to arrange for more than a handful of early Kelsenians, such as Leo Gross, Erich Hula and Eric Voegelin, to study in Britain and the United States on Rockefeller grants. Over the years, this morphed into a formidable transatlantic network of scholars and intellectuals, on which the Europeans could capitalise when darker times forced them to flee (Feichtinger 2009; Ehs 2010; Ehs and Gassner 2014). Kelsen cared as much as for the study of law as he cared for the students of law. In 'What is Justice?', he (1957a: 24) makes it very clear – 'science is my profession, and hence the most important thing in my life'.

He cannot be accused of being ivory-tower, though. His candid advice to his research assistant, who by that time was in his late twenties (and actually replaced Tucker at the Naval War College), reflects his position rather well: academia comes first. Back in Vienna, Kelsen's parents had instilled in him the essence and value of a good *Bildung*, or education, and so throughout his life and career he supported all serious efforts for everyone to receive as good an education as possible. Going beyond the core of the academic world, he was not only an early advocate of adult education programmes, but actually a teacher or lecturer at a so-called Viennese *Volkshochschule* (Ehs 2009b). He was a man who helped where he could; and thus it came about that what his research assistant Lowenstein eventually did was to go first to Harvard Law, and only then join the State Department to embark on a diplomatic career.

In total contrast to what the Schmittians say about him, Kelsen never was the type of scholar to be disconnected from the real world. This flies in the face of substantial conceptual evidence (of which more in Chapters 3 and 4), and also in terms of his own biography. In Kelsen's life, theory and practice intersected in many ways. For example, it was his work at the *k. u. k.* War Ministry that really propelled his university career, for even though Kelsen was at the time a widely recognised jurist and scholar, it is true that both the Kaiser and the War Minister had backed his bid for a professorship at crucial moments. And one might also say that, decades later, the world of scholarship and war intersected once again, at yet another crucial moment in his life and career: that is, from his expert work for both the FEA and the War Crimes Office, to his achieving tenure at Berkeley and securing for himself a reasonable US pension.

Well versed in realist literature and philosophy, surrounding himself by Freudians and no-nonsense economists, he had always been quite a bold theorist. Looking back at the time when he was working on his *Habilitation* thesis, Kelsen (1947a: 41) made it plain enough how he felt about what he was really doing: 'I was quite intoxicated by the sensation of breaking new ground in my academic discipline.' And certainly, as the Schmittians know full well, whenever there was an intellectual or theoretical battle to fight, the gloves came off. British legal philosopher H. L. A. Hart (1999 [1962–3]: 70), a very eminent Western thinker, recalls this telling episode (see Vinx 2007). It was at the end of a public lecture in 1961 at Berkeley, where the two intellectual giants were debating legal philosophy, 'when upon Kelsen emphasizing in stentorian tones, so remarkable in an octogenarian (or in any one), that "Norm is Norm" and not something else, I was so startled that I (literally) fell over backwards in my chair.'

As Hart (and many others) can vouch for, Kelsen was without doubt an intellectual streetfighter. And naturally so, for that is what the creation of the Pure theory was all about in the first place: it was to be used as a critical tool.

And, Kelsen did use the Pure theory of law, state and international legal order. That is, throughout his life and career, and for us to use in reality, there was a great deal of real theory, and there was a great deal of applied theory or real practice: Kelsen advising the War Minister in times of war. Drafting the Constitution for a new Austria. Sitting as a justice on a Supreme Court bench. Doing work for American foreign intelligence in yet another war. Doing even more serious work in the context of what is perhaps the most vicious and foggiest of all realms: trying war crimes and atrocities.

One might say, then – or perhaps half-conclude at this point in the book – that he was both a Pure positivist and quite a realistic bureaucrat–scholar. He has proved to be a man who was at ease, and very good, in two spheres that, today, appear to be far too distant from one another: the safe and smooth college campuses over here, and the frontlines of government and politics over there. Unlike many of the Schmittians and some of the (pseudo-)realists out there, Kelsen had a foot in either camp. A calm and gentle man he surely was, but he was not naïve about the political. He saw the problem of violence and mischief in this world as clearly as Dante. With Freud and Weininger, and Schopenhauer and Nietzsche, he shared a profound form of human nature realism. And rooted in what is a strong individualism, methodological and otherwise, with the likes of Wieser, Mises and Schumpeter, he was less concerned with ideas than with the powerful role that interests play in all social life. To Kelsen the political realist, it really is about You and Me, then.

CHAPTER 3

KELSEN'S FREUDIAN MOMENT

'A little in heaven, a little in hell'

Miles Hollingworth (2013)

Four days after he had learned from the *Kölner Stadt-Anzeiger*, a daily newspaper from the Cologne/Bonn metropolitan area, on Good Friday, 14 April 1933, that the Nazis had removed him from his prestigious post at Cologne, effective from Maundy (Holy) Thursday, Kelsen was back in Vienna.[1] He knew that he was a target – a prime target. He was one of sixteen university professors to be dismissed in what was Hitler's most immediate, or first, wave of academic cleansing. And he certainly feared Germany's postal and telegraph surveillance capabilities. So, from his mother's apartment at Marokkanergasse 20, in the Third District near the Lower Belvedere, and aided by his friend Mises, he reached out to some foreign contacts and colleagues. The situation was very clear to him: he must leave Nazi Germany. As quickly as possible.

He needed to act swiftly. And he had to be extra-careful. News reached him that the Nazis wanted to revoke the passports of all the sacked professors. Hitler feared that they could otherwise escape to London or Paris, or to Switzerland or the United States. The Nazis were worried that these fine and able intellectuals would then push back against the *Führer* from abroad. After a few days in Vienna, Kelsen went back to Cologne and immediately started to prepare for the Kelsen family's escape. The situation, Kelsen (1947a: 80) recalled, seemed 'quite hopeless', and had it not been for a little helper in the university administration, actually a member of the National Socialist Party

(NSDAP) with good contacts at Cologne Police Headquarters, who secured the necessary paperwork for Kelsen to leave Germany legally, it is all but certain that he would have eventually been sent to a 'concentration camp'.

The Nazis hated him. And Carl Schmitt, the Third Reich's *Kronjurist*, hated him. To them, Kelsen was not a human being, a Mensch, a scholar, a democrat. Driven on by their hate, these Nazi Schmittians saw in Kelsen just what they wanted to see: *einen Juden*, and *einen Marxisten*, and *einen Feind* of the *Deutsches Reich*. And to be sure, Kelsen saw it all clearly: if they had had their chance, they would have caught him. Imprisoned him. And killed him.

11 SPEAKING TRUTH TO POWER

To the Schmittians, he was a dangerous man. A Pure positivist of law and the state, he was a friend of democracy and the rule of law. And, likewise, he was a no-nonsense foe of autocracy in all its many guises. Throughout his life, Kelsen said what he meant, and meant what he said, which, in essence, was really a kind of political realism: as a scholar or scientist, the one true task – the one and only task, really – is to explain social reality, which in the social sciences, Kelsen (1937: 238) clearly sees, is necessarily 'political reality'. And since, in the 'sphere of the political', everything and everyone is either 'friend or foe', as he continues in 'Science and Democracy', a 1937 essay published in the *Neue Zürcher Zeitung*, the Zurich daily and Switzerland's leading newspaper, the yearning of all theorists and intellectuals for truth must sooner or later get in the way of real-world politics, which to him is the 'art of government, that is to say, the practice of regulating the social behaviour of men' (Kelsen 1937: 238).

Now, Kelsen the political realist is correct about what is in analytical (not normative) terms a kind of Schmittian-style understanding of politics, and about the role of intellectuals in this political reality. Surely, politics is in the final analysis nothing but a vicious day-to-day struggle for power. The political pits political friends against political foes. It is a very serious game, in which everyone, from a party's top leadership down to the rank and file, knows that there is only one goal in political life: to accrue power after power, as much as one can, so as to bring the party or its elected officials into a true governing position from which it is possible to shape society in the party's image. Let us not fool ourselves: a party, or any other political organisation, that did anything less than strive for a maximum share of power would not really be worth a vote. As former British Prime Minister Tony Blair (2020), largely yet unfairly remembered as the one key European ally who backed George W. Bush in the 2003 invasion of Iraq, recently put it in an opinion piece for *The Guardian*: the 'task' of a party (he meant Labour) is 'to win power'. The real question in Western democracy is not the *if*, but the *how*. What are the rules of this game that most of us play? How do we not pursue power blindly or unrestrainedly, but wield it responsibly and wisely? And as to the question of the role or standing of the intellectual in political life, Kelsen is right again: every no-nonsense scholar or serious scientist is invariably taken to be either a friend or a foe.

He was, all in all, more of a foe. The way that Kelsen had spoken *truth to power* by means of his newly created Pure positivism had not been seen at the time he started doing so, and had therefore really unnerved the Schmittians and other pseudo-democrats on the left and the right. To show the scale, scope and depth of Kelsen's progressive penetration of enemy territory, it is useful to bring Morgenthau back in here for a moment; this *Schüler* of Kelsen serves as a useful starting point for unpacking Kelsen's positivist project and its continued and timely relevance.

Thanks to more than a decade of revisionist readings of Morgenthau (and, for that matter, pretty much all so-called classical realists from Niebuhr to Carr), it has now been proven in many ways that this fine political theorist and candid public intellectual, whom Joel H. Rosenthal (2004), longstanding President of the Carnegie Council for Ethics in International Affairs in New York, calls the 'father of modern political realism', was by no means an aficionado of power, let alone an apologist for it. Morgenthau was as critical as you can be: of McCarthyism, of Vietnam, and of what he feared was the 'new moral force of nationalistic universalism' (Morgenthau 1967 [1948a]: 323). Morgenthau was extremely serious, as William Scheuerman (2009, 2011) has shown, about global reform, and envisioned a world order beyond the thick walls of the nation-state, which he called a 'blind and potent monster' (1962a: 61).

Morgenthau was firm in his view that any theory of international politics, and a realistic one in particular, must be able to understand what really drives foreign affairs but also what might lead us beyond our mutual killing. Political realism, Morgenthau (1967 [1948a]) says, is built around two concepts: power and peace. Has he become soft over the years? Not really; he just lived for what to him was the realistic yet critical study of power and peace in American foreign policy and world politics. He survived all the many beatings from the left and the right in the 1960s and early 1970s, and stayed the course as a sharp political theorist and public intellectual. In many ways, it was exactly as Herz recalled. It was the annual convention of the International Studies Association, held in Los Angeles in March 1980. Herz debated with his old comrade, both schooled by Kelsen in 1930s Europe, at a session that was themed 'Realism Revisited', about which title the ageing Morgenthau, who died only a few months later, quipped: 'Why revisited? I never left it' (quoted in Herz 1981: 182).

Morgenthau did struggle. He had a hard time in the United States, and particularly in Washington, for two reasons (Morgenthau 1984b: 378). One was, as he put it, that in terms of intellectual outlook and persuasion, he 'was quite unprepared for the United States'. Perhaps he was at times a bit too candid and frank. Rather undiplomatically, he pointed out that even though he had read, in German translation back on the Continent, the work of William

James, one of America's leading philosophers, psychologists and pragmatists, working from Harvard and with an extraordinarily wide reach in Western thought, Morgenthau said he 'had found him rather flat, commonsensical, and not particularly interesting'. And he added, quite correctly to be sure, that he 'had been influenced by such people as Max Weber and Hans Kelsen'. All of this really translated into what was a heavy critique of American thought. As Morgenthau put it: 'I was quite taken aback by the optimism and pragmatism characteristic of the American intellectual tradition.'

But Morgenthau (1967: 9), to me anyway, had yet another self-inflicted intellectual streak working against him: his very vision of realist political thinking, paired with his views on what makes an intellectual or, let us say, what makes a public intellectual. To him, and as noble as his view may be, it all comes down to this one aspect: the all-important quality of an intellectual, old and new, he says, is the 'discovery of truth and the presentation of truth'. And what is more, according to Morgenthau, all intellectuals are either 'discoverers of truth' or 'they are at least purveyors of truth'.

Now, that is all well and good, and most certainly sounds very noble and impressive. But Morgenthau, the political realist, misses the point. The real problem, going back to the Greeks and the polis, is most likely a quite different one. It is also a much more practical one. In fact, in an important 2017 essay on Kissinger and Morgenthau (and Trump), written for the *National Interest*, Barry Gewen, editor of *The New York Times Book Review*, pointed out that the real question, the moral question, is 'whether intellectuals should get their hands dirty making policy, or preserve their integrity at the price of influence'. And so, the real reason why I am bringing up what is perhaps one of the thorniest of all issues at the intersection of academia and government, the so-called theory/practice divide (Desch 2019), is to pave the way for really juxtaposing Morgenthau and Kelsen. I want to have these two men, with their biographies and their ways of political thinking and political acting in the real world, sort of side by side in front of us. Not only is this interesting in terms of intellectual history, but, more importantly, it helps me show, in a comparative way, why Morgenthau the political realist may not have been that realistic after all, and why Kelsen the so-called naïve idealist really has been what I would call a true political realist.

Morgenthau acknowledged the influence of Kelsen, who taught him how to speak truth to power on two prominent occasions. One was in 1970, as I have pointed out, when Morgenthau dedicated *Truth and Power* to his former teacher, mentor and friend Kelsen (Morgenthau 1970a, 1970b); the other occasion was when Kelsen turned ninety, with Morgenthau sending him quite a heartfelt letter, promising that he would really follow his lead. But then there is something very peculiar to the case of Kelsen – in a very positive way – that Morgenthau was seriously lacking, in terms of both biography and intellectuality. As I see it, from my own subjective vantage point as a political and IR theorist and a Critically inspired foreign-policy practitioner, Kelsen managed to be, at one and the same time, a great deal more practical and realistic, as well as more theoretical and critical, than Morgenthau.

Psychology may have done its fair share. Kelsen's self-image was that of a pure scholar, so in the eyes of politicians and bureaucrats, he did not arouse too much suspicion in terms of being an agenda-driven political actor. He was a low-key, or low-profile, almost reclusive figure: always there but never really seen. Morgenthau was, in many ways, very different. He would seek the lime-light. He was on a mission to change the course of American foreign policy. To be sure, no one at the very top in politics and government is too keen to hear from the sidelines about what may be best for the country, or what may, or may not, be in the national interest. While trying too hard or doing too much to be at the centre of the action, Morgenthau would end up with very little: he found himself, eventually, on the very fringes of American politics. The way he was, or operated, it must have hurt him when President Kennedy said to him, after Morgenthau had written a critical piece: 'You should sit where I do' (quoted in Gewen 2017). But then, of course, Morgenthau was not sitting in the White House, and that is what makes all the difference.

That is not to say that Morgenthau was not conscious of the problem that he, as an (over)ambitious public intellectual, was facing. He knew very well that, come the time when intellectuals must look real power in the eyes (raw as they are), there are essentially four options, of which one must be chosen (Gewen 2017). One is to retreat: that is, to hide oneself behind the walls of the ivory tower, pursuing knowledge relentlessly, thereby keeping one's ethos of theoretical purity and logical consistency. Second, one might go on the attack: that is, to criticise, using whatever it takes, any other government policy – which is to say that this or that policy is wrong in substance, or goes against better fac-tual knowledge, or is based on myths, or is a total lie. A third strategy is playing along: that is, to surrender or align oneself, against one's better judgement, with a party line or a government policy, thereby becoming, at worst, a propagandist, a sort of in-house intellectual. Finally, says Morgenthau, intellectuals might join in: that is, enter the political process by working in governmental apparatuses as bureaucrats or specialists, learning the trade of compromising on one's methodi-cal deductions for the sake of real results.

Morgenthau wanted to be what he called an intellectual streetfighter. He wanted to see his colleagues marching to the battlefield, and have them make clear, as he put it, on which side of the barricades they stand when the actual fighting begins. That is noble and touching. But, then, how did he fare? Of the four options, he played attack, though this was not of his own choosing. He never wanted to be a Washington outsider, but had 'hoped to burst the bounds of the academic community and leave his imprint on American foreign policy' (quoted in Gewen 2017). Yet that was not meant to be. It is almost tragic. He may have been the one man who did more than any other mid-twentieth-century political and IR theorist to establish the Realist study of international politics on college campuses across America, and *Politics among Nations* was widely recognised as a classic text on war and peace, read by students and national security professionals alike (White 1996). But then, once Vietnam was heating up, he was to become 'the most relentless critic of the war' (Zimmer 2011: xvi). Nowhere near the inside of things (where Professor Kissinger was), Morgenthau was in fact totally on the outside. Quite tellingly, the obituary that *The Washington Post* published, a couple of days after he died at Lenox Hill Hospital on Manhattan's Upper East Side, reads 'Hans Morgenthau, Vietnam War Critic' (Weil 1980).

Compare that to how *The New York Times* (1973) had reported the news of Kelsen's death, a day after he passed away at what is today the Orinda Rehabilitation and Convalescent Hospital, in Contra Costa County, San Francisco Bay Area: 'Dr. Hans Kelsen, Legal Scholar, 91; Expert on International Law and Jurisprudence Dies'. It is quite clear: the focus is on Kelsen the scholar, the jurist, the expert. And quite rightly so, for this is exactly how he saw and presented himself. Science was his profession, and all the professional rest of it, to him at least, was a side-show. Now, what if Kelsen had been as critical of Vietnam as Morgenthau? Would *The New York Times* have chosen a different headline? That is a non-question. He just was not a Morgenthauian-style Vietnam critic. In fact, to the best of my knowledge, he did not comment on America's war efforts in South-east Asia, though I suspect, from all that we know about him, he was surely critical of it. But then, that is the point: he did not say, not least because he chose his battles wisely. And even if, for whatever reason, he had wanted to say something about Washington's Vietnam policy, he most likely would have done it differently from how Morgenthau voiced his criticism.[2]

So, to get a grip on the intellectual style of Kelsen the political realist, how then did he speak truth to power? Though he was not afraid of going on the offensive, he was not, per se, in the attack camp, and he was clever enough not to get boxed into that particular corner. Neither was he the type simply to play along: as a Pure scholar, being seen as a propagandist or the extended brain of any political party would have been the worst to him – which is not to say that he did not have any political views or clear moral compass. As Martti Koskenniemi (2001: 245), a Finnish jurist and former diplomat, writes in *The Gentle Civilizer of Nations*: 'He made no secret of his democratic and left-liberal preferences or of his cosmopolitanism.' He certainly was a political man, and he certainly did his fair share of politics.

Yet, the specific way that he operated on the intellectual and political scene was to do all the streetfighting from two standpoints, keeping them separate.

He was good in both roles or techniques: retreating and joining in. There were, of course, the walls of the ivory tower, behind which he retreated in quite fascinating ways, and on the other hand, there was the real world of power and government in which he joined in, however temporarily. There was theory and there was practice. And in some peculiar way, he was so theoretical and had such an aura of being a real yet pure theoretician of law that it allowed him at times to be very practical without arousing too much suspicion as to his intention. His strong footing in theory reaffirmed his standing in practice, and vice versa. Through his *Habilitation* thesis in legal theory and his Pure positivism he was known as a methodical legal technician who could solve legal problems, such as drafting a constitution from scratch. It was exactly the kind of hyper-Purity of the Kelsenian project that made Kelsen the legal theorist so very valuable for the bureaucracy, with the added benefit that everyone knew where he stood: nowhere!

It was all rather brutal – a disillusionment, really. As Kelsen (1967 [1934a]: 106) put it, 'the Pure Theory is a radical realistic theory of law, that is, a theory of legal positivism. The Pure Theory refuses to evaluate the positive law.' To the politicians and bureaucrats who were to hire him for work, then, he must have appeared purely methodical and theoretical, and in essence also a-political. As Kelsen (1967 [1934a]: 106) was keen to point out, 'the Pure Theory refuses to serve any political interests'. All of this is to say that Kelsen the legal theorist must have appeared unsuspicious. From the point of view of his strict legal positivism, what he was required to do, by his own rigid standards, was to uphold the strict methodological separation between a legal–political is and a legal–political ought. As a Pure technician of law, his one and only task was to analyse law for its internal legal structure, not for its political efficacy or moral quality. In many ways, Kelsen was a much sought-after juristic problem-solver. No more, no less.

Of course, he did *not* stand nowhere, as we have seen with respect to his own political and moral convictions. But then, even though his core juristic–methodological withdrawal from the political and the moral has been bitterly contested from the very beginning of the Pure theory of law, state and international legal order, it has served a very fundamental aim: to have, for theoretical and practical purposes, a genuinely critical science of law, freed from ancient myths and always ready to spot hidden ideologies of natural law, God or Nature at once. Put differently, the very Kelsenian project of a Pure positivism is *speaking truth to power*. No matter if you retreat or join in, as a Kelsenian you will be unmasking power posing as truth, and you will be doing what Copernicus, Darwin and Freud were doing. As Matthias Jestaedt (2014: 11) put it: he who, in the Enlightenment spirit, wants to dis-illusion his contemporaries will really cause just that: dis-illusionment.

12 LAW AND STATE

Kelsen knew how hard his Pure positivism was on his contemporaries, and in many ways he paid the price for it. To be sure, for Kelsenians, to dis-illusion is a necessary and healthy way of trying to rescue ourselves from what Kant had called our self-imposed nonage. Yet to others, to dis-illusion is to offend, equalling a threat – a political threat.

Calm and modest in style and tone, the Preface to the first edition of the *Pure Theory of Law*, published in 1934 by Franz Deuticke, well known for being Freud's publisher, shows how Kelsen the political realist sees quite clearly that creating a Pure theory of law, state and international legal order has made him more foes, and not many friends. Fascists fear what they see as Kelsenian liberalism. Liberals and Socialists fear what they see as Kelsenian quasi-Fascism. Communists fear what they see as Kelsenian capitalism. Capitalists fear what they see as Kelsenian Bolshevism. Others fear what they see is a Kelsenian-style Catholicism, Protestantism or Atheism. 'In short', Kelsen (1967 [1934a]: 6) writes, 'there is no political orientation of which the Pure Theory of Law has not yet been suspected. But then, this only proves, even better than it could do it on its own – its purity.' Surely he was very well aware that to appear on the intellectual scene and say to the entire world, accustomed as this world had been for centuries to believe that there is law and there is state, that they got it all wrong because law *is* state, state *is* law, must be nothing short of shocking.

He was totally right on two counts, and had seen it all coming. First, the time had been ripe for creating a Pure positivism, and taking on the Schmittians and natural law ideologues on the left and the right, who were primarily interested in holding on to power at all costs, was much overdue (see also Feichtinger 2010: ch. 4.8). Second, the backlash against him and the notion of Purity in law and politics was not only swift but also vicious, if not at times irrational. It was all about what the law *is*, and what the state *is*, or about how law and state relate to one another. It was about disillusionment and destruction. For what he wanted his colleagues in jurisprudence and political philosophy – and us all – to understand is that there is no theoretical or practical distinction between what makes a legal order and a so-called body politic. What he set out to do was to overcome the dualism of law and state, and bring us to a point where we can talk about the state freed from ideological and metaphysical baggage. In terms of critical depth, he was similar in spirit to three men who preceded him. Copernicus told us we inhabit what is only a tiny speck in the universe. Darwin was perhaps the most brutal, saying that we are not really that divine but in fact are rather apish creatures. Freud completed the destruction of our naïve self-love, shouting out loud that our ever so reasonable ego is not master in its own house (Freud 1917: 143; see also Weinert 2009).

What makes Kelsen such a valuable addition to this illustrious group is the fact that his scientific advance was theory at its most original, and that it radically changed our view of politics and power, legality and authority. Just as Freud was not the first in the history of the human sciences to speak of the unconscious, Kelsen was not the first legal positivist. But just as Freud could claim for psychoanalysis to have come up with a new method for holding the mirror up to ourselves, it was Kelsen whose strict positivist method, rooted in an even stricter methodological individualism, helped destroy and deconstruct the notion of the reified state. As Clemens Jabloner put it, he replaced what was at the time a powerful myth of German *Staatslehre* with a new general – or new scientific – theory of 'the state as a legal function' (Jabloner 2016: 333). What the 'iconoclast' Kelsen did, in the words of Alexander Somek (2006: 753), a Vienna-based legal theorist, was to 'deontologise' the state.

It was all very theoretical. And of course, his idea of a Pure positivism was primarily driven by epistemological and methodological concerns. Yet at one and the same time, it was all very practical and critical – and what is more, Kelsen's project was deeply political. He worked out all the details pertaining to the most serious legal concepts, and how they relate to one another in the realm of a positivist view of law and a modern legal science. But then, if one looks at his *œuvre* from a more political standpoint, it at once becomes clear that what he was really after was to confront You and Me with the problem of the use, and abuse, of power. He feared the mass appeal – or, let us say, the mass trap – of ideological pseudo-theories posing as scientific truth. From his critical standpoint, which was much informed by a heavy dose of Freudian human nature realism, it was all too obvious that 'ideologies are not aimed at deepening cognition, but at determining the will' (Kelsen 1967 [1934a]: 286); it was clear to him that we must guard ourselves against the (political) fact that the 'aim of the dualistic "theory" is not so much to understand the essence of the state, but to strengthen the state's authority'.

One might say Kelsen knew that the question of how power is wielded in any given society is too important to be left to ideologues posing as legal theorists (and, I might add, posing as political and IR theorists). And therefore he sought to mount a scathing attack on what he argued was a dangerously dualistic theory of the state, by which he meant, of course, the two-sided and self-obligating theory of the state. To him it is bad enough to think, and insinuate in the political arena, that the state is a biological, social or psychological mass, not least because that style of thinking gives way to all sorts of ugly speculation about who the real people in this very real mass actually are, or who they are not (us/them). It becomes much worse, though, if one argues that the state is an extra-legal body politic that has the sovereign power to make the law and then – in what is, so to speak, a second step – voluntarily subjects itself to it; if human history teaches us anything, it is that any social and political order is, by and large, a function of coercion, not of self-obligation. And it surely is the worst thing, if not also the most dangerous, to think of the state not only as a person, but as a living creature – or, as Kelsen (1967 [1934a]: 285) says, 'as a meta-legal being, as a kind of powerful macro-anthropos or social organism'.

Now, Kelsen agreed with Georg Jellinek, back then the doyen of German-speaking public law professors – though he found him 'dull and unoriginal' (Kelsen 1947a: 40) – that we reject all ideas that have 'the state as a permanent natural structure alongside or above men' (Jellinek 1929: 175). Both men saw the problem quite clearly: pretty much the whole body of nineteenth-century German legal thought was rooted in Hegelian ideas of the state. In turn, this meant that these ideas were either authoritarian or organicist, or both. Yet Kelsen took it further, arguing that any legal and political philosophy that claims to be a modern and scientific one must free itself from reifying the state as something real, or must free itself from deifying the state as a meta-legal power reservoir. What Western philosophy and political thinking require, as he put it succinctly in *The Sociological and the Juristic Concept of the State*, published in 1922 (and not yet translated into English), is really a 'theory of the state – without the state' (Kelsen 1922b).

While the Hegelians and the Schmittians of course saw in Kelsen their prime target, he equally kept them under close methodological and political watch. From his Pure positivist standpoint they were quite dangerous, to say the least. If they really do separate law and state from one another and see them as two different spheres, the one as a system of norms or imputation and the other as a system of nature or causality (Kelsen 1950c; Kelsen 1990 [1979]), this would perpetuate the myth of the state as some sort of grand and aggrandised Being that is endowed with a sovereign Will *extra legem*. Unless you believe in the goodness of human nature, this must be quite scary, for what you really do is place a huge bet on our individual and collective reason. You would wager that the organs of the state, and each one of us with our political and private interests, will obey the law because we all feel obliged to do so. This is naïve, and exactly what Kelsen was saying from first to last. Where law and state are not seen as one and the same, where the concept of the state is seen as something essentially different from the legal order, then whoever wields enough power, claiming to represent the state, is bound to sabotage this very state or law.

His foes will, quite naturally, see this totally the other way round. They will say, as they have in the past, while waving their flags and singing their national anthems, that the state cannot be reduced to the idea of being merely some sort of systemic hierarchy of positivised norms reflecting positive interests. For a Hegelian, it must seem absurd that one 'reduces the union of individuals in the state . . . to something based on their arbitrary wills': that is, to 'have transferred the characteristics of private property into a sphere of a quite different and higher nature' (Hegel 1942 [1821]: §75, 258). Edmund Burke, the British philosopher and statesman so adored by conservatives to this very day, argued similarly. A state is much more 'than a partnership agreement in a trade of pepper and coffee, calico or tobacco, or some other such low concern'; it is rather a partnership in 'all science', in 'all art', 'every virtue', 'all perfection', a partnership 'not only between those who are living, but between those who are living, those who are dead, and those who are to be born' (Burke 1986 [1790]: 194–5). And what is more, they will of course say this: where the state is a legal order (Kelsen 1967 [1934a]: 286; see also La Torre 2010); where state equals *Rechtsstaat* equals *Machtstaat* (van Ooyen 2017: 25); where the state wills what positive law wills; where law is created not by 'God, nature or reason', but by positive law, by 'human acts' (Kelsen 2007 [1945]: 392; see also Turner 2016); that is to say, where all these elements of a Pure positivism become political reality, are we not then facing the real danger that what may be willed by us, in a certain place, at a certain time, under a certain condition, might be something quite different to the ideals of *life, liberty and the pursuit of happiness*, or *liberté, égalité, fraternité*?

He knew the risks, and never sought to sugar-coat the realistic possibility that the Pure vision of the rule of law might lead us to the worst of all social and political orders: away from hard-fought democracy, possibly even toward the extreme point 'where one single individual rules in an autocratic or tyrannical way' (Kelsen 2007 [1945]: 186). He spoke out loud and clear: the idea of the *Rechtsstaat* has no intrinsic preference for any specific social and political order. If it had any such in-built preference, Pure positivism would have surrendered itself to a philosophy and style of political thinking that it has sought to overcome: the idea of natural law. And thus, the very idea of the *Rechtsstaat* is no more and no less than the idea of 'a state governed by law' (Kelsen 1967 [1934a]: 312). It does not say anything about the specific content of a specific constitution or specific law; and whether any specific legal norm is, from a moral point of view, either just or not, and whether this or that norm ought to be obeyed or not, these are entirely different questions. And thus, the case against Kelsen, put so vehemently by the Schmittians on the left and the right, that the Pure theory of law and state is in itself a political ideology, is a very weak one. What has always been very strong, however, is their fear of having their *Machtpolitik*, or their use of extra-legal power for their own political ends, whatever these ends may possibly be, exposed by Kelsen or Kelsenian positivist methodology.

Rejecting natural law, pushing hard for positive law – there was no doubt in his mind that this is what needs to be done, methodologically and politically. It was also an epistemological postulate, fanned by Freud and some other notable figures such as Ernst Mach and Ernst Cassirer, that what Kelsen wanted to do with the concept of the state was to progress from primitive thought to modern science. He wanted to rid Western thought from the animistic assumption that the state was of real substance, and bring us to a point where we would conceive of the state as a function (Feichtinger 2010: Ch. 4.16). A Pure positivism would help lift us, he argued, from the bottom of metaphysics, or a dangerous political theology of the state, up to the level of sound scientific enquiry. No more should 'we imagine behind the law, its hypostatised personification, the State, the god of the law' (Kelsen 2007 [1945]: 191).

Without doubt, fighting one's way through his Continental-style work of conceptual definition after definition is, at times, quite painful (Wacks 2017: Ch. 4), but then, it is not as if what he has been trying to enlighten us about, in a Kantian spirit, is in any way antiquated material. Not only are the Schmittians still around; so is much of exactly that kind of thought and theory that Kelsen was reacting against in his own time, and for which he gave us a timeless method that we can apply in ours.

And so from the perspective of a Kelsenian-style political realism in contemporary political and IR theory, let me ask you this: being mindful of the fact that human nature is, *grosso modo*, nowhere near as good as some would have us believe, would you really trust any scheme of thought and theory that says, or insinuates, that there is some sort of higher law somehow and somewhere sitting above positive law-making? Or, when you hear one of today's top IR theorists seriously argue that 'states are real actors to which we can legitimately attribute anthropomorphic qualities like desires, beliefs, and intentionality' (Wendt 1999: 197; see also Lerner 2020), then would you really sit still? Let us have Robert Kagan, a fine political commentator, writing in *The Return of History and the End of Dreams*, speak for himself here: 'Nations are not calculating machines. They have the attributes of the humans who create and live in them, the intangible and immeasurable human qualities of love, hate, ambition, fear, honor, shame' (Kagan 2008: 80; see also Welsh 2017). In light of many of such instances of premodern myth-making; forms of hypostatisations of mass, peoples and nation; zoomorphic projections of state behaviour paralleling the animal kingdom; and, worst of all, in light of what has been detected as a form of 'organismic, collectivist, or volksgeist-related bias' (Escudé 1997: 23) in much of contemporary political thinking, should we not be on high alert, and ask with Kelsen why that is so?

He saw clearly how seemingly innocuous ideas of the state inform political practice. Just think of his Weimar battle with Carl Schmitt: here the Schmittian decisionist, the-*Führer*-protects-the-law political theology (Schmitt 1940), and there Kelsen's own insistence on constitutional jurisdiction. And think also of the many other instances or situations in which Kelsen shuttled back and forth between the ivory tower and the real world, always insisting on what was the very core methodological principle of Pure positivism: there is no such thing as the state, there is only law. To be sure, then, he is as timely as he ever was, and Kelsenian methodology can aid us in exactly what Chris Brown (2005: 349), Emeritus Professor of International Relations at LSE, has cautioned us to do in plain language: 'As always, it is important that we all keep our bullshit-detectors on line.'

And thus I want to suggest that Kelsen provides us with effective analytical tools, or methodological weapons really, to confront two currents in contemporary IR theory. One is the Wendtian advance into social theory, which, fascinating as it may be, has (mis-)led some of us to believe, and quite seriously, that 'states are people too' (1999: 215). The other one, perhaps even more problematic, is the way that Waltzian-inspired neorealists have been arguing, ever since the publication of *Theory of International Politics*, that there is no need to bother about the concept of the state, for the behaviour of state is anyway a function of systemic top-down pressures in the realm of international anarchy (Waltz 1979). On both counts, though, Kelsen knew better, and for that matter, the classical realists were not as unreflective about the conceptual problem of the state as today's Wendtians and Waltzians have proven to be in many ways.

Kelsen the political realist and the classical realists were refreshingly honest and realistic about the symbols and dramas of a Freudian human nature in politics and international relations. Flags and nations, projections and identifications, myths and longings, interests and ideas: this is the stuff of which international politics is made. E. H. Carr (1939: 159) feared that *man* pretty much always seeks to compensate 'for his own lack of power to assert himself in the vicarious self-assertion of the group'. Niebuhr (2001 [1932]: 93) warned in *Moral Man and Immoral Society*, a classic study in ethics and politics, that

> The man in the street, with his lust for power and prestige thwarted by his own limitations and the necessities of social life, projects his ego upon his nation and indulges his anarchic lusts vicariously.

And thus, similarly in style and content, Morgenthau (1967 [1948a]: 98–9), in *Politics among Nations*, warned us that

> Not being able to find full satisfaction of their desire for power within the national boundaries, the people project those unsatisfied aspirations onto the international scene. There they find vicarious satisfaction in identification with the power drives of the nation.

It does not have to be this way, to be sure. And contrary to much popular wisdom and fast talk of a Mearsheimerian pseudo-realist pessimism, these classical realists did not say that we could not possibly, at some point, get beyond Westphalian sovereignty and the nation-state system. This is not to say, though, that they thought it easy to shake off the many shackles of individual and mass psychology. And, make no mistake, Kelsen too cautioned us on more than one occasion that we cannot fully escape who we are: more of this theme later (in Chapter 4) when we explore Kelsen's position on nationalism and the world state. Be forewarned: expect a great deal of Kelsenian foreign-policy realism.

That said, in the wake of a new Kelsenian conception of the state, this earlier generation of political realists has distinguished carefully between what makes the political in terms of human nature or otherwise, and what makes the state. We might casually refer, with Hobbes (1996 [1651]: Introduction), to the state as a Leviathan, as 'this Artificiall man', or 'indeed a "mortal God"'. This is all well and good as long as it is clear that there is no real state-personhood, or real personality of the state. As E. H. Carr (1939: 189) made clear in *The Twenty Years' Crisis*, 'its personification is a fiction'. Niebuhr (2001 [1932]: 54) too pointed out, in *Moral Man and Immoral Society*, 'The nation is an abstraction.' Or, as Morgenthau (1967 [1948a]: 97) argued in *Politics among Nations* for good reason: a nation is 'obviously not an empirical thing . . . cannot be seen. What can be empirically observed are only the individuals who belong to a nation.'

Totally agreed. And what is more, Morgenthau (1964: 212, 223) really does sound like a Kelsenian when he writes that the concept of the 'modern state' is 'synonymous with *Rechtsstaat*'. Or as Morgenthau (1967 [1948a]: 489) puts it in *Politics among Nations*: the state

> is but another name for the compulsory organization of society – for the legal order that determines the condition under which society may employ its monopoly of organized violence for the preservation of order and peace. When we have spoken in the preceding pages of the compulsory organization and of the legal order of society we have really spoken of the State.

This, in fact, is what Kelsen has really been saying: the state is a legal order, and thus is a *Rechtsstaat*. But then, the organs of the state have real power, and so the state is at one and the same time a *Machtstaat*. Let us have no illusions, then, as to what the Kelsenian equation of law and state really means: coercion and politics.

13 COERCION AND POLITICS

'It is one of the lasting merits of Hans Kelsen's theory of law and state to have demonstrated the unity of the legal and political order,' wrote Hans Morgenthau (1964: 210) in a *Festschrift* on the occasion of the thirtieth anniversary of the first, German edition of the *Reine Rechtslehre*. And for that matter, it was a few years earlier, in 1960, working in Berkeley, that Kelsen published what was the second, revised and enlarged, German edition: in it he conceived the all-important *Grundnorm*, or basic norm, as a fiction in the sense of Hans Vaihinger's influential philosophy of *as-if* (see Duxbury 2008: 55–8; see also Kletzer 2015: 23–9; Schauer 2015). And then, also in the 1960s, the jurist and writer Max Knight, once Max Eugen Kühnel, a former student of Kelsen's in

Vienna and, after emigration, longstanding Principal Editor of the University of California Press in Berkeley, produced the first English translation (see Kelsen 1967 [1934a]; 2017 [1960a]).

What the identity of law and state, or the unity of the legal and political order (as Morgenthau put is), means from a theoretical point of view is that there is nothing that separates the nature of the *legal* from the nature of the *political*. Of course, the cognitive or analytical emphasis is different: the Kelsenian jurist focuses on legal norms – that is, on the hierarchy of ought-propositions in the whole system of norms. The Morgenthauian political theorist focuses on political power – that is, on the distribution of the material means of control among political actors in the whole system of power relations. But then – and that is an important *but then* – the difference between the two positions is one of degree, not kind, for there is one element that unites law and the state, the legal and political, norm and power, and that is the fact of coercion. It is a truism that everything *legal* is at one and the same time *political*. As Kelsen (1941: 82) the jurist and political realist put it in 'The Law as a Specific Social Technique', a remarkable essay written for the *University of Chicago Law Review* at a time when he was a research associate at Harvard, shortly after he had fled Europe for good: law means state, and the state 'is defined as a political organization, that is only to say that it is a coercive order; the specifically "political" element consists in nothing but the element of coercion'.

One of the many reasons why I am inclined to think of Kelsen as a real political realist, then, is exactly because there is this common thread running through his philosophy and political thinking – and which, to me anyway, tends to be neglected. It is Kelsen's smooth yet sustained Freudian human nature realism, opening the door for liberal realists, or realist liberals, to balance a political reality as it *is*, with a political progress as it *might be*, or possibly *can be*. As to the former, he is as hard-line as any other political realist that I know of in the history of Western thought: wherever there is society, there is – or better, there must be – law. To be sure, in the eyes of Marxist–Leninist theory this kind of thought must look like any other bourgeois myth, as Grigory Tunkin (1974), Soviet jurist and one of the Soviet Union's leading international lawyer–diplomats, once put it. But of course, Kelsen is unyielding. To him, what it all comes down to in the final analysis is really this: it is a universal fact in time and place, in any culture and economic system, that all earthly societies cannot but coerce their members into compliance.

He has argued more eloquently against what he saw as all too idealistic notions of human nature and society, of course, but the style of social and political realism that we can take away from his analysis and conclusion is actually all the same. As Kelsen (1941: 82) puts it, 'History presents no social condition in which large communities have been constituted other than by coercive orders.' It is just a fact – a historical one too, he says – that even 'the social communities of the most primitive peoples' are rooted in law; they are rooted in the mechanism of a 'religious coercive order', and the fact that we do not refer to these forms of 'legal community' as a state is 'because the necessary degree of centralization is still lacking' (Kelsen 1941: 82). According to Kelsen, then, what really makes society is the political fact that it is being regulated: through law, which is tantamount to saying through coercion. And thus, Kelsen (1941: 75) says, the very 'function of every social order is to bring about a certain mutual behavior of individuals – to induce them to certain positive or negative behavior, to certain action or abstention from action'. It is a sheer impossibility for You and Me that we will ever have a community without an element of force, and so Kelsen (1941: 79) writes that the law, or the state, is in fact our 'coercive order monopolizing the use of force'.

Unless, of course, you believe in natural law, or unless you want to believe in the power of a natural law (in the true meaning of the term), a kind of higher law that can definitely sanction You and Me into obeying this or that set of norms, or this or that kind of 'desired social conduct' (Kelsen 1941: 79), make no mistake that, to Kelsen, the *withering away* of law or state, or of politics or the struggle for power, is all but a pipe dream – a beautiful one, perhaps (depending on where you stand), but none the less a dream about to be brutally shattered. Recall Kelsen the political realist, the Freudian, the Nietzschean, the Darwinian: left unchecked, 'the big fish will swallow the small ones', one by one. What is required in all social life is therefore law with teeth, and such a law must, out of necessity, be positive law: that is to say, law is a specific social technique to regulate – by means of coercive power – human behaviour in any given legal and political order, national and international. 'Law is a specific social means, not an end' (Kelsen 2007 [1945]: 20).

This is not to say, though, as we shall see, that the Kelsenian notion of law is purely formalistic or functional. This is also not to say that he was so naïve, philosophically and politically, as to believe that we have to have fought it out: norms in one corner, power in the other one, with reason as a sort of impartial referee. And what is more, I suggest that the Schmittians, old and new, take a fresh look at the house that Kelsen built, notably at its foundation, so that one day they might recognise that it is actually their decisionist political theology that is totally against human nature, *not* Kelsen's relativistic philosophy and political thinking.

It is striking how much Kelsen invested in putting the Pure theory of law and state on a firm footing, though without making it a kind of Schmittian prisoner of a narrow metaphysics or political theology. While he speaks in rather technical terms about law as a specific social technique, as if it were a device, such as a social contract designed to leave a Hobbesian state of nature where all life is solitary, poor, nasty, brutish and short (Hobbes 1996 [1651]: Ch. xiii), Kelsen, of course, rejected social contract theory as not only false but also naïve. To him, the very idea of a law-less state of nature is obscure; as he put it in *Collective Security under International Law,* 'Men have probably always lived in society, and where there is society there is some kind of law' (1957b: 3). And even if we had ever faced a situation of a total lack of security or total anarchy, would we have ever trusted in a social contract to get out of it alive? The Roman maxim *pacta sunt servanda* is all well and good, one might say, but what is really required to reach a point of at least relative security, he says, is the fact of coercion: nothing but coercion.

All else, short of coercion, is futile. What we cannot wish away, according to his Pure positivism and political realism, is human nature. We can have only little hope, if not no hope at all, other than that we seek to cope, as best as we can, Kelsen (1941: 84) writes, with a social situation or human condition that is marked not only by the 'innate urge to aggression in man', but by the fact that 'the happiness of one man is often incompatible with the happiness of another'. And thus, to understand Kelsen the political realist properly is to understand the not-so-nice image that he had of You and Me. Speaking of an image of human nature, though, let us be clear that it was not his image, not his invention. It was not dreamt or conjured up by him. And neither was it the result of a Kelsenian quasi-pathological anthropological pessimism. Forever seeking to escape both metaphysics and mythology, Kelsen the political realist was a scientist, and he sought, wherever and as best as he could, to move past the point of any story-telling about man and society. And thus, quite naturally almost, he had turned to Freudian psychoanalysis in this matter, for the one man who, back in the heyday of Viennese Modernism, provided the latest facts and data on human nature was, of course, Freud.

And so one might say that very fundamentally, or at a very basic and almost anthropological level, Kelsen's normative construction of law and state is really informed by a realistic conception of human nature and mass psychology. Rooted in a fascinatingly detailed yet also political reading of Freud, he tells us that we must not be naïve. Never. For what Morgenthau (1967 [1948a]) would later call the 'struggle for power and peace' really is a fact of all social life, domestic and international. Where there is society, there is law; where there is law, there is the state; where there is the state, there is coercion; and where there is coercion, there is power. But let Kelsen (2007 [1945]: 190–1) speak for himself:

> Speaking of the power of the State, one usually thinks of prisons and electric chairs, machine guns and cannons. But one should not forget that these are all dead things which become instruments of power only when used by human beings, and that human beings are generally moved to use them for a given purpose only by commands they regard as norms. The phenomenon of political power manifests itself in the fact that the norms regulating the use of these instruments become

efficacious. 'Power' is not prisons and electric chairs, machine guns and cannons; 'power' is not any kind of substance or entity hidden behind the social order. Political power is the efficacy of the coercive order recognized as law.

All of this, Kelsen (2007 [1945]: 191) says, really translates into this: 'The problem of the State is a problem of imputation'. Thus the problem of political power is a problem of what *ought to be* in a society, implying by necessity a 'relation of superior to inferior'.

Not bad for an alleged idealist! And to be sure, the best of Kelsen the political realist is yet to come. But first things first. It is, of course, standard for foreign-policy realists, such as Benjamin Frankel (1996: xviii), a former editor of *Security Studies* and of two excellent volumes on political realism, to say that 'States rely on the use of force or on the threat to use force to protect their interests and enhance their security.' And in a similar vein, Matt Sleat (2013: 61), a British-based political theorist of a fine-tuned realist persuasion, writes correctly that 'All political associations will involve coercion of some sort and no proper form of political understanding can eschew the truth that forms of coercion will be necessary for political order to be possible at all.'

To be sure, just as E. H. Carr (1939: 297) used to say that 'Power is a necessary ingredient of every political order,' Niebuhr (2001 [1932]: 3) was equally accurate and timeless when he wrote that the 'coercive factor is . . . always present in politics'. That surely is a standard theme in all political realism, old and new.

But then, let us take another look at some of these political realists. Niebuhr (2001 [1932]: 6), for example, says that 'only a romanticist of the purest water could maintain that a national group ever arrives at a "common mind" or becomes conscious of a "general will" without the use of either force or the threat of force.' And Sleat (2013: 61) argues, also similarly:

> Of course, more often than not the threat of coercion is sufficient to ensure individuals' obedience and allegiance. But for this threat to provide sufficient solidarity it must be backed up with effective institutions of law and its enforcement agencies such as a police force, judicial system, legal processes, etc.

Now, is Niebuhr implying here the possibility that, as a function of the maximum use of force, we could possibly have a political situation, however temporary, in which all members of any given social order share one and the same *ought*? And likewise, is Sleat implying here a duality of law and state, and that the question of solidarity plays any role when it comes to the political?

At least the Kelsenian answer to these important questions must be clear. Never, ever give in, not in the slightest, to the illusion of any form of a common ought. Impossible, no matter how much force is used. And what is more, the state is not the realm of solidarity or legitimacy or the like but, in the final analysis, the realm of power. Pure power. As Sandrine Baume (2012: 1), a political theorist and historian of ideas at Lausanne, has shown with clarity in *Hans Kelsen and the Case for Democracy*, the Kelsenian mind rejects even the slightest inkling of something like 'the "general will", of political oneness, and of the objective interest of the state'. Not in theory, and no less in the day-to-day reality of government and international affairs – as bleak as this may seem to natural-law idealists on the left and the right – are there any means, devices, formulas or tricks out there in social life that could move You and Me past 'the fight for the realization of interests' (Kelsen 1949: 513).

Politics is here to stay. Whether we like the struggle for power, and over interests, or whether we do *not* (why would we not?), to conceive of any social or political order that could possibly escape positive law and the fact of coercion, as Kelsen (1957a: 21) puts it, is an 'irrational ideal or, what amounts to the same, an illusion'. And thus all the power struggles are here to stay. We cannot escape a world that is inescapable: which is to say, from the 'point of view of rational cognition, there are only interests of human beings and hence conflicts of interests' (Kelsen 1957a: 21). He was very strict on that point, squashing any Hegelian or Marxist hopes for an altogether different world: there is no law of historical evolution. Says Kelsen (1948a: 19) in *The Political Theory of Bolshevism*: Hegel praised 'the state as a god' and Marx cursed it 'as a devil' and yet what both got wrong – one *with* the state, the other *without* – is that at some point in history, magically, there will be one Truth, Justice or Ought to be shared either between the divine, spirit and flesh (Hegel), or among the proletariat in a post-class society (Marx).

To Kelsen, this is all laughably idealistic, while proof of a dangerously anti-democratic style of philosophy. From the point of view of scientific enquiry, he argues in the aptly titled article 'The Natural-Law Doctrine Before the Tribunal of Science', published in 1949 in *The Western Political Quarterly*, any kind of philosophy, or any kind of recourse, overt or covert, to some sort of natural law, 'whether it presents its results as deductions from a law of nature in terms of jurisprudence or as deductions from a law of evolution in terms of sociology or history', is not only 'logically erroneous', but also 'entirely worthless'. And as to the danger of it all, Kelsen the political realist is equally clear: it is all a big lie. Babbling about any higher law, or any higher justice, surely is 'useful to the government' and it is a 'very useful lie', to be sure, for what it really does is help ensure 'obedience to the law'. Yet no matter the purpose or intention, good or bad or ugly, in the end, every form of natural-law doctrine is a big make-believe – 'a lie' (Kelsen 1949: 513).

He is pretty Hobbesian: not in terms of social contract theory (which Kelsen, of course, rejects), but regarding the degree and depth of an almost total subjectivity in our deeds and preferences, and relentlessness in the quest for securing our interests. He would agree with Hobbes (1996 [1651]: Ch. vi) that whatever it is that You and Me want to obtain in each of our lives for whatever reason, and whether we call this or that interest that we pursue either good or evil, these interests are, first and foremost, 'words' – no more, no less – that 'are ever used with relation to the person that useth them: there being nothing simply and absolutely so'. Kelsen would also approve of Hobbes's important point that 'there is no such *Finis ultimus*, (utmost ayme,) nor *Summum Bonum*, (greatest Good,) as is spoken of in the Books of the old Morall Philosophers' (Hobbes 1996 [1651]: Ch. vi). This is not to say that he did not recognise that social orders are not totally atomised. 'In reality', as Kelsen (2007 [1945]: 185) puts it in his *General Theory of Law and the State*, 'the population of a State is divided into various interest-groups which are more or less opposed to each other'. And so, yes, we will have to battle it all out.

Yet, we will not have to battle out our conflicts of interests through mere force or the violence of the stronger, but through the organs of law and state: through positive law understood as 'a specific order or organization of power' (Kelsen 2007 [1945]: 121). That is to say: the battle is one of influencing how political power is distributed in any given legal order, be it a primitive or a highly centralised one. Surely, forever the Pure positivist as much as the political realist, Kelsen (1957a: 21–2) is clear enough on the fact that we can seek to solve the perennial problem of conflicting interests among members of any given social order by two means, or in two ways: 'by satisfying one interest at the expense of the other, or by a compromise between the conflicting interests'. One leads us down the path to brute autocracy, the other to liberal democracy and open society ideals. Either way, though, the root problem remains the same: You and Me.

14 Roots of Authority

Kelsen, one might say, is a Freudian human nature realist in a dual sense. One concerns what, in German-speaking political and IR theory, has traditionally been called *Politische Anthropologie*, or political anthropology. In the case of Kelsen, it is in many ways how he has sought to warn us against natural-law doctrines on the basis of what was his sustained focus on the darker traits or drives lurking in You and Me. The second sense, while rooted in the first one, is less philosophical in nature and outlook. Surely we must not be naïve in matters political, and neither must we be intellectually or cognitively lazy. When the chips are down, and come the time that we must choose between different ought-propositions, what we tend to do, says Kelsen (1957a: 22) the Kantian psychoanalyst, is attempt to shift the burden from our own conscience 'to the government, and, in the last instance, to God'.

Sapere aude – where and when? And how? To Kelsen, shutting one's eyes and ears like this will make us none the wiser, of course: not as individuals, not as society. And thus we cannot let all the many different natural-law doctrines out of our sight, for with one of them we might be lured or tricked into an unhealthy intellectual and political relationship that does not involve You and Me. Perhaps we are hoping that through Nature, or God, or Reason, we can kill two birds with one stone: that is, arrive at a most satisfying moral and political outcome, while not taking any responsibility for it. But then, of course, this is just naïve, a self-confession of one's own authoritarian mind and self-myths. And so Kelsen (1927: 54) has sought to warn us (see also Dyzenhaus 2000: 20):

> The question on which natural law focuses is the eternal question of what stands behind the positive law. And whoever seeks the answer will find, I fear, neither an absolute metaphysical truth nor the absolute justice of natural law. Who lifts the veil and does not shut his eyes will find staring at him the Gorgon head of power.

What he is really telling us is that in all social life, no matter where and when, for *Us* there is no escaping from the fact of power. There is no choosing for us whether we want to live in a world rid of politics and power struggles, or in the real world. The one real choice is 1between accepting that fact, or fleeing to the pseudo-safety of the venerable form of self-deception that all natural-law philosophy, old or new, actually is. The Kelsenian answer must be clear enough by now, but to back it up, the analytical task at hand is to explore the roots of authority.

Why should we obey the law or the state? Who likes to be ruled, and for what reasons? From what I have been saying thus far in the book, biographically and conceptually, these questions can be answered swiftly: the roots of authority are the early Freudian dramas of primitive societies. Freudian human nature realism explains the obedience problem. And to be sure, no person wants to be ruled by another person. All this needs explaining; and since this is complicated territory – notably, Kelsen's almost legendary concept of the basic norm – I should add a couple of disclaimers here. First, recall that I am a foreign-policy realist trained in political and IR theory, not in jurisprudence; relying on the relevant law literature required for my purposes here, I leave the basic norm as is, not discussing any technical juristic problems, which are surely important themes for jurists but not here. Second, and perhaps even more importantly, from the very start my discussion of authority and the obedience problem will distinguish carefully between what is Kelsen's legal theory and what I see as Kelsenian political thinking on this matter, not trying to synthesise the legal and the political into one (which may be a future task for someone else).

From the Pure positivist's standpoint, or from the rigid point of view that Kelsen (1957c: 259) liked to call the 'science of positive law', the very fact that we should obey the law is a juristic postulate, not a moral one. In a short yet concisely written essay for his seminal 1957 essay collection *What is Justice?*, 'Why Should the Law Be Obeyed?', Kelsen (1957c) starts out by saying this: positive law ought to be obeyed because it is valid law, and the very fact that we ought to obey valid law, which in turn is binding law regulating individual and collective behaviour through coercive acts, is to be 'presupposed by a theory of positive law' (Kelsen 1957c: 257). What he leaves us with here is, of course, a pure legal positivism: law and coercion require us to obey the law, not any morality or justice. This means that if we decide, out of any ethical concern, that we will not obey the law, we may (or may not) be morally right in this, while none the less paying the juristic price for our disobedience, of course. Positive law, as the truism has it, is not necessarily morally just law. And thus the question is: why ought we obey any given legal norm?

One set of answers is, naturally enough, totally out. From a broadly Kantian critical perspective, both Nature and Justice, as well as God, are not helpful. It makes little sense to propose that we ought to obey legal norms because Nature commands us to. Norms are ought-propositions, while Nature is firmly the realm of causality and therefore cannot have any will; nor does Nature have any ought, and saying otherwise would be 'animistic superstition' (Kelsen 2007 [1945]: 191). Likewise, resorting to natural-law ideas of Justice will not provide a satisfying answer. As much as any Lockean, seeing individual property as a natural right, will not be willing to obey the legal norms of a Communist government, the Marxists, viewing private property as inherently unjust, will give any capitalist legal order 'no chance of being recognized as a valid law which its citizens ought to obey' (Kelsen 1957c: 259). To have positive law follow natural-law ideas makes legal norms meaningless, as what it really does is say that it 'is solely the norms of natural law which men ought to obey'. Similarly, to say we ought to obey positive law because God tells us to does not answer the question of why we would owe any obedience to this or that earthly legal norm, for then the 'question arises why men ought to obey the commands of God' (Kelsen 1957c: 260).

The obedience problem, says Kelsen the Pure positivist and political realist, cannot be solved by natural-law philosophies, and in fact, it should not be solved in quasi-mythical and anti-democratic ways of thought. No wonder he has few friends in these circles. He is unmasking them as variants of one 'metaphysical hypothesis', and says we must recognise natural-law ideas for what they are: 'highly subjective value judgements of *their* various authors about what *they* consider to be just or natural' (Kelsen 1957c: 259). What Kelsen wanted to do, and wants us to do, is to justify positivised norms regulating our living-together on their own terms: that is, solely from *within* positive law. As much as he sought to end the dualism of law and the state, Kelsen (1957c: 258) wants us to do away with the dualism of natural law and positive law: there is no kind of law – heavenly or otherwise – that could or should ever be 'superior to positive, man-made law'.

And so the problem of the roots of authority is intimately intertwined with the specific – and bold yet cautious – way that Kelsen has confronted the obedience problem through the concept of the basic norm, which is all fiction, a hypothetical concept or, later, an *as-if* construction. Keeping an eye on his natural-law foes, he knew of course that the battle is now hypothesis versus hypothesis, or fiction versus fiction. None the less, as he saw it, there was a big difference between the two camps: while he felt that he had laid all his cards on the table, the natural-law philosophers kept on with what he felt was a cover-up of ideology posing as Truth. Against this background, his conception of a positive legal order as a 'supreme, sovereign order' (Kelsen 1957c: 261), a hierarchically structured one, is key. Its very basis is the constitution, written or unwritten; based on it are statutes enacted by law-makers, and based on statutes are norms created by courts and administrative organs. Put differently, we should obey norms because of statutes; statutes because of the constitution; the present constitution because of the prior one – it is a pyramid.

He takes us back to the idea of a very first constitution. Arriving there, eventually, means this: the Kelsenian basic norms stipulate, as Neil Duxbury (2008: 52), Law Professor at LSE, neatly put it, that 'citizens ought to obey legal norms validly created in accordance with the historically first constitution'. But then, as to nature and purpose of the basic norm, let us hear Kelsen in his own words. The very norm, writes Kelsen (1957c: 262), that

> we ought to obey the provisions of the historically first constitution must be presupposed as a hypothesis if the coercive order established on its basis and actually obeyed and applied by those whose behavior it regulates is to be considered as a valid order binding upon these individuals; if the relations among these individuals are to be interpreted as legal duties, legal rights, and legal responsibilities, and not as mere power relations; and if it shall be possible to distinguish between what is legally right and legally wrong and especially between legitimate and illegitimate use of force . . . It is the ultimate reason for the validity of positive law, because, from this point of view, it is impossible to assume that nature or God command obedience to the provisions of the historically first constitution, that the fathers of the constitutions were authorized by nature or God to establish it.

For almost fifty years, the basic norm was a fundamental hypothetical concept that Kelsen (1967 [1934a]: 215) 'presupposed in juristic thinking'. In the early 1960s, due to his methodological concerns, Kelsen (1986 [1964]: 117) re-conceptualised it as a '(*figmentary*) act of will', a fictitious norm in the Vaihingerian *as-if* sense. Yet, for the present purpose, it suffices to say that the Kelsenian core positivist logic stayed very much the same. We do not need Nature, Justice, God or any other similar natural-law ideas, for it is the basic norm, Kelsen (1967 [1934a]: 195) makes clear, that provides us with the 'highest reason for the validity of the norms'.

You and Me – in a strictly juristic sense (not necessarily a moral or ethical one) – should obey today's legal norms because we should obey the provisions of the historically first constitution. Now, with regard to legal logic within the intellectual realm of legal positivism and beyond, surely Kelsen (1957c: 263) saw clearly that the basic norm 'may or may not be accepted' – and yet, to him, it makes a difference, methodologically and politically, whether we rely on a juristic–scientific hypothesis or on a metaphysical–mythical one:

> the validity for which the basic norm of legal positivism furnishes the reason is the inherent validity of the positive law, whereas the validity for which the basic norm of the natural-law doctrine or that of Christian theology furnishes the reason, is the validity of a natural or a divine order.

In other words, translated into the language of politics, one hypothesis shows us the way to constitutionalism, whereas the other one leads us down the road of political theology.

But then, what *if* Pure positivism's story of the basic norm is not a hypothesis? Let me pause here for a moment and reiterate briefly my two disclaimers: juristic thought versus political thinking, and no intention to synthesise them. So in this sense, while the what-if question is rhetorical, it is none the less important, and has its roots in what the jurist Clemens Jabloner (1998: 383), a very intimate interpreter of Kelsen, put to us two decades back: 'Kelsen made an extremely bold attempt as a legal theoretician to apply Freud's theory of totemism – collective consumption of the same sacrificed animal by the tribal community as an act of identification – to legal theory.' More recently, he commented that it was 'rather surprising that Kelsen's critique of ideology found its inspiration not least in Sigmund Freud' (Jabloner 2016: 333). Taking up Jabloner's challenge from the perspective of political and IR theory, I will say that Kelsen saw in Freud a most useful ally in debunking natural-law ideas as problematic anti-democratic myths.

As both an intellectual streetfighter and a political realist (my attributions), he needed to attack the Achilles heels of his natural-law foes relentlessly, and protect with as much power as was available his own weak spots. Theirs were the many different forms of metaphysical speculation, as well as various kinds of hypostatisation with a quasi-religious spin; and his own was, of course, the hypothesis of a basic norm. And as before, Freud was the go-to man. As Kelsen the human nature realist saw it, Freudian psychoanalysis provided a combination of offensive and defensive weaponry that would perhaps help him win his many intellectual battles.

A jurist through and through (though a reluctant one), he proved to be extremely well versed in the psychology of the day, and in what to take away from Freud in terms of legal and political thinking. In the early 1920s, at a time when Kelsen used Freud's *Group Psychology and the Analysis of the Ego* (1921) to de-ontologise the state (1922a, 1924), in 'God and the State' (Kelsen 1922/3; 1973), he used Freud's *Totem and Taboo* (1913) to de-ideologise the obedience question. In what could be seen as actually coming from Freud, Kelsen (1973: 61) leaves the reader in little doubt as to where he is going:

> The religious problem and the social problem exhibit a remarkable parallelism, and do so, in the first place, from the psychological point of view. For if one analyses the mode and manner in which God and society, the religious and the social, are experienced by the individual, it appears that in broad outline his state of mind is in both cases the same.

That is the key starting point, and by means of explicating the political psychology of authority, it leads him to one key conclusion, which elsewhere Kelsen (1941: 82) spelled out as loud and clear as possible: 'History confirms the saying: *ubi societas, ibi jus.*'

There was never total anarchy. Rather, in all social life, past and present, there has always been law. A primitive law or decentralised law, to be sure, but law none the less. Even God's commandments, or what we thought were the commandments of God, have always been conditional and relative: that is, in our consciousness there is nothing like a God's absoluteness when it comes to the question of regulating our behaviour and living-together. What Kelsen (1973: 62) was saying, with Freud's help, is that God – no more, no less – is perceived to be a 'normative authority'. In many ways, and to many people, seeing God this way is, of course, like dropping a bombshell, most notably because it paves the way for doing exactly the kind of clinical deconstructing that Kelsen had chosen to do: a Freudian-style unpacking of the whole concept of authority, seen as a psychological process of identification.

And thus once again in the work of Kelsen we really can see how important it was to him that we are all very clear about human nature as it actually is. To be sure, from today's point of view, Freud's studies at the intersection of psychology and anthropology might be 'scientific myth' or 'phylogenetic fable' (Jabloner 2016: 333). But, in the Vienna of their own time, Kelsen used it, quite understandably, as the latest science on the subject. So in lieu of looking into every nook and cranny of Kelsen's Freudian house, it seems far more important to focus on what was the result of all this in terms of political thinking. To be sure, tracing religious and social authority back to the same root – the authority of the father: that is, the primal father of the primal horde – is to attack the dualism of natural and positive law. And indeed, as soon as Kelsen had allowed Freudian psychoanalysis a place in his philosophy, there was no escape: You and Me, we will be having our battles, within us, and no less between us. And since the situation will be fairly similar to the one in which Schopenhauer's porcupines find themselves (we cannot do with each other, nor without), the only realistic chance of having a relatively stable and just political order is to have a democratic government.

Taking human nature as it really is, as Pure positivists do, Kelsen knew there are no easy solutions to the problem of authority and, for that matter, government. It is perfect enough that *The Essence and Value of Democracy*, written by Kelsen in the 1920s – his 'most important text on democracy' (Invernizzi-Accetti 2015: 247), now available in English translation (Kelsen 2013 [1929b]) – begins with heavy human nature realism. 'In the idea of democracy', Kelsen (2013 [1929b]: 27) writes,

> two postulates of our practical reason are united and two primitive instincts of man as a social being strive for satisfaction. First and foremost, there is the reaction against the coercive nature of the social condition: the protest against the subjection of one's own will to the will of another and the resistance to the agony of heteronomy.

And then Kelsen (2013 [1929b]: 27) moves on to what is familiar territory for anyone acquainted with the core logic of Freud's *Civilization and Its Discontents* (1930):

> Nature itself demands freedom and, thus, rebels against society. The more one man's primary feeling of self-worth depends on the rejection of any other man's higher worth, the more he perceives the foreign will, which the social order imposes upon him, as a burden. The more elementary the relationship between the subject and the master, the more likely the former is to ask: 'He is a man like me; we are equal! What gives him the right to rule over me?' . . . For society and the state to be possible, there must be a valid normative order regulating mutual behavior of men, i.e. there must be rule. But if we must be ruled, then we only want to be ruled by ourselves.

The fundamental antagonism between what is willed by You, and by Me, and at one and the same time, what any legal and political order demands from *Us* in terms of coercion and obedience, is unavoidable.

The antagonism is also unsolvable, though – for each and every state in general, and in particular the Schmittian one.

15 A MOST REALISTIC STATE

Is it not Kelsen's point that law and the state are one and the same? Is it not one of Kelsen's ground-breaking endeavours to have shown their normativity? And is it not one of Kelsen's lasting influences (1967 [1934a]: 1) to have constructed a science of law that was totally against 'methodological syncretism' or 'the uncritical mixture of methodologically different disciplines' from first to last? In other words, and from the point of political and IR theory, what does it mean to say that in Kelsen we find a most realistic state? And for that matter, if these were Kelsen's scientific goals and intellectual ambitions, why is there so much Freud – this 'duplicitous, egomaniacal fraud' (Rorty 1996) – in Kelsen's philosophy and political thinking?

He has sought to warn us, irrespective of time and place: we will always have to reckon with those voices in intellectual and political life that claim, through Nature, Reason or God, to possess the final answers to age-old questions. In light of natural-law philosophy's naïve idealism, we will ignore what a Freudian human nature realism tells us, at our own peril. And faced with Schmittians old and new, we will challenge what political realism teaches us about law and state, politics and power, only at the risk of a monumental failure.

That is all well and good. But then, really, all this with Freud? To be sure, given the way that Freud has been treated ever since he started psychoanalysis in Vienna's Ninth District, it really looks as though 'the Freud Wars will never end' (Kirsch 2017). Too much criticism and critique, good and bad, back and forth from all sides, old and new, and I say that to recall one of my three methodological disclaimers stipulated in the Introduction: unless otherwise stated, I explore Kelsen's life and thought from the perspective of his own time. As Miles Hollingworth (2013: 1) put it so well with regard to all great thinkers: 'We, of course, have the advantage of knowing how it all turns out.' But *they*, of course, did not. As to Freud, then, psychoanalysis was new science, and of course Kelsen used it.[3] No more, no less.

Now, on the face of it, there is no immediate connection between Kelsenian delicts and Freudian drives. And there should not be one, at least not from the rigid standpoint of Pure positivism. Yes, without any doubt, the state *is* the law. It is a 'legal order', says Kelsen (1948b: 226), that

> prescribes a certain behaviour, or what amounts to the same, imposes upon a person the obligation to behave in a certain way by providing a sanction in case of contrary behaviour, which thus is made illegal or a 'violation' of the law, a 'delict'.

As I have been saying, as a trained IR theorist and foreign-policy realist, I will not at all challenge anything in what is core Kelsenian jurisprudence. And in fact I do not even want to because what we can all learn from him – for our own methodology and for our own politics – is to be strict in, well, methodology and politics. That is, the fact that the state is a normative order, firmly in the realm of imputation and ought-propositions, does not mean that the Kelsenian state is not also a very realistic one in the sense that it is a nice one.

Given You and Me, the Kelsenian state may be best understood as a legal order with real power. The state is the law, and the law is the state. And to understand why Kelsen was so strict about ridding ourselves of the ancient dualism of law and state, one must work through the many pages of his jurisprudential writings. They are often dry, but fascinating none the less, and all very valuable, for what you come to see is how he really tries to tell you, in a calm yet bold way, that the state is a coercive order, and that the organs of the state have but one task: to coerce us into a certain behaviour. What lies behind each and every single clarification, conceptual or formalistic, in Kelsen's juristic way of thinking is a very strong – yet equally calm and bold – form of political realism. Could Kelsen have arrived at this political realism without Freudian psychoanalysis? Perhaps so; but then it helped him to ground his conception of law and state, coercion and politics, authority and obedience, in a robust view of human nature, a Freudian science of human nature.

As soon as one begins to peel off layer after layer of what many critics scorn as Kelsen's abstract formalism, one comes to see, ever more clearly, a sketch of Kelsen the progressive political realist. And in the process of digging deeper and deeper into core methodological Kelsenian territory, thereby clearing away one metaphysical notion of natural-law philosophy after another, what was clearly visible as a sketch eventually turns into an ever sharper picture of him as a man, and what he really thought of social and political reality. We come to see a passionate man of science who was really speaking truth to power: in the real world, and on each and every single page of his writings.

We may lament the so-called tragedies of politics as often as we like. Kelsen will not take away from You and Me the responsibility for confronting the dynamics of democracy and its power struggles. From the first page to the last, he keeps on telling us that a Freudian human nature realism is inescapable – and so is foreign-policy realism.

CHAPTER 4

KELSEN'S FOREIGN-POLICY REALISM

'A problem from hell'

Samantha Power (2002)

Kelsen was no softie. Neither was he a pacifist (at least not in the strict sense) – and he knew that he had to get rid of his gun. It was the spring of 1933. One day in April, most likely, perhaps immediately after he learned that the Nazis had sacked him as law Professor at Cologne, where he was director of the international law programme. At the time, he was living in what is today the German state of North Rhine–Westphalia, and had already acquired Prussian citizenship.

Gone were the days when he was operating out of the Dom Hotel, an old-world place situated right next to the cathedral, where a young Herz had knocked on Kelsen's door asking if he could be his doctoral student. Nowadays, the Kelsen family was residing in Cologne's Second District, Rodenkirchen, at Mehlemerstraße 26, located in the Marienburg villa quarter bordering the Rhine. He was frightened. In the social and political climate of rising Fascism and anti-Semitism, he feared an imminent house search by the Nazi police – a realistic prospect. And so, what he actually did was to take his old *k. u. k.* service revolver, which to him was nothing more than a memento of a bygone time, wrap it in a banana peel, and then, after what must have been a quick walk of ten minutes or so, throw the old gun into the Rhine. Not into the Danube. Life was such that it was the Rhine.

16 THE KELLOGG–BRIAND PACT

To speak of an imperial service revolver in the hands of a liberal Professor of International Law, at the time of Hitler's rise and the politics of fierce nationalism, is to speak about realism versus idealism; and since we are in the inter-war period, so succinctly called by E. H. Carr (1939) the 'twenty years' crisis', we might as well ask, who would not have wanted to have a global peace pact in place?

The reader will know where I am going with this: of course, we did have such a pact, signed in Paris in the summer of 1928, on 27 August. And to be sure, who would not agree that it was all huge and grand? As Oona A. Hathaway and Scott J. Shapiro (2018: xi), two law Professors at Yale, have written in *The Internationalists: How a Radical Plan to Outlaw War Remade the World*, a passionate plea for defending the post-war liberal international order:

> The entire ceremony took less than an hour. At 3:57 p.m., a Swiss Guard banged his halberd on the floor, the cameras stopped rolling, and, for the first time in the history of the world, war was declared illegal.

It was the Kellogg–Briand Pact. And it was a masterpiece of international diplomacy. The treaty between the United States and France, also including Great Britain, Germany and several other major and minor powers, and providing for the renunciation of war as an instrument of national policy, stipulated the following in no uncertain terms: first, get rid of Clausewitz, and stop using war as bargaining tool or an extended means of foreign policy. Second, settle all disputes and conflicts 'by pacific means'.[1] This was quite a lot. Or depending on where you stand, it was very little. It could be said that Kellogg–Briand was the worst of all worlds.

Feelings run high about this pact, as they usually do when it comes to the question of whether it is possible to relieve the world of war, and through what means. And in many ways this is how it should be, at least if the debate is focused enough to be a reasonable one. Writing this at a point in history when the United States, Russia and China seem to be entering into a new arms race; when the end of the Intermediate-range Nuclear Forces (INF) Treaty risks placing Europe back in reach of Russian and American missiles; and when, what makes it all so much more dangerous, neither the North Atlantic Treaty Organisation (NATO) nor the European Union is in a stable condition, I am more certain than ever that it is important to have all these informed foreign-policy debates and intellectual battles old and new, and make them accessible to the public.

Now, what have we learned from the Kellogg–Briand Pact? It would be a grave mistake – *foul play*, really – to insinuate that its supporters refuse to have a realistic view of how it all ended: 'You don't have to be an expert in international relations to know that the agreement . . . failed to end war' (Hathaway and Shapiro 2018: xv). That hits the nail totally on the head. Sadly so. Look at all the wars we have been fighting since that mild summer's day, where inside the Clock Room at 37 Quai d'Orsay, Aristide Briand, the French Foreign Minister, his American colleague Frank Kellogg, the forty-fifth US Secretary of State, and no fewer than thirteen plenipotentiaries from West and East, including the Global South, signed the accord to a great deal of international fanfare. What we have really learned though, is that there will be blood. And, actually, there was going to be even more blood than there had ever been before. It is perhaps one of the biggest ironies of the twentieth century, and surely the deadliest one, that during the course of the Second World War, 'with the exception of Ireland, every one of the states that had gathered in Paris to renounce war was *at war*' (Hathaway and Shapiro 2018: xv).

No wonder, then, that the Kellogg–Briand Pact has such a bad reputation. Even Kelsen was unhappy. A liberal, a jurist, a Pure theorist of law, who cared so deeply about the big questions relating to the causes of war and a realistic means for peace, he was more than unhappy. His overall verdict was a damning indictment. Everyone who wants to hold in his hands a theoretical and practical argument *against* international law in politics among nations, Kelsen (1944a: 18) says in *Peace through Law*, should take a look at everything that is wrong with this treaty, and when you are finished with doing exactly that, chances are that you will never want anything to do with 'a legal approach to the problem of peace'.

In ways similar to Kelsen, but not identical, present-day realists join in the chorus of how these internationalists – or idealists, as they appear to ridicule them – could have been so foolish or naïve. To see where Kelsen fits in, let us take a brief look at how the contestants have positioned themselves. It is nothing new but it will be important for the rest of this chapter, and what is more, for the Conclusion, and the questions of whether Kelsen was a progressive political realist, and if so, what that might mean for us today.

The supporters of the Kellogg–Briand Pact raise its virtues, or positive real-world impact, to new heights. The signatories, and their successors, may not have renounced war, it is, of course, conceded. But – and this is odd – as Hathaway and Shapiro (2018: xix) write, the 'Pact outlawed war'. And they go on to say – and this is worth quoting at length – that the pact

> did more than that. By prohibiting states from using war to resolve disputes, it began a cascade of event that would give birth to the modern global order. As its effects reverberated across the globe, it reshaped the world map, catalyzed the human rights revolution, enabled the use of economic sanctions as a tool of law enforcement, and ignited the explosion in the number of international organizations that regulate so many aspects of our daily lives.

That is quite something to digest for everyone in the field of politics and IR, but for foreign-policy realists it is almost like having a bombshell dropped on their head. Lots of talk about norms and transformation. Little on history and power. And as power-focused as realists are, they do not take such claims lightly.

A realist response cannot but point to the question of cause and effect, and the problem of correlation and causation in diplomatic history and world politics. The critical issue is, what accounts for the real decline in frequency of inter-state war since the Pact was signed? It may have been caused by the Pact. It may have been caused by the legal or normative constraints that the signatures have since put upon world leaders, so that they fight less frequently than they used to do. But then, surely, the independent variable that has made for a more peaceful world may have also been one of the following: increased economic interdependence; blossoming democracies; growing repugnance toward institutionalised bloodshed; or a combination of all of them. And the list of variables goes on. Perhaps, at some point, one comes back to the basics of foreign-policy realism: to the core logic of military power – that is to say, to the logic of anarchy from which the contracting parties wanted to escape. As a result, then, the actual decline in war and conquest may have been caused by the fact of strategic deterrence, the (strange) reality of nuclear weapons.

Thus there is a gentle way of saying it and there is a more provocative one. Stephen Walt, Robert and Renee Belfer Professor of International Affairs at Harvard and today one of the most outspoken neorealists in the United States, if not the West, has chosen a combination of the two: analytically driven, not shying away from a good polemic and with a good political punch line. Directly responding to present-day internationalists regarding the Kellogg–Briand Pact, which he says is just a picture-perfect example of the 'misplaced idealism' so prevalent in the inter-war period, Walt (2017) makes it very clear what he thinks of all this: 'Sorry, liberals – just saying "no" to war doesn't stop it' (see also Drezner 2013; Menand 2017).

Gentle or provocative, the analytical key message is the very same; and what must also be the same is the normative message to foreign-policy-makers. It is one thing to invest in legalistic diplomacy. If you are lucky, it might even secure you a place in the history books: that is, in 'a mostly irrelevant footnote' (Walt 2017). It is quite another to get something out of an effective legalistic diplomacy, or out of what Kelsen (1967 [1934a]: 211) would call an 'efficacious' international legal order. And so unless we can do the latter, we might want to stick with what Morgenthau (1967 [1948a]: 545) suggested in *Politics among Nations* as the fifth rule (of nine) of what makes good diplomacy: 'Give up the shadow of worthless rights for the substance of real advantage.'

Actually, Morgenthau did understand Kelsen. He did not agree with what he thought was his mentor's way to unpolitical legalism but, unlike Herz, he was one of the few foreign-policy realists who did grasp that the *Pure* jurist was unconvinced by any Wilsonian conception of international politics or world order. In 'The Machiavellian Utopia', Morgenthau's (1945: 145) short piece published in *Ethics* and dealing with the flaws of what he called a 'liberal rationality', he saw in Kelsen quite a useful ally. Morgenthau was critical of Dumbarton Oaks, or let us say, he was critical of the political thinking behind it. And in some ways, he was right to implicate Kelsen in his own fight. From the conventional realist's standpoint, Kelsen may have relied too heavily on judicial organs in the quest for peace. But then, Morgenthau says, Kelsen none the less carries an important strategic lesson for us, which is a timeless one: it is that all attempts at devising an efficacious collective security regime are bound to fail, unless there is a centralised, coercive power that has the real means to execute its decisions.

Herz was not so kind. He appears to have been less thoughtful vis-à-vis his *Doktorvater* than Morgenthau, and that is a bit awkward. One would expect that Herz, precisely because he had been a doctoral student of Kelsen's in Cologne, would be more nuanced toward his mentor's public international law theory. But he just was not.

It is odd. In 'The Pure Theory of Law Revisited: Hans Kelsen's Doctrine of International Law in the Nuclear Age', Herz's essay for Kelsen's 1964 *Festschrift*, edited by Salo Engel, a close follower of Kelsen since their Geneva years, he refers to Kelsen's theory of international law as 'the most sophisticated natural law theory which has been developed during this century in the field of international affairs' (Herz 1964: 108). Certainly, he goes on to qualify this by stating that he did not mean it in any Thomistic way, saying that Kelsen was really driven by the question of what the nature of the law is. You might say I am being over-sensitive here, but Kelsen's almost super-critical stance toward 'natural law doctrines' (Kelsen 1949: 486) was so widely known (if not feared too) that it seems awkward that Herz would use this kind of language.

The same goes for the term doctrine. Kelsen the Pure positivist, the moral relativist, the political realist – one might say – dreaded doctrines, or doctrinaire thought and politics. Why, then, would Herz use this term? It may very well be because the term doctrine is, after all, a realist fighting word, a *Kampfbegriff*: a weapon used by political realists to shoot at any style of philosophy or political thinking that they deem idealistic or dangerous, or both. Morgenthau (1967 [1948]: 540–1) liked to quote a line from the ground-breaking and vibrant William Graham Sumner (1934):[2]

> If you want war, nourish a doctrine. Doctrines are the most frightful tyrants to which men ever are subject, because doctrines get inside of a man's reason and betray him against himself.

Not that Morgenthau or Sumner or any other foreign-policy realist is wrong about this. Doctrines in politics, and foreign affairs, really are just that: very dangerous. But to insinuate, as Herz does, that Kelsen's Pure positivism is a doctrine is awkward, to say the least. To be sure, the Pure theory of law, state and international legal order has its flaws. Of course, it has; and depending on where one stands, perhaps it even has many flaws. Which theory has not? Saying, though, that Kelsen's legal and political thinking is doctrinaire or quasi-ideological is, to me at least, false.

This is where the Kellogg–Briand Pact comes back in. If one goes through Herz's *Festschrift* essay, and for that matter, through his *Political Realism and Political Idealism* (recall how Kelsen successfully promoted Herz's book for the 1951 Woodrow Wilson Foundation Award of the American Political Science Association), you will grasp at once what Herz's key message, theoretical and strategic, or key criticism is: that there is a direct line from, a sort of intimate intellectual connection between, the ideas of Kelsen and the ideas of the League, Kellogg–Briand and the United Nations. Needless to say, in the eyes of Herz, all these schemes are idealised stuff: dangerous politics, naïve. And what is more, and what also explains the use of the term doctrine, Herz (1964: 108) writes that the sum total of all 'Kelsen's "should-be's"' is – and be warned – 'expressive of what one may call "legal imperialism"'.

Now, you will find no foreign-policy realist who either was, or is, or will ever be totally happy with how Kelsen sought to juridify world politics, and thereby sought to create a more just world order. What you will find, though, is that there have been political realists, such as Robert Tucker, who seem to have understood the Kelsenian project of a positivist law, a progressive politics and a relative justice in foreign affairs a great deal better than others, many of them pseudo-realists. This is, of course, a theme to which I will return at length in Chapter 5, for it is really *the* theme. It is this book's *raison d'être*, how one – from the point of view of a liberal foreign-policy realism – might make sense of Kelsen's political thinking, thereby recovering it for our time.

It is, then, safe to say that no foreign-policy realist loves Kellogg–Briand, as much as no one loves a political realist (Gilpin 1996). In *The Twenty Years' Crisis*, E. H. Carr (1939: 40) condemned it as one of the era's 'utopian dishes', and saw the Pact as yet another 'symptom of the growing divorce between theory and practice'. Kelsen would not object. In *Moral Man and Immoral Society*, Reinhold Niebuhr (2001 [1932]: xxi) speaks of 'the romantic over-estimate of human virtue and moral capacity in our modern middle-class culture' that gives 'such ventures as the Kellogg Pact . . . a connotation of moral and social achievement which the total facts completely belie'. Kelsen would agree. And, in 'About Cynicism, Perfectionism, and Realism and International Affairs', Morgenthau (1962b: 127) recalls how he 'was called a cynic for the first time in 1929, after the signature of the Kellogg–Briand Pact'. Why cynic?

As he wrote, he was apparently one of those who 'pointed to the impotence of a legal formula in the face of the formidable social forces which make for war'. That is not cynicism; it is *speaking truth to power*! Ask Kelsen.

He was as fierce and direct about what he called an 'international legal instrument excluding war from international relations' (Kelsen 1944a: 18) as he ever was when he looked at something and thought it to be lacking logical consistency. In *Peace through Law* (1944a) – where he successfully applied the Pure theory to concrete world events (Olechowski 2016a: 61) – he comes right to the point. Never one to mince words, Kelsen (1944a: 18, 32) begins by saying that the 'so-called Briand–Kellogg Pact, ratified by almost all the nations of the world', is – you will surely have guessed by now – a 'failure'; and a little further on in the book he even calls it a 'complete failure'. It is about time, then, to bring back in the veil of ignorance: not for human nature, though (see Chapter 1), but rather with regard to his stance toward the Pact. If we knew little other than what Kelsen said about this treaty, which is, after all, seen in many quarters as a signature achievement of world politics, Kelsen could easily pass for quite a foreign-policy realist. This, of course, needs explicating.

To begin with, who would come up with the idea of outlawing war *without* replacing the use of force with an effective or efficacious alternative sanctions regime? Surely, in reference to Stephen Walt's point, *Yes*, just saying *No* is not enough. Kelsen (1944a: 18) was taken aback by the fact of 'prohibiting any kind of war, even war as a reaction against a violation of law, without replacing this sanction of international law by another kind of sanction, and internationally organized sanction'. Doing that – that is, *not* doing that – was a disaster waiting to happen.

He would, of course, couch it all in the scientific language that was so typical of such a methodical man of Pure legal technique. For example, Kelsen (1944a: 18) would say that the Pact did, in the end, suffer from 'its own technical insufficiency', meaning: only if you are either a naïve idealist or a rigid pacifist would you not take into account what is going to happen if you make war illegal, while putting nothing in its place that would compensate for what is war's positive function. What the Pact did, in fact, was rob the politics among nations and international law of what surely was a most important juridified sanction mechanism in world politics – war. It was a decentralised one, to be sure. But it is better to have the use of force as a legal, however decentralised, sanction regime than to have no coercive regime at all. What about a war of self-defence?

Here is some more political realism in general, and yet more from the realm of foreign-policy realism in particular. Writes Stephen Walt (2017), short and sweet, and also quite correctly: 'I use the 1928 Kellogg–Briand Pact as an example of a misplaced idealism that failed to stop the slide to war' and – very important now – that 'may have made it a bit more likely'. Agreed. Compare Kelsen. Let us begin with his softer version. The 'Pact attempted too much' because it abolished a coercive sanction, while creating for us all, intentionally so, a void. And what this very void actually did, Kelsen (1944a: 18) continues, was '[favor] States inclined to violate the rights of other States'. That is Kelsen speaking, not Walt or any other one of the foreign-policy realists.

That brings us to the more outspoken version of his criticism. 'The Pact undertook too little', he adds to the foregoing, 'by obliging the States to seek pacific settlement of their disputes without obliging them to submit all their conflicts without any exception to the compulsory jurisdiction of an international court' (Kelsen 1944a: 18). Here is the problem of the void again. Of course it is. Call Morgenthau a cynic, or call me or Kelsen one. But, Kelsen (1944a: 32) says, to really think that you can have quarrelling powers and states – major, medium-sized or small – voluntarily submit themselves to whatever kind of 'pacific' mechanism for settlement of their conflict – that is, without providing any 'obligatory procedure' for it –is just one thing: 'dangerous'.

To Kelsen – and who among the foreign-policy realists would not agree? – the idea of abolishing war is surely a noble one. But if we do this and we declare war to be illegal in international relations and law, while literally at one and the same time *not* following through with the second and much more important element, which is the element of compulsory juridifying for a settlement, this means that we end up with the worst of both worlds of realism and idealism. In fact, as Kelsen (1944a: 32) the foreign-policy realist writes, following true realpolitik logic: it is exactly that kind of void in world politics which provides for nations and states 'the greatest temptation for settling the conflict by the employment of force, even if force as means of settling the conflict is forbidden by a special treaty'. For what really is a treaty, or what really is a norm, without any coercive element attached to it?

Of course, we have been there: human nature, law and the state, coercion and the political understood in terms of power and interests, roots of authority and obedience. And to be sure, all these Kelsenian elements of political realism make Kelsen the foreign-policy realist very much aware that You and Me are even worse in international life.

17 ANARCHY AND WAR

You might think that I was a bit too polemical in the way that I presented Kelsen's criticism of what he thought was public international law done very badly. And be forewarned (as I said in the Introduction): I will be even worse in Chapter 5, a lengthy conclusion about what Critically inspired progressive political realists can take away from Kelsen's style of political thinking. It will include an imagined dialogue in which a Kelsenian realist will battle it out with a warm-hearted idealist. For now, though, let us do the groundwork, and explore Kelsen's take on what surely are the basics of foreign-policy realism old and new – the twin problem of anarchy and war.

What is it, as the saying goes, that keeps political and IR theorists, and most notably practitioners of national security and foreign affairs, up at night? The answer is clear enough: it is risks and threats, minor and major, and especially those kinds of strategic risk that are perceived to be threatening one's national security, understood in terms of the national interest. Here is what makes up the list, at the time of writing: great power competition, conflicts and instability in key regions, migration, cyber and influence operations, terrorism and proliferation of dirty weapons, energy security and economic resilience, disruptive technologies and demographic change. And on it goes. Such lists tend to be living creatures, their scope depending on whatever strategic logic or political reason there is to have to deal with some threats at any particular point, and not so much with other ones.

But then, of course, the core strategic issue behind all these other issues, real or imagined, is a structural one. The international system has been designed in such a way that wars can occur at any time and in any place, exactly because there is nothing to prevent them from doing so.[3] So say realists. So say neorealists. And so says Kelsen too.

One might say he is in good company. It might be intuitively so but he does share this core analytical assumption of sustained international anarchy with an illustrious round of realists – or, as others have said, with a treacherous group of neorealist IR theorists. The expert reader knows where I am headed: 1984. Ashley. Neorealism.

To me at least, anyway, the late Robert Gilpin, inaugural Dwight D. Eisenhower Professor of International Affairs at Princeton's Woodrow Wilson School, had done the right thing. Mocking the man who was then a sort of critic-in-chief of the neorealists, Gilpin (1986: 301–2) the foreign-policy realist wrote with a wink that he could not understand why someone else would speak of foreign-policy realists as 'card-carrying members of an insidious and rather dangerous conspiracy that, like Socrates, is indoctrinating the youth (read graduate students) in false and dangerous ways of thinking'. What had happened was, in 'The Poverty of Neorealism', Richard K. Ashley (1984: 258), a former Associate Professor in the School of Politics and Global Studies at Arizona State, sought to cut neorealism to bits, arguing that this new realism was 'an "orrery of errors", a self-enclosed, self-affirming joining of statist, utilitarian, positivist, and structuralist commitments'.

What does Kelsen have to do with any of this? This was, and still is, an ongoing internal IR theory debate about important epistemological issues of structuralist theorising. And to be sure, if you add Freud – who will, of course, re-appear later as part of Jean Bethke Elshtain's Freud – what you have at the table is quite an explosive, though fascinating, mix of thinkers and theorists. Let me start, though, one by one, and take it one step at a time.

To begin with, Hans Kelsen and Kenneth Waltz – and, for that matter, John Mearsheimer – make an odd trio. Here is the idealist jurist, or so they say. And over there are two frontline political scientists, widely recognised as foreign-policy realists. Waltz, a giant in the study of world politics, a key founder of neorealism in IR theory and a so-called defensive realist, holds that states do not attempt to accrue maximum power, but rather seek to maintain their position in the system's power hierarchy (Waltz 1979). And then there is Mearsheimer, or 'Mearchiavelli', the R. Wendell Harrison Distinguished Service Professor of Political Science at Chicago, without doubt one of America's boldest and perhaps also most combative foreign-policy theorists, thriving on unpopular truths, at least as he sees them; he is a so-called offensive realist, arguing, contra Waltz, that states are prone to a much more aggressive stance, going for maximum power wherever they can (Mearsheimer 2001, 2018).

What is so interesting is to look at where these men have seen the root cause of how states behave. Or, taken to the most serious form of foreign-policy behaviour, where they have seen the root cause of war – which is, needless to say, the most vexing question for all of us. Only if we get the analysis of *why war?* at least reasonably right, might we be able to come up with ways and means, strategic and operational, for *how peace?* – or at least, for making a temporary peace more sustainable. And so what I now hope to show, from the standpoint of my liberal foreign-policy realism, is that Kelsen, not unlike Waltz and Mearsheimer, has proved to be quite a third-image theorist of war – a peculiar one, to be sure, but no-nonsense none the less. Where Waltz has discerned three images of war, then I would see Kelsen as being in the same third spot that Ashley, and legions of critics of neorealism, identified as a sort of pseudo-(neo)realist hell, where the evil of anarchy is reified over and over. As usual, of course, matters are much more complicated, yet it is very much worthwhile exploring them for the present purpose. First things first.

It all goes back to Waltz's dissertation at Columbia, published in 1959 as a game-changing little book entitled *Man, the State, and War: A Theoretical Analysis* and re-published in late 2018 in a sixtieth anniversary edition (Waltz 2018 [1959b]). It is a breathtakingly concise statement in the study of philosophy, political science and IR. What Waltz did was look systematically at the history of Western philosophy and political thinking, and try to make sense of how we were explaining war. Waltz said, in three ways, that we had three images of war. Rooted in this kind of analytical work at the intersection of political and IR theory, Waltz helped instigate what political scientist Ashley J. Tellis (1996: 3), a Senior Fellow at the Carnegie Endowment for International Peace, aptly called political realism's 'long march to scientific theory'.

Kelsen was not involved in these debates, at least not directly. And why would he have been? He was a jurist and they were the political scientists. They all had an interest in war: that is, in stopping wars from occurring and in making the world more peaceful. Who would not want more peaceful international relations? But then they were of two different disciplines, each one wrestling with its own fundamental questions, conceptual bases and methodological tools. As have seen, Kelsen was very strict on that point. Never mix what must not be mixed; never commit the error of any 'methodological syncretism' (Kelsen 1967 [1934a]: 1). Waltz also sought to make the field of IR more rigid, more scientific, more explanatory. In other words, Kelsen's two realist students from former times, Morgenthau and Herz, were on the watch for Waltz, for two reasons: one concerns the role of human nature (Morgenthau), and the other concerns the constitutive role of the security dilemma (Herz).

Kelsen was what many political and IR theorists, perhaps including Waltz, would call a human nature pessimist, at least if they were following my argument about Kelsen being a Freudian-inspired man and thinker. Rather than calling him a pessimist, my own preference is to call him a human nature realist. That is: first, he was a realist about the dynamics of human nature. Second, he was a realist about what human nature means for us: sustained conflicts of interests. Third, he was a realist about what human nature does *not* mean for us: there will never, ever be any harmony of interests among individuals in social life, or among nations and states in international life. Sad but true. And in broad brushstrokes this looks quite similar to how Morgenthau (1967 [1948a]: 4) had seen things: unless we reach a point in history where there is a *new man* – chances are we never will – we are stuck with all the struggles for power and interests that we have seen since 'the classical philosophies of China, India, and Greece endeavored to discover these laws'. And then Waltz (1959) came along, questioning in the later 1950s whether human nature has anything to do with why states fight wars.

The outcome is well known. With the ascent of Waltz, as Stefano Guzzini (1998: 127), a Swedish-based professor of political science, had put it, realism got 'rid of the first image'. Waltz was neither the first challenger to Morgenthau's style of political realism, nor the only one. But then, Waltz was very fine-tuned, and also an early scientific critic from *within* the realist tradition. In *Man, the State, and War*, Waltz (1959) put Morgenthau, Niebuhr, Spinoza and Augustine in the first-image camp, saying it is pointless to search for the cause of war 'in the nature and behavior of man' (42). What all these classic thinkers had done was to commit the 'error of psychologism: the analysis of individual behavior used uncritically to explain group phenomena' (28). And what is worse, they do not do proper theory. Explanatory power? Predictive value? Nothing. The first image, concludes Waltz, amounts to nothing more than 'the simple statement that man's nature is such that sometimes he fights and sometimes he does not' (29). Case closed.

Ever since Waltz's famous criticism of what he called the first-image pessimists, the realist study of foreign-policy and international relations has sought to move on. It has attempted to shift from 'realist thought to neorealist theory' (Waltz 1990b). And it did move: toward the so-called third image (Waltz 1959a: Ch. vi). Leaving behind the concept of human nature, these new (neo) realists or structural realists started to focus on the structure of the international system. And what they found, soon enough, was systemic anarchy: a real lack of a central political authority, as realists have it, or a real lack of a centralised coercive order, in Kelsenian parlance. In other words, anarchy is seen as the core reason why war is an ever-present possibility.

Where the core cause of war is anarchy, then it is clear – put the other way round – that as long as we have a world order of systemic anarchy, there will be war. That is it. Sad but true. You and Me, we may be evil, or not. Who cares? It is the structure of the international system – its nature, if you wish to call it that – that forces the major players in this system to behave in certain ways; war is one these ways. And so, with an eye to Ashley and other Critically inspired critics of neorealism, does that kind of political and IR theory make Waltz – and, for that matter, Mearsheimer and the neoclassical realists – really a bunch of co-perpetrators and co-perpetuators of anarchy and war? I am not so sure, at least not when it comes to Waltz, who, a decade ago, said something very important: 'I certainly believe that, as long as the world continues to be anarchic, the theory that I developed will maintain its direct relevance. One cannot expect the world to change unless the structure of the world changes' (quoted in Schouten 2011). He is (about) right, so do not shoot the messenger.

Herz was a forerunner of this type of realist logic. In *Political Realism and Political Idealism*, he spoke for the first time of a tragic situation that has come to be known as the security dilemma. Wrote Herz (1951: 3):

> Whether man is 'by nature' peaceful and cooperative, or aggressive or domineering, is not the question. The condition that concerns us here is not an anthropological or biological, but a social one. It is his uncertainty and anxiety as to his neighbors' intentions that places man in this basic dilemma, and makes the 'homo homini lupus' a primary fact of the social life of man.

As we have seen in the context of Kelsen's human nature realism, Herz surely, like Morgenthau (and Kelsen), was not convinced that we are all saints, or that we were, are or will be any time soon full-blown reasonable Kantian rational animals (Kant 1991a [1784]). But then, that may be beside the point anyway (at least for now), because in the relations among nations, where the logic of balance of power dominates strategic thinking, what would count is to have a central coercive order. And like it or not, we do not have one internationally.

Thus it has all unravelled. Morgenthau was seen as being increasingly out of touch with what was required of a new behavioural-style political science of IR – theories and testing, models and hypotheses, variables and maths. There was little, if no, room any more for the hullabaloo of a Nietzschean *animus dominandi* or the like. And it was a style of political thinking that was not really understood anyway. 'Human nature realism', Mearsheimer (2001: 19) says with regard to Morgenthau, 'is based on the simple assumption that states are led by human beings who have a "will to power" hard-wired into them at birth.' Surely Morgenthau never said, meant or implied what Mearsheimer is saying in this grossly over-simplified take on Morgenthau's so-called classical form of foreign-policy realism. In fact, Morgenthau saw clearly that the real problem of world politics, war and peace, is lack of world government.

But then, *Politics among Nations* is hardly a kind of theorising in the new mould of social science (Morgenthau 1967 [1948a]). It was Waltz (1979) who filled the void. In *Theory of International Politics*, a second major coup, he explained international outcomes by looking at how capabilities are distributed within the anarchical ordering principle of the international system. Years later, Mearsheimer took it to yet another level, arguing in *Tragedy of Great Power Politics* (2001) that it is the mix of anarchy, distribution of power and lack of knowledge of each other's strategic intentions that forces states to seek maximum power: to reach the point where one is 'the biggest and baddest dude on the block' (Mearsheimer 2002). Surely, it is all part of how Herz (1951) had conceptualised the security dilemma: what are one side's defensive measures are taken by the other as aggressive, thereby triggering a vicious circle of measures and countermeasures in the form of an arms race. And whatever you make of Mearsheimer (2001: 33), we should all take it very seriously when he cautions: 'Add to this the "911" problem – the absence of a central authority to which a threatened state can turn for help – and states have even greater incentive to fear each other.' All this is serious material, a quite thorough political realism. And, in fact, the way from one of the most controversial IR theorists of our time, 'Mearchiavelli', back to the allegedly 'idealist' jurist Kelsen is a short one.

As someone who has been critical of neorealism myself (Schuett 2010b; and see Ch. 5), make no mistake, there is a great deal in the philosophy and political thinking of Kelsen on the one hand, and in the neorealist theory and politics of Mearsheimer on the other one, that separates them, keeping their intellectual projects quite apart from one another. Mearsheimer totally and expertly recognises the problem of anarchy and self-help, yet in the final analysis his solution to the problem appears to be that he wants to see more self-help. That is to say: he keeps calling upon politicians and policy-makers in Washington to do away with what he sees as a sort of liberal internationalist wish-wash, and start anew with a grand strategy featuring a shrewd balance-of-power politics based on two pillars: strategic deterrence and offshore balancing (Mearsheimer 2018; also Walt 2018). This is not Kelsen's intellectual and political mindset, though.

Kelsen wants to put the brakes on anarchy not through more self-help, but through less and less power politics, and through more and more public international law. From his legal point of view, though – and, I should add, from the standpoint of his foreign-policy realism – more and more norms in international law are not enough: what would make all the difference is to have ever more efficacious international law in the form of an ever more centralised international legal order. In terms of barricades, then, Kelsen and the neorealists are most certainly standing on different sides. My point is, though, precisely because I can already hear these (pseudo-)realists mutter idealism, legalism, naïve and the like, that it is absolutely not that Kelsen was unaware of all the harshness of sustained power politics. Of course, they differ in their prescriptions or political *ought*. But in terms of the *is* – which is to say, in terms of the root cause of anarchy and great power conflict and war – they see almost eye to eye. I should add that, to me at least, Kelsen even appears to be the more clinical and stronger foreign-policy realist.

So let me put it like this: who in our time invented the concept of anarchy in international relations? Or, to be more precise and clear here, who in the eyes of the structural neorealist Mearsheimer (2006: 234) was the 'first great structural realist' in the modern West? It was not him. It was not Waltz. Nor was it Morgenthau, nor – spoiler alert – Kelsen. None of them. It was Goldie! To Mearsheimer, it was none other than G. Lowes Dickinson, the brilliant British philosopher and political theorist, publicist and poet, humanitarian and pacifist, member of the Bloomsbury Group and the Labour Party, teacher at Cambridge's King's College and a core protagonist of the League of Nations. I like that very much. Mearsheimer has chosen a man, as *New York Times* writer Percy Hutchison (1934) put it, 'whose deep resolve and lifetime passion it was "to discover reality and help mankind"'. One might say he was a man of realism *and* idealism.

As to the analytical side, or realism bit, Mearsheimer's choice seems perfectly understandable. In *The European Anarchy*, published in the midst of the Great War in the April of 1916 and 'written in the hope [it] might be read and considered by the more reasonable section of the British public', Dickinson (1916: 5) comes across as a third-image type of intellectual at his best. Writes Goldie with spectacular clarity: the tragic turning point in European history was Westphalia. What it meant for all of us was the 'emergence of the sovereign State at the end of the fifteenth century', and what it brought was the 'definite acceptance of international anarchy' (Dickinson 1916: 13).

What then happened was that, in the wake of tragic Westphalia, along came all the Machiavellians – I cannot resist the temptation to add here: all the

'Mearchiavellians' – and they were the ones, as Dickinson (1916: 13–14) goes on to note with bold clarity, who just 'could not, indeed, practice anything else'. And so, let me quote him at length so as to allow him to speak his political realism:

> For it is as true of an aggregation of States as of an aggregation of individuals that, whatever moral sentiments may prevail, if there is no common law and no common force the best intentions will be defeated by lack of confidence and security. Mutual fear and mutual suspicion, aggression masquerading as defence and defence masquerading as aggression, will be the protagonists in the bloody drama; and there will be, what Hobbes truly asserted to be the essence of such a situation, a chronic state of war, open or veiled. For peace itself will be a latent war; and the more the States arm to prevent a conflict the more certainly will it be provoked, since to one or another it will always seem a better chance to have it now than to have it on worse conditions later. Some one State at any moment may be the immediate offender; but the main and permanent offence is common to all States. It is the anarchy which they are all responsible for perpetuating.

What is there to add, really? It is all in there, loud and clear. The fundamental cause of war is anarchy. That is the same as saying: as long as we have anarchy in general, and a kind of Westphalian anarchy in particular, there will be war.

And that, of course, is where Kelsen the political realist comes in. This is also and exactly his own position, or is his foreign-policy realism too. In *Collective Security under International Law*, his juristic theory of collective security written when he was Naval War College Chair of International Law in 1953–4, Kelsen (1957b: 4) makes it clear that in the final analysis there is no essential distinction between national security and international security. It is merely one of degree, not kind: it is a 'police problem'. Neorealists, of course, will frown upon Kelsen as he brings in here the theme of police – read: world police. But then, what is so different to what the neorealists are saying? Mearsheimer has it right that there is no kind of international emergency number available for nations and states to dial when their dealings with one another get messy. And in some ways Kelsen (1957b: 8) was even quicker to point out that, without any emergency number of this kind in general, and without any policy to come to our rescue in particular, we are all trapped in an anarchic situation, which is one of our own making and where one principle prevails: 'the principle of self-help'.

As much as the analytical side or realism bit is both straightforward and similar, however, the real test, of course, is the normative side or idealism bit. To Mearsheimer (1994–5), there is nothing really that would not make international law a 'false promise'. And today, while recognising the many advances and forms of progress and reform in the sphere of national security and international relations, a Kelsenian observer would be hard pressed not to share the former view of Kelsen (1957b: 49), that 'to date the international organizations which have been established for the purpose of collective security have not been effective enough to prevent war'. Why do we not make the world safe for democracy, then (Wilson 1917; see Perlmutter 1997), or even better, why not get rid of anarchy altogether and have a world state?

18 Democracy and Peace

Kelsen was not easily tricked, nor fooled. Never. At least I cannot think of anything really in his philosophy and political thinking that strikes me as either particularly idealistic or naïve. The whole point of this book is: Kelsen, a man of realism, political realist and foreign-policy realist too. So let us explore this further by testing him against Waltz's second image.

In *The Advancement of International Law*, a stimulating book, Charles Leben (2010: 168), Emeritus Professor of Constitutional Law at Panthéon-Assas University in Paris's Latin Quarter, argues that it 'is necessary to sketch out a side of Kelsen that is little known to legal scholars, that of political militant for democracy within states and for peace in the international community'. As much as I agree that there is so much more to explore in Kelsen, most notably political, the less I am convinced that it is fair, or doing Kelsen any good, for Leben to put the label *militant* on Kelsen. Bold as a theorist? Yes. Sharp as a razor on methodology? Sure. Passionate about democracy? Certainly. A no-nonsense intellectual streetfighter for open society ideals? Absolutely. But a militant type of a man or character he was not.

What is good and valuable, though, is that Leben has two fundamental concepts of political and IR theory in one and the same sentence: democracy and peace. And then the question becomes, or has been all along, only too obvious: was Kelsen a democratic peace theorist? Or couched in Waltzian (1959a: 81) terms: where in the first image war is explained through human nature, and where in the third image war has its roots in anarchy, champions old and new of the so-called second image claim that 'the internal organization of states is the key to understanding war and peace'. So can we imagine Kelsen saying democracy makes for peace? From what I have been writing in the last section about the problem of structural anarchy in world politics, the answer is bound to be in the negative – even more so if we recall what he said about the utopianism of socialism, and of course human nature.

But then, because Kelsen is conventionally associated with Kantian philosophy, it would be awkward to neglect the second-image question – and as we shall see, it would be false to say that in the Kelsenian logic, democratic governments are unimportant for pacifying international relations or for soothing the struggle for power and peace. To be sure, a world of anarchy, even it were full of democracies large and small, would be, in the final analysis, well, a world of anarchy: an anarchical arena where war is still endemic. Without any doubt whatsoever in Kelsen's mind, though, where autocracy is always a realistic chance of politics, it really comes down to this with regard to democracy: the more the merrier. For reasons both moral and political, rather than fewer it is surely better to have more democracies around in world politics.

Kelsen is none the less, and clearly, not a second-image theorist. What Waltz, more than half a century ago, called the second image in political and IR theory is today an incredibly rich body of work, stemming from pretty much all fields dealing with questions of globalisation and world politics in one way or the other: most notably politics, law and philosophy, and also history, sociology and economics (see Hall 2014; Parashar, Tickner and True 2018; Taliaferro 2019). These questions coming in so many different forms and shades, it is impossible to test Kelsen against all of them. And truthfully, I do not think it is even necessary. A small selection will do to show where he stands, and I will take them one by one.

Of all the many different 'liberal dreams', as Mearsheimer (2018) has recently – and disrespectfully – called them, the most important is democratic peace theory. Its theoretical backers say that democracies tend not to fight one another, and so practitioners say that if we work towards a point in history where we have a world society composed only of democracies, humankind will forever be rid of the disease of war, which we have brought upon this planet ourselves (Brown, Lynn-Jones, and Miller 1996). As Kant, professed to be the 'greatest of all theorists of international relations' (Brown 1992: 95), who found Hobbes 'quite terrifying' (Kant 1991b [1793]: 84), put it nicely in *Perpetual Peace*: 'The republican constitution [. . .] offers a prospect of attaining the desired result, i.e. a perpetual peace' (Kant 1991c [1795]: 100). And at the end of the Cold War, when spirits were high and the *end of history* in sight, Francis Fukuyama (2006 [1992]: 262) was convinced of the 'fundamentally un-warlike character of liberal societies'. And years later still, at the turn of this century in *The Law of Peoples*, John Rawls (1999: 48) said 'when liberal peoples do go to war, it is only with unsatisfied societies, or outlaw states'.

Unsurprisingly, of course, foreign-policy realists of all stripes, classical, structural or neoclassical, and defensive or offensive, find second-image theories in general, and democratic or liberal peace theories in particular, quite simply 'seriously flawed' (Mearsheimer 2018: 195; Walt 2018). Sadly, and most dangerously, as the data show, democracy as we have come to know (and appreciate) it in the post-war liberal international order has been in global decline in recent years (see Achen and Bartels 2016; Diamond 2019; Krastev and Holmes 2019; Plattner 2020). And even if things were not dictated by Trump, Orbán and their like, and even if we did rebound to a more reasonable and less Schmittian politics (as I am sure we will eventually), and even to the point of us as Rawlsian peoples, we could not bet on the assumption that democracies do not wage war with each other – not least because the past has proven that they did fight (see Layne 1994; Friedman 2015; Mearsheimer 2018). So, where does Kelsen fit into the picture?

In 'Foundations of Democracy', he sounds like a democratic peace theorist – indeed, like a very committed and very liberal one. He devotes one section to the question that he calls 'Democracy and Peace' (Kelsen 1955b: 32–3). It is not a long one but it gives you everything you need to know about his views on a democracy's foreign-policy-making. He starts out like a Wilsonian. There are two types of government, he says, and each one of them – democracy versus autocracy – leads to two types of foreign-policy behaviour: there is in each bureaucratic type a 'pattern of internal policy' whose different set of values and culture 'corresponds to a definite standard of external policy' (32). And thus it happens that a democracy is 'decidedly inclined to cherish a pacific ideal', and a government of 'the autocratic type shows unmistakable symptoms of imperialism' (32). Surely it all sounds rather Kantian, if not fairly deterministic too. Hence one might be tempted to brush Kelsen aside as a hopeless idealist.

Yet I count two reasons why that is false. First, Kelsen was, without doubt, a progressive man with left-liberal leanings, a democrat through and through, and an early advocate of everything that came to be known as open society ideals. At one and the same time, though, he has proved to be a Freudian no-nonsense human nature realist, and above all else, a Pure positivist who was keen on methodology and scientific knowledge. Why would he, all of a sudden, change course and become a natural-law-ish type of freedom fighter? Second, as a Pure positivist and foreign-policy realist he never said that democracies do not fight. They do. They even 'have waged wars of conquest' (Kelsen 1955b: 32). It is a non-starter to claim that democracies will bring us perpetual peace: only an efficacious international legal order with a centralised sanctions regime can do that. In democracies, the bar to go to war is higher, the 'political inhibitions to overcome much stronger' (Kelsen 1955b: 32), but they will find ways and means. And thus, even though he clearly favoured democracy over autocracy for many reasons, Kelsen can hardly be associated with the theory, and politics, of the democratic peace thesis.

Neither was he one of those second-image theorists who would put their hopes, so to speak, in a Socialist foreign policy of peace. When it comes to the question of world peace, to him the democratic or liberal peace thesis makes no sense, and even less so any type of socialist peace thesis. And it cannot be otherwise. Since the whole philosophy and political thinking of a Socialist utopia are flawed, not least because they are built upon totally utopian premises regarding human nature and the political, it is obvious to him that any Socialist type of government could never achieve in the realm of international society what it cannot achieve at home. Any claim that society, domestic or international, could be freed from coercion is not only a non-starter but a total non-starter.

As he saw it as a Pure positivist and political realist, there is never any intrinsic element or such like that would really link any type of government to any type of behaviour, or to any type of intrinsic ideology. What we can do, as historians or political and IR theorists, is identify some such patterns or parallels, if they exist at all, but never really any laws, and still less any natural laws. The struggle for power, politics, is contingent to the core. And thus Kelsen argues that there is nothing natural or intrinsic that would link any specific political or economic system or ideology of resource allocation and resource ownership to the notion of a Kantian perpetual peace. That is to say: in the most fundamental question of world politics, how to achieve peace, economics plays little role. Not that it plays no role: it can make war less likely but not eradicate it.

For a start, he was rather uncompromising in his analysis that 'democracy as a political system is not necessarily attached to a definite economic system' (Kelsen 1955b: 94). Contra Lockeans and Marxists, and unnerving many intellectuals in the West and in the United States in particular – quite a list, to be sure – Kelsen (1955b: 94) finished his 'Foundations of Democracy' on this prototypically positivistic note, writing that all

> attempts at showing an essential connection between freedom and property, as all other attempts to establish a closer relationship of democracy with capitalism rather than with socialism or even the exclusive compatibility of democracy with capitalism, have failed.

Recall that we are in the mid-1950s, and the FBI and McCarthyites were, of course, totally suspicious of everyone, intellectual or worker, who was not fully behind what they saw as the twin ideas that make and shape America: freedom and property.

Kelsen was right, though. If you take legal positivism seriously, as seriously as he as a Pure theoretician would do; and if you take political realism seriously, as seriously as he as a Freudian-inspired one would do, then you cannot but come to the conclusion that the system of legal norms of a democracy, this one or that one or any other one, can shape the (legal) norms of our economic and business dealings in many different ways, leading to either a quite centralised economic system, a libertarian economy or forms of mixed systems (the latter seems to be Kelsen's preference). And what is more, according to Kelsen (1955b: 70), it is

> an undeniable fact that policies for the realization of religious and nationalistic ideals have obtained the enthusiastic, even fanatic, support of the great masses regardless of the most severe restrictions of their economic welfare imposed upon them by these policies.

The point is that not only are politics and economics not intimately tied to another, but they also do not necessarily work in what may be reasonable ways. Or, as one might say, Kelsen was very well aware that economic rationality, in the sense used by his friends of the Austrian School of Economics, is one thing, and the fact of mass irrationality, which his friend Freund had so expertly unearthed at the Berggasse, is quite another.

The elephant in the room, clearly, has been the question or debate as to whether the realisation of a socialist economic justice is, or might be, the one royal road to world peace. Or, as the line of argument has been, as long as we continue to divide the world into essentially two social groups, the 'haves' on the one hand and the 'have-nots' on the other, there will be conflict and war. What we need to do, we are told, is remove this one economic cause of war and then we are all good: we would have created social justice. We would have made war vanish from the earth. We would also do away with law and state as a coercive order: the popular idea is, as Kelsen (1957b: 23) put it, that the 'future would be a stateless and lawless society'.

In *Collective Security under International Law*, Kelsen (1957b: 23) tells us that this is all wishful thinking: peace through Communism is 'utopian'. It goes against all the facts of human nature, and the argument 'that violations of a social order are caused only or mainly by its economic insufficiency is contrary to all our social experience'. For, irrespective of the concrete circumstances of economics and ideology and order, what there will always be in us, and in society, is this: our 'hunger', our 'ambition', our 'sexual desire'. Forever the Freudian, Kelsen goes on to say that if it were true that we could, miraculously, remove the economic aspect of conflict and war, it would possibly mean that our yearning for prestige and pleasure would become all the more vicious. It is, he (1957b: 23) cautions us, 'an illusion to believe that, even if it could secure the satisfaction of all economic needs, a social order could prevent all its violations . . . and thus make the legal use of force, as a sanction, superfluous'. From where he stands, he just cannot see any type of second-image peace, be it a democratic or a Communist or a Marxist–Leninist one.

He sought to buttress his position not only through Freudian psychology and the facts of history, but also – hugely interested as he was in this topic – through the field of economics. At the forefront of economic analysis back then, Kelsen seems to have been particularly impressed by Lionel Robbins, Liberal Economics Professor at LSE, a committed anti-Marxist and British advocate of the Austrian School. He thought of him as 'an outstanding English economist' (Kelsen 1957b: 253), and hence relied on *The Economic Causes of War* (Robbins 1939), a 'masterpiece of sound analysis and clear exposition' (Woolbert 1940). In it Robbins has shown, as Kelsen (1957b: 253) writes, that 'although it would be an exaggeration to say that wars have no economic causes or to deny that conflicts of national economic interests may lead to war, these conflicts are not the root cause'. Kelsen read widely in general, and particularly when he needed intellectual allies to make his point. And since he was a man of science, he read science widely: here an important economist of the day who helped him argue that the root cause of war is neither domestic politics nor economics, as second-image theorists would have it.

Back then, it was not, of course, just a theoretical debate. Together with other realists (I dare use the term), he was reacting against what, in inter-war Europe and in the immediate aftermath of World War II, was 'a strong tendency to consider economic circumstances as the main causes of war' (Kelsen 1957b: 23). He wanted to warn us, notably Western and American intellectuals and foreign-policy professionals, to beware of the 'danger' of over-estimating economics as a cure-all for the pressing problems of the day and the future. There are no magic bullets in political and international life.

Yes, economics is a factor in the day-to-day struggle for power and peace. But then, it is all too obvious that there is much more to the question of war than the quarrel over energy, investments and new markets. Kelsen (1957b: 253), quoting Robbins, believes it is evident that the

> ultimate condition giving rise to those clashes of national economic interest which lead to international war is the existence of independent national sovereignties. Not capitalism, but the anarchic political organization of the world is the root disease of our civilization.

And thus, from that perspective, it is clear enough why, through yet another direct quotation from Robbins the economist, Kelsen (1957b: 253) concluded in such strong terms: 'We know today that unless we destroy the sovereign state, the sovereign state will destroy us.'

So, then, how realistic is it for us to get rid of the sovereign state?

19 Nationalism and the World State

Can we not skip this section? Is it not clear enough by now that Kelsen was no naïve idealist? Would he not say that if a world state were possible, we would already have seen it at some point in history?

He is basically saying this to us: given human nature is what it is, the core logic of having You and Me locked in a coercive legal order does not stop at the water's edge. Where law and the state are required to keep us at bay through the centralisation of force, it cannot be different in international life: hence the world state. And in *Peace through Law*, concerned with how to 'eliminate the most terrible employment of force – namely war – from inter-State relations', Kelsen (1944a: 4–5) wrote that no answer seems to be more self-evident than this: to unite all individual States or, at least, as many as possible, into a World State, to concentrate all their means of power, their armed forces, and put them at the disposal of a world government under laws created by a world parliament . . . There can be no doubt that the ideal solution of the problem of world organization as the problem of world peace is the establishment of a World Federal State composed of all or as many nations as possible.

Who would disagree? This is straightforward if/then-logic, put forth by a Pure positivist and proven political realist. If anarchy is the cause of war, then we must get rid of anarchy, by the same method: through a pacifier!

In *Collective Security under International Law*, Kelsen (1957b: 30) pointed out that the only real pacifier – from the point of view of Pure legal technique – is the world state, in the form of either a centralised world state or a world federal state. And even if the states comprising such a world federal state were allowed to keep their means of force, then what would happen is that any real act of aggression by one state against any other would be dealt with by the world federal state's centralised police force, who would enforce world law, including illegal acts of 'internal' aggression, formerly known as war.

But then, of course – from the standpoint of political and international life – who would give up their own sovereignty? What about nationalism? And national egotisms? To be sure, Kelsen the foreign-policy realist clearly saw all these stumbling-blocks to world pacification. The centralisation of force, having taken tanks and other guns away, comes at a price, one that, in the eyes of all too many peoples, nations and states, is considered way too high. As they see it, limiting a nation's right to self-determination while posing a direct threat to national identities, the problem of the world state in whatever form, as Kelsen (1944a: 11) writes, is that it would probably demand too much, not least because it will simply

> comprise nations so different from one another in respect to language, religion, culture, history, political and economic structure, and in their geographic situation as are States of the American and States of the European continent, nations of western and nations of eastern civilizations.

This is not to say or imply that Kelsen was giving in to any form of Hegelian–Schmittian nationalist sentiments (of which he as a man disproved), but only – as he himself put it – that we have to 'reckon with this phenomenon as with other decisive facts' (Kelsen 1944a: 10).

Among these so-called other decisive facts is – quite naturally, given Kelsen's Freudian style of philosophy and political thinking – what one might call human nature writ large, or even will to power writ large. Since I have discussed what I called Kelsen's Freudian moment in Chapter 3 at length (and also in the two chapters before that), I will not repeat here the psychoanalysis of how You and I and We appear to identify ourselves with the power of the nation or the state, but will confine myself to showing how serious he was about the problem. It is perhaps in 'God and the State' that Kelsen (1973: 66–7) is most outspoken about the problem of identification in politics and international relations:

> Just as the primitive at certain times, when he dons the mask of the totem animal which is the idol of his tribe, may commit all the transgressions which are otherwise forbidden by strict norms, so the civilized man, behind the mask of God, his nation or his state, may live out all those instincts, which as a simple group-member, he must carefully repress within the group. Whereas anyone who praises himself is despised as a boaster, he may still unashamedly praise his God, his nation or his state although in doing so he merely indulges his own conceit; and whereas the individual as such is in no way thought entitled to coerce others, to dominate or even to kill them, it is nevertheless his supreme right to do all this in the name of God, the nation or the state, which for that very reason he loves, and lovingly identifies with, as 'his' God, 'his' nation and 'his' state.

Written in beautiful prose, it is an ugly yet realistic picture of You and Me in social, political and international life – making the world state or, for that matter, any other form of world society all the less likely.

And if that were not enough with regard to the depth of sovereignty and nationalism, in addition to the challenges posed by self-determination and identity, as well as by human nature writ large and identification processes, there is a third decisive fact that works against the setting up of a world state: national egotism. Why would a state be willing to give itself up for something like a world state? That would be committing 'State suicide' (Kelsen 1944a: 10). It is hardly conceivable, writes Kelsen, that any one state or government would ever do anything of real substance that is not in the national interest: As Kelsen (1957b: 48) put it in *Collective Security under International Law*: 'No matter how a state acts, its action is motivated by egotism.' And – as could have been written by Morgenthau or Mearsheimer, or any other foreign-policy realist – he keeps on pushing this strongly: 'That all actions of a state are motivated by its egotism is an undeniable fact and the ascertainment of this fact is a truism' (Kelsen 1957b: 48). Where is the idealist now?

But of course, Kelsen would not be Kelsen if he did not have a positive note attached to his style of foreign-policy realism. By positive I do not necessarily mean optimistic, but rather positivistic as in Pure positivism. And it is here, at exactly this point in the book, that I want to begin, slowly but surely, to re-balance our perspective of Kelsen back to, let us say, a kind of middle ground, to be explicated further in Chapter 5. What I was doing up to this point, as I kept emphasising from the beginning, was focusing on *the other Kelsen*. Too long has he been wrongly treated as a quintessentially naïve idealist, so that the analytical task seemed necessary to identify elements of political realism and foreign-policy realism in his biography and thought. Have I been eclectic? Yes. But then, so have many of his critics. My hope is that the reading I have presented here will help someone at some point to synthesise Kelsen the Pure jurist and Kelsen the political realist into a more comprehensive view (perhaps in the form of an intellectual biography) of Kelsen the political philosopher! The present book is not the place; nor is the author qualified for such a task. What I can and must do, though, in the rest of this book is to balance out the progressive and realistic bits in Kelsen.

Now, as to the scepticism of having a world state any time soon, or hav-ing even a budding form of world society, Kelsen was in good company with some of the most illustrious mid-twentieth-century realists. You might find the following statements cynical or elitist, or both, but at the time (emerging from Fascism and Nazism) they were not wholly inappropriate. Surely George F. Kennan (1993: 77–81) hits the nail on the head in *Around the Cragged Hill*, when he writes that romantic nationalism was a 'pathological form' of a 'mass emotional exaltation to which millions of people . . . appear to be highly sus-ceptible'. Nor is it false when Walter Lippmann (2008 [1915a]: 60), in *Stakes of Diplomacy*, states in equally Freudian fashion that national sentiments are

> a cluster of primitive feelings, absorbed into a man and rooted within him long before conscious education begins. The house, the street, the meadow and hill upon which he first opened his eyes, the reactions to family and strangers which remain as types of his loves and hates, the earliest sounds which brought fear and pleasure – these are the stuff out of which nationalism is made. They constitute the ultimate background of the mind, its first culture and the most tenacious one.

And of course Kelsen not only agreed, but also was as frightened as they were that nationalism was here to stay for a long time.

Why would nations wither away? One might say that pretty much all of the classical foreign-policy realists writing at the time were scared to death (recall that Morgenthau and Herz were Jewish) of what a Schmittian-style mass poli-tics of exaltation and emotion might mean for their own life, and for political and international life more generally. And so of course, and understandably, Kennan (1993: 82) had an 'extreme dislike of all masses'. Yes, the notion of the 'omnicompetent, sovereign citizen' is as realistic, as Lippmann (1993 [1925]: 29) said, as for 'a fat man to try to be a ballet dancer'. In this regard, E. H. Carr (1936: 854) questioned the 'limited capacity of the elephant for aviation'. And Niebuhr (2008 [1952]: 169) warned that 'collective man always tends to be complacent, self-righteous'. In this sense, then, Piki Ish-Shalom (2006), Chair of the International Relations Department at the Hebrew University of Jerusalem, was right when he spoke of a so-called triptych of realism, elitism and conservatism relating to human nature and change.

But then, this earlier generation of realists never said that change is impossible. Of course, Kelsen agreed with them about their scepticism toward You and Me, and interestingly enough, he and Morgenthau almost saw eye to eye on the question of progress and reform in general, and on the idea of the world state as the one real or efficacious pacifier in particular. What is remarkable is how Morgenthau was hoist by his own petard: by the positivistic conception of the national interest.

In *Collective Security under International Law*, in the section aptly called 'The Opposition to International Security', Kelsen (1957b: 42–52) forces his friend and former student Morgenthau into a hidden dialogue. I say hidden because most of Kelsen's critical remarks are hidden in the book's notes. Not long, it is revealing none the less. He takes a swipe at Morgenthau's (1967 [1948]) core point in *Politics among Nations* that international politics is necessarily the realm of national egotism, and for the insinuation that virtually all systems of collective or international security are 'doomed to failure' because the 'only motive of national policy' is to 'serve its own national interest' (Kelsen 1957b: 47).

Now, as Kelsen (1957b: 47) sees it, short and sweet, Morgenthau's line of 'argument is fundamentally wrong'. And what follows is almost like Kelsen giving Morgenthau a quick lecture in political and foreign-policy making. Without any doubt, 'No matter how a state acts, its action is motivated by egotism' (Kelsen 1957b: 47). To him that is almost too trivial to mention. It is as if he was saying that there would be something wrong with the government if it did something that was not in the national interest. But then, eying Morgenthau, it is quite another thing to say or insinuate that the national interest is always, like a natural law, or like a government on autopilot, against each and everything internationalist or globalist. For the national interest, says Kelsen the Pure positivist, who has always been clear-eyed about power struggles domestic and international – or let us say, the fact of what is *in* the national interest at any given time – 'is the result of a highly subjective value judgment' (Kelsen 1957b: 48). It is certainly trivial, but Kelsen (1957b: 48) goes on (for all the right reasons) to make it as clear as possible that

> in the opinion of one government of a state a policy may be in the interest of the state, while in the opinion of another government of the same

state under another political party, this same policy may not be in the interest of the state.

And thus there is nothing 'objectively verifiable', he argues, that could have us say that the national interest does not allow for more international law, effective regimes of collective security or an ever-more centralised international legal order, if not also for a world society and world state (Kelsen 1957b: 48).

One might say we have pitted one positivist against another here, and my point about these two men seeing almost eye to eye concerns how Morgenthau conceptualised the national interest in *Politics among Nations*. There he did it in a way that is much in line with Kelsenian positivist methodology: the national interest, like the norm, is not a product of Nature, Reason or God but 'depends upon the political and cultural context within which foreign policy is formulated'. Thus he is clear enough: 'The goals that might be pursued by nations in their foreign policy can run the whole gamut of objectives any nation has ever pursued or might possibly pursue.' And exactly because he does *not* think that the 'conditions under which foreign policy operates . . . cannot be changed', he is forced to reach this conclusion:

> Nothing in the realist position militates against the assumption that the present division of the political world into nation states will be replaced by larger units of a quite different character, more in keeping with the technical potentialities and the moral requirements of the contemporary world. (Morgenthau 1967 [1948a]: 8–9)

That is quite a statement, all too often forgotten or neglected, innocently or not, by today's pseudo-realistic Schmittians and Schmittian-style pseudo-realists of doom.

And so what Kelsen and Morgenthau shared was not only a sustained human nature realism and clear view of anarchy as the real cause of war, but also the analysis that the world state would be the most efficacious pacifier of world politics. What Kelsen the rigid Pure positivist seems to have been a bit worried about is that his friend Morgenthau did not make it clear enough that the national interest has nothing to do with natural law. Surely this is wholly important for us too, for only if it is clear whether we are talking about the *is* or any (disguised) *ought*, do we find real answers to the question that William Scheuerman (2011: Ch. 6) put to us so neatly in *The Realist Case for Global Reform*, which becomes all the more urgent: 'Who's afraid of the World State?'

20 A Most Realistic World Politics

'I wish Walter Lippmann would forget Freud for a little – just a little,' complained Harold J. Laski (quoted in Steel 1980: 173), the British socialist and

Political Science Professor at LSE, in a letter dated 20 November 1916 to Justice Oliver Wendell Holmes, the legendary American jurist. A year earlier, in 'Freud and the Layman', published by *The New Republic*, Lippmann (1915b: 10) had said of Kelsen's Viennese friend: 'I cannot help feeling that for his illumination, for his steadiness and brilliancy of mind, he may rank among the greatest who have contributed to thought.'

Lippmann's Freudianism was too much for Laski, and two decades later he complained that Kelsen was doing too little. Laski was not referring to Kelsen's Freudianism, but repeating what was a standard charge against Kelsen: too much formalism, too little reality. As D. A. Jeremy Telman (2016a: 3), a law Professor at Valparaiso, has it in *Hans Kelsen in America*, a volume that was long overdue, 'echoing Oliver Wendell Holmes' famous dictum that the life of the law is not logic but experience, Harold Laski denounced Kelsen's legal theory as a sterile "exercise in logic and not in life"'.

In light of Laski, my hope is that you will not say the same about me, for of course I will be bringing Freud back in here yet again. But for a good reason: against Laski. What he has been saying flies in the face of all evidence: if we test Kelsen against Waltz's three images of war, as I have done this chapter, what emerges is the image of Kelsen the foreign-policy realist.

The critics of the strategic idea of a 'Permanent League for the Maintenance of Peace', whose covenant he drafted in *Peace through Law* in 1944, will perhaps always say, in the language of Mearsheimer, that this is all a great delusion, a liberal dream bound to fail badly in light of international realities. Fine. Let them call it dreamy, wishy-washy, legalist, naïve or unrealistic. The point they do not want to see (at least so it appears to me) is this: why would Kelsen argue for a kind of a world state? The answer is clear enough: because if we do not have one, chances are we will keep killing each other for whatever it is that makes it to the top of the list of our *national* interests. That to me is a most realistic kind of foreign-policy realism. Seen the other way round, to say that we need to work toward a world state is not only the most logical in terms of legal thinking but also the most logical when one takes a clear-eyed look at the core condition of a Westphalian world order: an anarchic arena of sovereign equality where great powers seek to have their way through decentralised force. What else can the solution be other than centralised force? And of course, it is close to impossible to achieve all this without the great powers. Yes, so we have heard. We have been there before; it is almost too trivial. Let me simply say, it is still not impossible.

In *Man, the State, and War*, Waltz (1959b: 238) is clear about how the three images hang together and form a coherent piece of political thinking on international relations: 'The third image describes the framework of world politics, but without the first and second images there can be no knowledge of the forces that determine policy.' Or, amounting to the same thing: 'the first and second images describe the forces in world politics, but without the third image it is impossible to assess their importance or predict their results'. Surely the reader will have spotted long ago why I have been working my way through Kelsen alongside these three Waltzian images: because my point was to show that we will find Kelsen in all three of them – and certainly *not* as an idealist.

I find it useful to think of Kelsen's philosophy and political thinking in ways similar to how Jean Bethke Elshtain (1989) presented her Freud, in what is one of the most subtle treatments of Freudianism in political and IR theory. In 'Why War?', the 'sterile so-called discussion with Einstein' (Jones 1957: 187), Freud (1933: 207) makes a perfect Kelsenian pitch for peace: 'Wars will only be prevented with certainty if mankind unites in setting up a central authority to which the right of giving judgement upon all conflicts of interest shall be handed over.' Continues the Viennese doctor: 'There are clearly two separate require-ments involved in this: the creation of a supreme agency and its endowment with the necessary power' (Freud 1933: 207). But as to the causes of war, Freud is a bit harder to grasp, and here it is Elshtain's (2009: 295) reading of Freud that is so helpful. Freud 'transgresses' Waltz's three images. It is not one image, but all three at one and the same time. So – at least to Elshtain (1989: 55–6), anyway, and I am agreed – to 'the question "why war?" then, Freud would reply: "man, the state and the international system"'. So I have little doubt as to Freud's response, and I have even less doubt about Kelsen's response, for to him, of course, the problem of war has its roots in all three images. But then, if he were pressed to say clearly which single one of the images is the most important factor in the dramas of international life, he would most certainly say without any hesitation: anarchy!

Nowhere is his third-image view of the causes of war, and the strategic prob-lem of world politics, more clear than in his scathing attack on the Kellogg–Briand Pact. To wish for something either to happen or to go away, in international poli-tics or in all political life, is a recipe for disillusionment. To outlaw war without (literally) at one and the very same time putting coercive measures in place to settle the disputes through compulsory jurisdiction, is useless and dangerous, and at worst – see inter-war Europe – actually a driver for even more aggression, con-flict and war. In this sense, Kelsen the foreign-policy realist keeps reminding us of the truest meaning of the saying 'be careful what you wish for', once you start to interfere in politics among nations without having anything at your disposal that gives you real power in terms of a centralised coercion mechanism.

He has always been very clear where he stands: only if we were pure angels would we not need to be coerced by a centralised force monopoly. Only if all nations and states behaved like Rawlsian peoples would we not need to coerce them into a societal behaviour through either a balance-of-power play or a coercive international legal order. But then, of course, this is all wishful thinking, for it is not something that the reality of human nature, the state and world politics has in store for us from day to day. There is a reason why we have reached for the rock and flexed our muscles for so long in human history: because law had long been primitive, and had only evolved eventually to an ever greater degree of centralisation. And so we keep sending nuclear-powered aircraft carriers into blue water, and we seek to project power where we can, because international law is still rather primitive and decentralised. We continue this style of power politics because we know that we all face the very same permissive cause of war: international anarchy, lack of a world state or world force.

And lest we forget, Kelsen never said that a world state or real global reform is impossible. The jurist never ever said anything so absurdly *unpolitical*.

CHAPTER 5

KELSEN'S STYLE OF POLITICAL THINKING

'Practically anything is possible and fallibility reigns supreme'

George Soros (2019)

It was three years before the outbreak of World War II. The autumn of 1936, 22 October – a Thursday. The next day, *The New York Times* (1936) covered what had happened deep inside Central Europe in three short paragraphs – 'Jews in Prague Beaten; German Nationalist Students Rally Against Exiled Professor'. But then, better than no report at all. Three years earlier, as reported in the *Jewish Daily Bulletin* of 2 June 1933, German Nazi students had already protested against Kelsen's planned appointment: 'Out with Jewish professors!' At the time he was one the West's leading jurists, a liberal through and through, and a towering antipode to the Schmittians (see Olechowski and Busch 2009; Osterkamp 2009).

The university building was packed, as was the hall in which he was due to give his lecture. It was an unimaginably hostile atmosphere. From where did this raucous crowd of nationalists come? The majority were not even students, let alone at Prague. This was organised violence. Kelsen (1947a: 85) later recalled how incited the crowd had become by the nationalistic press and propaganda in the run-up to his lecture. Looking into their eyes, he spotted their 'hateful look'. He fought his way through to the lecture hall, and undeterred by their resentment, actually started his lecture, when suddenly someone shouted: 'Down with the Jews, all non-Jews must leave the hall' (Kelsen 1947a: 85). And almost instantly this whole nationalist anti-Semitic operation produced an ugly picture: friend versus foe. Kelsen was left in the hall, all alone.

He headed back to the Dean's office, filing a report about what had happened. On his way there, he grasped how violent the situation was. None of his students had attended his lecture because they were being beaten up badly, thrown down the stairs and the like. It was ugly in many ways. And it got worse. Weeks later, the Prague police had credible intelligence that Kelsen was on the target list of a violent Nazi student group. The threat was real and serious, and soon he was under police protection: this meant that when he was lecturing, one police officer sat in the front row, with a second one at the back of the lecture hall. It was, as he said, a 'grotesque picture of academic freedom' (Kelsen 1947a: 86).

21 KELSEN AND POPPER

What if Kelsen had not written a letter of recommendation for Popper in the mid-1930s? And why have George Soros at the head of this book's concluding chapter on Kelsen's style of political thinking?

It all took place in Paris, in the early autumn of 1935, at some point between 15 and 23 September.[1] Popper had travelled to France, where he was scheduled to give two lectures at what was the very first International Congress for the Unity of Science (Popper 2006: 552). The congress was organised by one of the Vienna Circle's leading philosophers and political economists, Otto Neurath, who had fled to The Hague in 1934, and thereafter to England, where he died unexpectedly in Oxford. The Congress was a success, and the list of participants – around 170 scholars pouring into Paris from around the world – reads like a *Who's Who* of the international philosophy scene back then. Together with the likes of Bertrand Russell, Rudolf Carnap and quite a few other twentieth-century heavyweights, Kelsen was a board member of the Congress's international committee – and he was in Paris, too.

At the time, Popper was pretty much unknown outside a core circle of a few philosophers of science. And as much as he was aware of the social and political direction in which Austria was headed, in terms of both rising anti-intellectualism and growing anti-Semitism, leaving him with little hope for a university career in the foreseeable future (even his life as a schoolteacher was becoming more and more difficult), he was not what one would describe as a well-connected man. If he ever needed to escape Vienna, though, he would need some contacts. In other words, he had never met Kelsen. Nor was he acquainted in any way with Hayek, who had left Vienna in the early 1930s, arriving at LSE on 22 September 1931 to take up a one-year visiting position, starting out on an impressive career as a Professor of Economics and Statistics that was to last until 1950, the year that he moved on to Chicago.

Popper was pretty much on his own. And he knew that the situation was not good, and so was determined to make it to England: to make it there as a philosopher and scholar, which had been his 'cherished dream' for many years (Niemann 2014: 11). We, of course, have the advantage of knowing how well it all turned for Popper. But back then, he could not be so sure. He did manage to reach London, right after the Paris conference, and even though he was operating out of a 'horrible' bedsit in Paddington (Gombrich 1999: Ch. 2), he liked it in England very much. He was desperate to stay: as Popper put it, he felt free, in many ways as if he could breathe fresh air, as if windows had been opened up. The term 'open society' stems from this experience.[2]

It was not meant to be, though. It did not work out, at least not this time, during what was his first stay in London in those nine months in 1935–6. He could not find a permanent lectureship and so had to return to Vienna. From there he eventually succeeded in securing a well-paid position at what is now the University of Canterbury, New Zealand. He arrived in March 1937, and there and then began to pen *The Open Society and Its Enemies* (1945). Written in the era of Hitler and Stalin, this was a timely and powerful wake-up call for Western politics: for a world that was emerging from two world wars and facing yet another major strategic confrontation. It was published in 1945, the year before he returned to Europe: to his beloved England, the LSE and Hayek.

It is odd that Popper cannot recall when he had met Hayek for the first time. After all, according to Malachi H. Hacohen (2000: 316), a historian at Duke and a specialist on Popper's formative years, the Hayek–Popper relationship was deep and long, and 'Popper's encounter with Hayek turned out to be one of the most important in his life.' Popper (1984) himself wrote in the mid-1980s that he saw in Hayek, who was actually only three years his senior, 'a kind of father figure'. Four decades earlier, in 1943 in New Zealand, he said he held Hayek in the highest regard: his 'kindness to me promises no less than to change the whole course of my life' (Popper 1943). Still, in a tribute to the life and work of Hayek, held at the LSE a few months after his death, Popper (1997 [1992]: 311) began by saying that his 'lifelong friendship with Fritz Hayek began in September or October of 1935, when I knocked at the door of his study here'.

And what is more, Popper, having just turned ninety, recalled precisely the man at the Paris Conference in the mid-1930s who had suggested that he go to see Hayek in London in the first place – and that man, of course, was Kelsen. As Popper (1997 [1992]: 311) put it: 'I had a letter of recommendation from Professor Hans Kelsen, then teaching political theory in Vienna. Kelsen had told me to visit Hayek, but had warned me that he and Hayek were not seeing eye to eye.' At the time Kelsen was no longer teaching in Vienna. Actually, he had already left Cologne for Geneva.

A year earlier, interviewed in the summer of 1991, Popper hinted at how Kelsen fits into the picture. And, as so often in life, it was the product of a piece of luck. On the surface the whole story sounds straightforward. Popper is on his way to England. He makes a stop-over in Paris. There, at the conference, Popper recalls: 'Julius Kraft introduced me to Kelsen and Kelsen gave me a letter to Hayek. And then in England I got to know Hayek' (quoted in Stadler 2015: 274). But, needless to say, it was not quite that easy, nor was it planned in any way.

Popper is quite right. Kelsen and Hayek were not on the same page. But still Kelsen knew full well how bad the political situation had become in Vienna, and in precarious situations like these, which are existential threats, who cares about who is friends with whom? And so, naturally enough, whenever Kelsen was in a position to help, he earnestly tried to do so. He knew how much weight his name carried, and he used it gently and very wisely (recall Morgenthau and Herz).

Still, from Popper's perspective, it was not straightforward at all. There was the case of Kelsen and Kraft, a relationship that could easily have gone off the rails years earlier. Kraft, a distant relative of Popper and a sociologist from Wunstorf near Hanover, died of a heart attack aboard a train from New Haven to New York in 1960; he had come to Vienna in the mid-1920s to pursue his *Habilitation* under Kelsen's guidance. Kraft and Popper spent a great deal of time together. They would discuss philosophy, talking about anti-Marxist philosophy as much as Kantian epistemology, 'often lasting into the small hours of the morning' (Milkov 2012: 146). But then, academic disaster struck. Kraft, who had come to Vienna from Göttingen, where the socialist philosopher Leonard Nelson was his *Doktorvater*, failed to achieve his post-doctoral qualification, and left after only two years for Frankfurt's Franz Oppenheimer. All this could easily have turned into an ugly teacher–student struggle. None of that happened, though, and instead of bitter disappointment and overt resentment, as Kraft himself put it, Kelsen became a lifelong friend.[3] And so it was possible, a decade later in Paris, for Kraft to introduce his friend Popper to Kelsen. And there and then, Kelsen's letter of recommendation of Popper to Hayek was written: apparently, on the spot.

Also, it really was the case that Hayek had a crude view of Kelsen's philosophy and political thinking. He was conciliatory at times, such as when he refers to him as 'my former Viennese teacher Hans Kelsen' (Hayek 2014 [1970]: 352), but then, on the whole, Hayek was highly critical of Kelsen. From the perspective of Hayek's libertarianism, Kelsen's Pure positivism was seen as the one single road to Socialism, crushing all individual liberties through an all-powerful Kelsenian state of coercion that seeks to regulate everything, large and small. Though Hayek's is surely part of the standard criticism levelled at Kelsen, no matter how often it is repeated, it does not make it any more correct.

Put bluntly, Hayek's criticism of Kelsen is false in many ways. Or as Judge Posner (2001: 41) put it, 'Hayek can't have known a great deal about Kelsen, or indeed legal positivism, to have said what he said about him.' If Hayek had cared more about the Pure theory of law and state, he might have understood the distinction between law and the rule of law. What Kelsen said was that all societies known to us, including those under the most despotic rulers, have operated on the basis of some form of codified law; it may have been primitive law, but it was law none the less. Kelsen never said that laws were necessarily decent laws, or that the mere existence of law is equivalent to a rule of law.

It is one thing to analyse law as it *is*. It is quite another to judge what legal norms *ought* to be. To insinuate, as Hayek did, that Fascism and Hitler might have been prevented if only a Kelsenian legal positivism had not spoken of Nazi law as a form of factual law, 'merely shows', as Posner (2001: 41) writes, 'Hayek's exaggerated belief in the influence of philosophy on society'. Hayek and, for that matter, Popper do not seem to have understood the Pure theory of law and state; nor were they realistic enough to grasp that it is interests defined in terms of power, through either force or law, that make the world go round, not ideas. What is more, Kelsen was *not* a libertarian because he was a legal positivist; he was a liberal socialist, and could have followed any other political persuasion, because he chose to be one. The whole point of Pure positivism is to separate the *is* from the *ought*. Judge Posner (2001: 41) is very clear: 'Kelsen's analysis of law is content neutral; and Hayek is interested only in content.' It is apples and oranges.

Now, I do not want to insinuate that Popper the great open society intellectual would not have existed if it had not been for Kelsen the compassionate old-world gentleman putting his name to this particular letter of recommendation in Paris. My point is a more trivial, yet perhaps also more powerful and liberating one. Life tends to be pretty contingent upon the shifting existences and concrete choices of You and Me, and – to me, anyway, at least as a Critically inspired political realist and foreign-policy realist – political and international life is exactly the same.

22 WIN SOME, LOSE SOME

In what follows over the next three sections I shall not try to summarise what I have presented in this book as *my* Kelsen. Instead, I want to come to an end – slowly but surely – through three Kelsenian themes relating to politics and international relations as I see them. Now that *the other Kelsen* is before us, my hope is that we are in a good position to note in a general way where a Kelsenian political realism might take us. Doing this will also clarify, I hope, a few points here and there that may still be in doubt.

Being a political realist, as I see it from a broadly Kelsenian standpoint, is quite uncomplicated. Not being wedded to any philosophical pessimism or progressive optimism, nor tied to any *Weltanschauung* or political idea, political realism in general, and foreign-policy realism in particular, is first and foremost positivistic, or content-neutral. In terms of political and IR theory it is a method of analysing politics, and in terms of the real world, it is one way of doing politics. It is not an art; it does not carry any 'timeless wisdom' (Buzan 1996). These are merely quasi-mythical images, ostensibly to aggrandise what is the most normal of all things in all political life: in Weberian language, to strive for a share of power, to influence how power is distributed in any given political order. And thus being a political realist means having a clinical view of government and international affairs – or a methodical view, in Kelsenian jargon – of how state organs relate to one another politically: who gets what, when, how and, above all, why.

What political realists do is analyse each and every policy situation from the vantage point of each and every stakeholder relevant to the political problem at hand (Heilbrunn 2015). And I would go so far as to say that there really is only one dictum, one maxim, always to keep in mind: no matter how morally abhorrent or ethically ugly one of these relevant stakeholders may be, take them seriously and see and listen to the concrete political problem through their eyes and ears. Or, as Morgenthau (1967 [1948a]: 543) put it with regard to the problems of international politics: 'look at the political scene from the point of view of other nations'. Easier said than done, of course: think of all the biases, good and bad, the dynamics of group thinking and collective hubris, our own will to power, and so on: all the stuff that clouds one's ability for sound analysis and assessment. To say that one leaves morality and emotions out of the equation is not due to the political realist's inherent viciousness or amorality, but speaks to the fact that what one must do is work one's way through the political problem methodically: that is, positivistically.

That, in turn, means this: once the political realist has managed to obtain enough credible intelligence about who actually is a relevant political actor on the scene in this or that specifically political situation (that is hard enough, to be sure), it is important not to waste time and money focusing on what these political actors, individuals or groups, *say*, or what they *write* in their strategic documents or policy papers. Helpful, to be sure, but in the end meaningless, or politically irrelevant. What counts – really counts – is what all these relevant political actors will bring – de facto – to the table by way of interests defined in terms of power (Morgenthau 1967 [1948a]). And surely, it is all about material interests and material power. This is not to say that soft power – or its uglier cousin, sharp power (Walker, Kalathil and Ludwig 2020) – is unimportant. It only means that although it may be interesting to hear them speak about where they stand on policy issues or what they intend to do politically, what counts is what these political actors can do in terms of political resources, and what they are realistically willing to do to pursue their interests, which may even include going to war.

And thus it is all rather trivial and complex at one and the same time. From the point of view of political realism, the political goal must be – let us say, in the domestic context of a parliamentary democracy – to have accrued more votes and seats than your political opponent has managed to win at the ballot box: it would be perfect, of course, to have the absolute majority of lawmakers. And, likewise, in terms of foreign-policy realism, in the specific context of international anarchy, the strategic goal of a nation or state, large or small, must be to protect its core national interests by whatever type of power politics; needless to say, in the context of the great powers, where the basic condition is that the chips are down, for them it is vital to have the regional and global balance of power tilted much towards them. As John Mearsheimer (2005) once put it: 'Better to Be Godzilla Than Bambi'. But then, of course, since absolute majorities or positions of hegemony tend to be very rare in political and international life, it might be better to have more friends than foes. This, in turn, can never be easy: one political actor can never be certain about the real motives or intentions of another (Morgenthau 1967 [1948a]; Mearsheimer 2001). Sad, but true.

And so whatever we might call political realism – a philosophy, *Weltanschauung*, persuasion, art, wisdom and all the rest of it – from my Kelsenian standpoint I want to suggest that the core political-realist logic is one driven by a rigid positivist methodology focused on the distribution of power and interests in any given political order. Make no mistake, however: one cannot wish away one tragic fact. Under the condition of imperfect knowledge, and as much as political realists try to work their way through the fog of politics and war through data, history and theory, more often than not the assessment or advice will be along these lines: better safe than sorry – or, with regard to international politics, better Machiavellian safe than Kantian sorry.

Now, from what I have been saying thus far about my Kelsenian-inspired take on political realism and foreign-policy realism, I can very well imagine that those coming out of the 'revisionist' or 'progressive' camp of recent realism studies may be disappointed. And in many ways I can relate to why they might think or say that I am just another self-styled custodian of a conservative-minded style of political and IR theory. Is it not quite clear that what I have been just saying about the centrality of power and interests in all political life makes me just another hopelessly out-of-touch realpolitik romanticist?

Let us keep this debate or dialogue, real or imagined, going for a little while. And let me ask them in return: what would you have expected me to say? After all – and I have laid my cards on the table, not only in this book's Introduction but also much longer ago too (Schuett 2007) – I am a foreign-policy realist. Of course, I may be a liberal or progressive, very much preferring Kelsen's expression liberal socialist; and of course in terms of political and IR theory I may be a Critically inspired political realist of a classical persuasion (Schuett 2011, 2015, 2018). Yet, to be sure, I am a foreign-policy realist none the less, so would you really have expected me to argue that we can do away with the problem of power and the struggle for security and wealth? Or that we can do away with the problem of interests and national interests? Or that if all us were as reasonable, rational and gentle as Kelsen seems to have been throughout his life, we could create a Kantian perpetual peace? Well, I must certainly disappoint you. Nothing of the sort. As former President Obama, who sought to transform Western foreign policy vis-à-vis the Middle East and Russia, once said: the problem of international politics is that it just does not work like 'Let's all hold hands and sing Kumbaya' (quoted in Rudoren 2015).

Kelsen, of course, had very much the same key message for us. We may dream as often as we like about a society from which the state has withered away, or about a world society from which conflict, violence and war have been eradicated. We may continue to believe that a time will come in which the forces or agents of Nature, Reason or God will have shown us the way for a communal living-together in absolute justice and earthly peace. Not going to happen, at least not any time soon; and if it ever is going to happen as part of a grand social experiment, chances are we are going to have, not less injustice and violence, but more. Even to imagine any form of communal living-together of individuals without positive law or politics, without coercion, is naïve – says Kelsen.

And if you wish to call it that – realpolitik – Kelsen has even more of it in store. It is inconceivable that we could ever create any type of political order, domestic or international, that would be freed from power struggles among political actors, thereby giving way to a harmony of interests, however temporary. No societal condition of that kind, be it a type of a natural harmony or a sort of a manufactured harmony (either through the most clever politicking or the most brutal force), is realistically attainable. There are no, and never have been any, Rousseauian (1997a [1755]: 151) noble savages out there, enjoying life in the wide forests in a so-called uncorrupted state of nature. And at the same time, one does not necessarily have to be a Freudian to see that we just are not those Enlightened enjoyable Kantians or any other saints that some philosophers and writers would have us believe we either were at some glorious point in the past, or could become once we have reached the sprawling coast of utopia (see Elshtain 2008) – which, of course, we never will. How could we possibly change You and Me?

All of this is not to say we ever should accept, both politically and morally, what is out there for us to see, particularly the violence and hatred, and most certainly not the daily cases of human rights abuses large and small, and war. As a Kelsenian-inspired political and IR theorist, and foreign-policy practitioner, I take it that the notion of realism – that is, human nature realism, social realism, political realism, foreign-policy realism – speaks to this fact of the human condition in the simplest terms: You and Me. We may not be as good as we tend to think of ourselves but we all want the same: we want to do different things at different times in different places! And so it may very well be that the only universalism there is in all political and international life is not the universalism of one common interest, or *summum bonum*, but the universalism of a solidarist pluralism of millions (or billions) of highly subjective value judgements about justice and happiness.

One might say that political realism, seen from such a Kelsenian angle, really and very fundamentally is about power and interests, and nothing else. Of course, I am very well aware of the fact that behind the masks of at least one or two *intellectual streetfighters* in the worlds of theory and practice are eyes full of personal ambition and a lust for power. Hobbes (1996 [1651]: Ch. xi) was probably quite right in his *Leviathan* when he postulated that we are driven by 'a perpetuall and restlesse desire for Power after power, that ceaseth only in Death'. Let us face it, one would not even succeed in becoming a small-town council member if one did not possess a certain liking for attaining power, keeping power and making the most of power. But then, I also take it that all of the real political realists, Kelsenian or otherwise, appreciate another real and fundamental fact: the political game we all play, whatever the position, is ultimately a powerplay over different *oughts* in life, and so the specific outcome of politics can take many different forms. As Kelsen would say, it is all man-made law.

And therefore I will put it to my critical (if not Critical) colleagues in the revisionist or progressive camp that a Kelsenian variant of political realism and foreign-policy realism may be useful for their own theoretical and practical battle, which is to separate out two kinds of political realists: one are the pseudo-realists, mostly Schmittian, who not really realists at all because they have a mostly conservative ideology hard-wired into them; the other are the real political realists exactly because they are, analytically and normatively, *political* through and through.

23 THE NATIONAL INTEREST

The pseudo-realists tend to be quite clever in how they hide their natural-lawish type of fixation on the status quo, or on what seems to them to be a glorious kind of past. From the point of view of a Kelsenian-style political realism, we know what is in their playbook: and typically, it is a three-part plot. But then, what if this playbook reveals a streak of naïve idealism?

To begin with, all the pseudo-realists seem to have is the concept of the national interest. And thus they keep repeating, as often as they can, just how important this concept is in political and IR theory, and in the practice of national security, diplomacy and foreign affairs. Rather fittingly, there is an otherwise fine foreign-policy quarterly out there, aptly called *The National Interest*, devoted to a return to realism in American foreign policy, a theme of which more soon.

In fact, it is Morgenthau who seems to be one of the worst offenders regarding this tutelage of the national interest. In his 1951 book – titled, sure enough, *In Defense of the National Interest*, and yet another of his frontal attacks on all things considered idealist, legalist and moralist (see also Morgenthau 1946) – the one path forward to a sustainable foreign policy of sound strategy and good diplomacy is made unmistakably clear. As Morgenthau (1951: 242) tells us:

> And, above all, remember always that it is not only a political necessity but also a moral duty for a nation to follow in its dealing with other nations but one guiding star, one standard for thought, one rule for action: The National Interest.

And, similar in spirit, the editors of *The National Interest*, justifiably regarded as one of the flagship magazines in the West of a realist persuasion, reiterated only recently: 'While it may be an old foreign policy concept, the notion of a national interest is not an antiquarian one . . . it has never possessed more relevance than now' (see *The National Interest* 2019). That comes over loud and clear – but is it really clear?

Now that the concept of the national interest is firmly established – aggrandised, really – as a core intellectual and political concern, the time has come for the second part of the pseudo-realists' playbook: all that counts is a Machiavellian-style *raison d'État*, narrowly conceived. And thus they keep emphasising, as powerfully as they can, just how important it is to have nothing but a clear-eyed view on state survival. Typically, this is played in two variants: one quite gentle, the other hard.

In the softer version, a distinction is made between two realms within foreign affairs: one is international politics and security, or high politics, where it is all about a nation's strategic concerns, primarily military and economic, vis-à-vis adversaries and peer competitors, respectively; the other realm is international relations and law, or low politics, which, as a sort of political catch-all, must deal with pretty much everything else that is deemed non-essential to the very survival of one's political order or polity. I would place Morgenthau in the softer category: without a doubt he was notably concerned with the study of so-called grand strategies relating to what makes good high politics, but then he never said that law (or morality, for that matter) would not play any role, let alone denying that international law 'has in most instances been scrupulously observed' (Morgenthau 1967 [1948]: 265).

If pressed, really pressed, I would reluctantly see Kelsen in this camp too: he was interested in the elevated questions of war and peace, while of course giving international legal norms their due in world politics (on the empirical side of international law, see Simmons 2009; Hurd 2019). Needless to say, Morgenthau was sceptical about the prospect of a world order juridified in a Kelsenian way.

The harder version of the *raison d'État* gibberish is, at least as I see it, today perhaps most closely associated with Mearsheimer's offensive realism. I must say that, much as I find problematic, if not dislike, his co-authored book about a so-called Israel lobby in American politics (Mearsheimer and Walt 2007), I find him a bold theorist and many of his assumptions and hypotheses can be helpful starting points.

That said, Mearsheimer's eyes are thoroughly fixated on power; there is little, if nothing else than power in his conception of the world. As Mearsheimer (1994–5: 13) put it: 'the balance of power is the independent variable that explains war; institutions are merely an intervening variable in the process'. The other way round, this of course means: nations do what they must, whenever, wherever, with whatever means necessary. As the legendary British statesman and twice Prime Minister Henry John Temple, third Viscount Palmerston (1848), had said: 'We have no eternal allies, and we have no perpetual enemies. Our interests are eternal and perpetual, and those interests it is our duty to follow.' Who would not like this? It is not that there is something wrong in the core strategic logic, but none the less it sounds like a political blank cheque.

And thus it is almost self-evident what the third part of the playbook of all pseudo-realists is: to divide us up in two groups, idealists and realists. That is to say: there will be one group containing all those in political and IR theory, and in government, who are unwilling or unable to grasp what it is that is so clearly in the interest of one's nation; and then there is a smaller, more select group of strategists who just know it all and have got what it takes. As Dan Drezner (2016), International Relations Professor at Tufts' Fletcher School of Law and Diplomacy, and a regular *Washington Post* contributor, quipped, 'Man, this club is exclusive!' Behind Drezner's witty comment are, of course, as I see it, two serious questions. Who is in this club? What makes a foreign-policy realist?

Now, let me give one quick example illustrating the playbook problem. In early 2016, the final of President Obama's total of eight years in office, Stephen Walt, certainly one of today's most distinguished academics and serious public voices on American foreign policy and international affairs (see my disclaimer regarding the Israel lobby book, though), set out to render his judgement – Obama was not a foreign-policy realist! Some say he was (Zakaria 2008; Scheuerman 2011; Kaplan 2014; Goldberg 2016), while others argue he was not (Bonicelli 2012; Gay 2014; Saunders 2014): all discussed in breadth and wide scope, as it should be in political and IR theory. Walt (2016) is clearly in the latter camp: 'If he had been, he might have avoided some of his biggest foreign-policy mistakes.' As Walt (2016) continues to make clear:

> Obama did not in fact run a 'realist' foreign policy, because he doesn't fully embrace a realist worldview, didn't appoint many (any?) realists to key positions, and never really tried to dismantle the bipartisan consensus behind the grand strategy of liberal hegemony.

Straight to the point, as it should be.

Speaking of as it should *be*, here is a list of what Walt (2016) the foreign-policy realist would have liked President Obama to have accomplished during his tenure in the White House. Get out of Afghanistan in 2009. Get things normal in the Middle East. Get NATO/Russia relations right. Get regime change ideas out of Washingtonians' heads. Get America's grand strategy back on the track of restrained offshore balancing. Clear enough. And, although tempted, I will not go through each policy item, assessing their relative political and strategic value for American foreign policy in the twenty-first century; nor will I discuss whether President Obama was a successful foreign-policy president, let alone whether he was a foreign-policy realist.

Yet let me say this here, even provokingly: what does it matter whether this or that statesman was a foreign-policy realist or not? As a Kelsenian-inspired political and IR theorist, one might say that in the realm of politics, personal and political philosophies and ideas come only second: first come power and interests.

In a short essay, aptly titled 'Freud, International Relations Are Calling', published literally one day after Obama's election win in the autumn of 2008, Amitai Etzioni, former Sociology Professor at Columbia, Senior Advisor to the Carter White House and now Director of George Washington University's Institute for Communitarian Policy Studies, put the problem so well (Etzioni 2008). Each one of us political and IR theorists, intellectuals, pundits, politicians and bureaucrats may insist as often as we like, as shrewdly as we can, in our articles, books, opinion pieces, policy briefs, speeches or briefings, that a new government should work on this or that, should scrap this old policy or that one, and should devise new and better strategies.

Yet the fact of political life – if not the uncomfortable truth – is this: as Etzioni, the political realist, writes, 'If we have a need and it is not responded to, it is usually not because nobody has ever noted it, but because there are powerful causes that block treatment' (Etzioni 2008). How right he is to have said it out loud. The challenge is not ignorance but interests. Lots of different interests – backed by power.

And thus from that angle, to me at least, Walt's assessment of President Obama's foreign-policy legacy is rather unrealistic, if not quasi-conspiratorial. Writes Walt (2016; note my italics): 'Of course, even if Obama had *explained* the logic behind this [realist offshore balancing] strategy carefully and followed it consistently, he might still have failed to *transform* the foreign-policy establishment's interventionist *mindset*.' There is more: 'After all, that [liberal] worldview is supported by plenty of wealthy individuals, powerful corporations, influential think tanks, and well-connected lobbies' (Walt 2016). For a start (more below), why so negative toward the so-called establishment? It cannot come as a surprise to a political scientist that some people are wealthy, corporations are powerful, think tanks are influential or lobbies are well connected. That is political realism: interest groups pushing with real power their real interests.

And so I am reminded here of what Ido Oren (2009), Political Science Professor at Florida University, so succinctly called the 'unrealism of contemporary realism'. Or to bring Dan Drezner (2016) back in: who can ever fit the neorealist bill? No one would, unless this future president 'got a PhD in international relations from the University of Chicago and then hired the ghost of George Kennan to be secretary of state'. Very true.

As a Kelsenian-style political realist, then, one has to stomach stoically – out of methodological conviction and perhaps as a matter of style – the fact that there is indeed much Schmittian and pseudo-realist-style idealism out there. Now, you might think I am merely another thin-skinned bureaucrat–scholar incapable of taking any criticism from the sidelines. Be that as it may. The point is this: it is one thing to have political and IR theory help solve real-world problems through the toughest of Critique (speaking truth to power) and best possible advice. It is quite another to insinuate that ever since the optimism of 1989, American and world politics have been held hostage by a liberal conspiracy, a 'dysfunctional caste of privileged insiders' (Walt 2018: 95), ostensibly a so-called establishment stuffed from top to bottom with liberals from so-called mainstream universities and think tanks, paid for by mainstream private and corporate wealth, and 'mandarins intolerant of dissenting views' (Heilbrunn 2018).

Even if matters were so, what would such a take on these matters reveal other than that their authors appear to be rather unrealistic about politics. They appear to be complaining about the most normal of all things in political life: the democratic struggle for power and influence in state organs, as Kelsen would have it.

All of this is to say, from a Kelsenian standpoint, that there is no such a thing as an eternal or timeless, or monolithic or self-evident, conception of the national interest, or *raison d'État*. One might say in Kelsenian language that the only thing that is clearly self-evident in politics is that nothing is self-evident in terms of interests. The state acts through its organs, carrying out what has been willed by its organs, and through its organs, which is the same as saying what the state organs of any given legal order will at any given time is nothing but a reflection of the specific distribution of power at this very moment.

Let us return, then, to the statement by Stephen Walt, quoted above at length, that even if President Obama had explained the core logic of a restrained grand strategy of offshore balancing, he might still have failed to transform Washington's liberal–interventionist mindset. Agreed, but really – explain? Transform? Mindset? Sounds fairly idealistic:

First, a president is not some kind of explainer-in-chief. The White House, 10 Downing Street, the Élysée Palace and so on are not lecture halls, but political powerhouses. This is not to start a juristic debate about presidential duties, as in Article II of the United States Constitution, but surely, to insinuate that explaining policy will win you any votes at the ballot box or sway foreign dip-lomats in your policy direction is naïve.

Rather, a Kelsenian-inspired political realism can have but one clear focus: the 'concept of interest defined in terms of power' (Morgenthau 1967 [1948a]: 5), for two reasons. One is to distinguish the political from the legal, economical, ethical and so on, and avoid methodical syncretism. The other reason is clear enough. Here is Morgenthau (1967 [1948a]: 8) quoting George Washington's famous dictum that it takes only 'a small knowledge of human nature [to] convince us, that, with far the greatest part of mankind, interest is the governing principle'. And no less clear, true to his Continental intellectual heritage, Morgenthau (1967 [1948a]: 8) lets Max Weber speak for himself: 'Interests (material and ideal), not ideas, dominate directly the actions of men.' What this means is, of course, as follows: without appealing oratorical skills, success in today's social media age is unlikely – but, as has ever been true in political and international life, without Machiavellian ingenuity, political success is impossible.

Second, neither is a president some type of transformer-in-chief. No one is. It may be the Schmittian dream, but in reality, no one state organ in any given polity can realistically be so powerful as to transform politics, law and society, let alone international society. And as a Kelsenian foreign-policy realist I must say that Keir A. Lieber (2009: 28), Political Science Professor at George-town's Edmund A. Walsh School of Foreign Service, has it right in *War, Peace, and International Political Realism*, that human nature does not allow for any 'grandiose plans to transform international relations'. Sad, but true.

And thus I would argue that it has been the very point of political real-ism from the very start – ever since 'Thucydides had once seen fit to reverse-engineer his version of political reality from the power and fact of the Athenian fighting machine' (Hollingworth and Schuett 2018: 1) – that we acknowledge analytically that power and interests are what make the world go round; and that we accept normatively that the fact of You and Me gives us a certain set of limitations within which we have to operate politically and strategically. As Kelsen the Pure positivist and political realist has sought to caution us: regard-less of whether we have natural law or positive law in front of us, or whether we are operating within the context of an antiquated autocracy or a liberal democracy, we must never, ever be blinded, by either its cruelty or its beauty, respectively, to the fact that what we are dealing with are *not* agents of power and interests.

To a Kelsenian, surely, where there is society there is law. And where there is law, there is politics. And what is more, where there is politics there are, in essence, two ways to solve or accommodate different claims to power, and to deal with different sets of interests. One is through compromise. The other is through force. Either way (not that they are equally acceptable morally), in any given legal order we are confronted with decidedly political situations: that is, confronted with a specific distribution of power over a specific distribution of interests so thick or impenetrable that the notion of a transformational politics or a 'peace through transformation' (Morgenthau 1967 [1948a]: Part ix; Schuett 2011) seems far-fetched.

Nothing of this is to say, as a Kelsenian political realist, that we are doomed to what we have in front of us at any given time or point in history. Where the national interest or *raison d'État* comes across as an ideologically charged fiction in the context of a certain distribution of power and interests in any political order, there surely is a better option than going for the Schmittian sword or taking refuge in quasi-conspiratorial myths about politics – go and change that very balance.

24 ... AND OTHER MYTHS

There are many reasons why political realism old and new, Kelsenian and otherwise, tends to be seen as 'an essentially negative doctrine' (Hollingworth and Schuett 2018: 1). If one breaks its analytics of the strategic situation of international life down to foreign-policy realism's hardened core, what one comes to see is an ugly picture of You and Me: as long as we live in a structural condition of anarchy, we are trapped in a Herzian security dilemma.

And as crude as it is, it has been quite rational of You and Me to separate out rocks and rockets, and to keep saying to ourselves: better safe – through a balance of power – than sorry. But then, is it not almost too trivial to question that very strategic logic ethically? Is peace through force – that is, a kind of perfected, mutually assured destruction – not merely a tragic theatre of the absurd? Or let me put it this way: it is Monday evening, on 7 September 1964. A minute-long TV spot. A little girl in a meadow. A man's voice counting down. The image of an atomic blast. Then President Johnson's voice-over: 'These are the stakes. To make a world in which all of God's children can live, or to go into the dark. We must either love each other, or we must die.' The daisy ad – except that it is not just an ad in a commercial break during a Gregory Peck movie, of course.

As a Kelsenian foreign-policy realist I am stunned every time I hear this nonchalant talk about nuclear deterrence as a strategic tool for stability and peace. But then, as the logic of anarchy has it: if you want peace, go for nukes. They have proved to be a 'tremendous force for peace' (Waltz 1990: 731). They may be weapons of mass destruction, but none the less are 'weapons of peace' (Mearsheimer 1990: 20; 2012). Surely the analytics behind the decision to opt for a robust nuclear posture are all too well known: where you have a condition of structural anarchy, the great powers must provide for their own survival. The proliferation of nuclear weapons makes 'the cost of war seem frighteningly high and thus discourage[s] states from starting any wars that might lead to the use of such weapons' (Waltz 1981: 3). This is not bad scholarship, nor bad strategic thinking. It is game theory, applied to You and Me.

So the core question cannot be wished away: would You and Me have the nerve, in an anarchical condition where there is no dialling the emergency services for help, just to sit there and trust Our lives to the hope that all other actors relevant to Our specific security situation will not attack, thereby leaving Us, at worst, to our death? The problem is not new, and of course the reader will know where I am headed: an earlier generation of political realists, among them notably Morgenthau and Herz, seem to have been far more subtle and reflexive about the twin problem of war – and peace – than some of their self-styled followers of today in the neorealist mould.

To be sure, as foreign-policy realists they reacted throughout their lives and careers against everything and everyone that they considered to be naïve and idealistic. And of course they did not get it always right: at times they were polemical through and through, and lost themselves in battles they could not possibly win – at least not how they fought them, especially in the case of Morgenthau and Vietnam. But no matter what, they knew that what was at stake was not so much the national interest, but the broader picture – the theme of peace.

Were these political realists some kind of peacenik? Not really. But they thought about peace as much as they analysed the causes of war. As scholars, and as men. In light of the Cold War's ever-present threat of nuclear annihilation, Morgenthau (1967 [1948a]: 373) made it clear in *Politics among Nations* that peace must be the 'paramount concern of Western civilization'.[4] And Herz (1964: 117–18) argued, in a Kelsenian quasi-legal spirit, that what we must achieve is the 'transition from jumbled, chaotic patchwork to a true and common law of man'. While Morgenthau (1967 [1948a]: 532–50) pinned his hopes on what seems to be an idealised diplomat–statesman, Herz's (1951: 250) vision of a realist liberalism, rooted in the ideal of freedom (of which Kelsen has spoken so passionately), hoped that an ever larger number of You and Me 'escape stagnant and passive attitudes'. In other words, says Herz the liberal political realist, or realist political idealist: use your power, for your ought.

Kelsen the Pure positivist, and for that matter liberal or progressive political realist, would have said the same thing: use your power, use it wisely and use it for your ought, but most importantly – use it! And to this I would add: use it for whatever ought you can, but bear in mind perhaps how a Kelsenian political realism sets a few limits or boundaries as to what can possibly done with real power.

One key pillar is to take You and Me as we really are, which is not to say that we must give in to our many fears and worst biases, only that a Kelsenian political realist has to have a realistic conception of human nature, not an idealised one. The second pillar is to take laws or legal norms as they ought to be, which by no means implies that the ought in any way is derived from an is (human nature). And the third pillar, perhaps the hardest part, is to balance out the is and the ought, and arrive at a position of a can. Then, in the language of Morgenthau, do your intellectual streetfighting, or as Kelsen would put it – surely softer in tone but conveying the same message: do real politics in terms of power and interests.

So, a Kelsenian-style political realism is not thoroughly pessimistic or negative, and it most certainly does not hammer out the message that we are doomed to a strategic reality of violence and war. Even though Kelsen was much inspired by Freud, and was not at all naïve about the dynamics of human nature, he was not of the view (as we shall see later) that, as Freud once put, most of us are 'trash' (quoted in Roazen 1969: 245). What is more, for every Freudian pessimist there is a Pinkerian (Pinker 2016 [2002]) optimist waiting around the corner. My point, to be frank, is that much of the optimism/pessimism play seems synthetic, if not useless.

For what does the human nature optimism/pessimism binary really tell us, let alone change for us? At best, it does not matter at all. At worst, though, in light of our chew-it-up, spit-it out, 24/7 online age, we have ended up with exactly what we have been so keen to avoid: a manufactured angst. I fear that breaking the (good) news that the 'homicide rate in England was 50 times higher in the 14th century than is today' (Weintraub 2018) is not going to impress Londoners in the current knife crime crisis. I do not doubt the number; my fear is rather that Schmittians populists will propagandise and accuse us of whitewashing. The case is similar, but not quite the same, with the (positive) fact that over the last several decades we have seen less and less inter-state violence (see Lebow 2010). So why has global defence spending risen so sharply? We seem to trust each other very little in political and international life, and it costs us billions and billions of dollars each year to keep a so-called peace through force (see Preble and Mueller 2014; *The New York Times* 2019). But of course we continue to live in the condition of international anarchy.

Kelsen's style of political realism, as I have come to understand it, gives us little, if not no, room into which we could comfortably or realistically escape: not into the realm of Nature, Reason or God. We are out in the open, and the spotlight is firmly on *You* and *Me*. To be sure – and it is not that we would not know – Westphalia is not the product of the impersonal forces of history. You might say that the Westphalian balance of power is as important today as back then (Kissinger 2014). Or you might think of it as 'Westfailure' (Strange 1999). It is clear that this new sovereignty-based international order was willed by the 235 official envoys and their staff who facilitated the signing of the three agreements known as the Treaty of Westphalia. And as trivial a statement as it is, the very core of what was willed in 1648 is still willed. By You. By Me. Fair enough.

In a very calm and profound way, Kelsen reminds us that all the good, and all the bad, and all the ugly out there in political and international life is nothing but a reflection of choices made or not made, power used or not used, roads taken or not taken, votes cast or not cast, deals done or not done, interests followed or not followed, and so on. In politics nothing is inevitable, as the ideologues would have us believe. We choose to pursue power after power. We choose to do parochial politics. We choose to be nationalists. And we choose to be Schmittians – or not.

Kelsen the Freudian-inspired political realist was certain that there is no such thing as utopia. But that is not because conflict and war are predetermined by human nature, natural laws or any other quasi-mythical invisible social forces. Instead, the rules and norms by which a society lives, and by which an international society functions, are the results of power struggles over interests being pursued by relevant actors on the political and international scene. Thus Martin Wight (1966: 26), distinguished British historian and pacifist, is about right when he says that international relations is 'the realm of recurrence and repetition'. I say about right because that is not a natural law, but it speaks to the fact that You and Me tend to act in similar ways when confronted with similar situations.

Hence any Kelsenian political and IR theorist, not necessarily even a foreign-policy realist, must already be speechless to hear that the state was a person, and totally flabbergasted to follow a serious line of argument claiming in all earnest that 'a world state will emerge whether or not anyone intends to bring it about' (Wendt 2003: 529). Make no mistake, Kelsen was up for an ever more central-ised coercive international legal order, but still he would have been shocked in light of this kind of determinism and complacency, both of which are very dangerous.

'Finality is not the language of politics' – so said iconic British Prime Minister Benjamin Disraeli (1859). And thus it is very dangerous in political and IR theory that so many no longer conceptualise the political in terms of a materialist–individualist struggle for power and interest, but rather flee into some kind of constructivist idealist–holist mode of thinking (nota-bly Wendt 1999). Ever heard that the only driving forces in the real world are You and Me, and Your Interest and My Interest? As Henry Kissinger (*Harvard Magazine* 2012) once quipped, the problem is that when statesman err, it is irrevocable; when academics err, they can write another book.

All of this is to say, more seriously, that as a Kelsenian Pure positivist and political realist, one must be very strict on the point that the political has no telos, no goal, no end. Kelsen did not repeatedly warn us about the is of human nature in order to spoil any longing for progress and peace as our ought. He did so to point out that all forms of pseudo-political political and IR theory will lull us into a false sense of security. Surely to be an optimist is good – but to be a deterministic optimist or idealist is almost unimaginably dangerous. Exactly because of the power struggles, all political orders are fragile, but this is most notably true of democracies: they are not big planes full of well-behaved passengers sitting still in their comfortable seats with their seat belts on, while being flown on autopilot to utopia.

As a man who had one foot in theory and the other in practice, Kelsen had simply seen way too much in his life not to be very wary of naïve natural-law-ish ideologues and Schmittians, who believe they can decide their way out of the daily power struggles over competing interests – the reflections of subjective value-judgements of different oughts. Kelsen saw clearly that one cannot, and must not, shy away from the political. Or as Leszek Kolakowski (1960: 58), the former Oxford-based Polish philosopher who helped inspire *Solidarność*, used to say: you have to accept that you just cannot walk through the bloody morass of history wearing your freshly polished patent leather shoes.

He knew that, in his time and thus in the future, politics in general, and world politics in particular, are a 'matter of life and death', as Robert Keohane, Professor Emeritus at Princeton's Woodrow Wilson School of Public and International Affairs, said, because they have 'a daily impact on the lives of people throughout the globe' (Keohane 1986: 1). He would listen carefully to Primo Levi (2017 [1986]), the Italian Auschwitz survivor, and what he said about the Shoah: it happened, and so it can happen again. And he would also take seriously the assessment by George Friedman (2015: 258), the Budapest-born American analyst: while the history of European integration is, by and large, a successful one, in light of the renewed great power competition and nationalism no one can say with confidence that not even the Europeans might choose war, come the time: 'Nothing has ended. For humans nothing significant is ever over.'

And that, of course, is the flip side of human agency through politics – changing the status quo through progressive politics is possible, but it can go so horribly wrong. There is as much or little linearity hard-wired into the status quo as there is into a quasi-teleological progress. And so Kelsen would say that we must never ignore what was perhaps his friend's core political message. What Freud (1915: 258) had cautioned in his time, in light of the horrors of the Great War, is in its essence as relevant today as it was more than a hundred years ago: we must always reckon with the possibility that it may not be so much that we have sunken so low when we choose to fight our wars for flag and country, but rather that we may never have been that high up on the civilisational ladder as some had thought or wished.

Where political progress is possible, Kelsen helps us keep in mind, so is political regress. From the standpoint of a Kelsenian Pure positivism and political realism, we cannot have the one possibility without the other. We may lament the fact of the political, with some taking flight into Nature, Reason or God, but there is no escaping; and although Kelsen was certainly not a hyperbolic or alarmist type of character, of course his works and ideas reflect a profound caution that societal, if not civilisational, regress can happen very fast. And it would not take too much for a legal order or polity to regress: a bit of populism and demagogy here; a breeze of social envy and ethnic resentment there; add a few state of emergencies every now and then; and keep a number of so-called unideological bystanders with their stagnant attitudes happy. It is not as if we have not been there before – and that worried Kelsen, as it should worry You and Me. As one might say, carrying the intellectual or cognitive burden of this kind of political realism is the price of a Pure positivism's freedom.

To the reader all this may be rather unsatisfying, if not disappointing: Where is Kelsen's grand plan for progress? And for that matter, what is his narrative (to use that dreadful term) for a bright future? From what I have been saying in this book, you will find none of that in the work of Hans Kelsen. What you will find, though, is something even better and more important: you will find a method and a mindset. One is rigid and strict, the other is open and progressive. Taken together, they form a realistic 'can', which is You and Me working, day in, day out, towards a realistic peace: legal and political.

It will be no surprise, of course, if the strongmen and the Schmittians (and some of the pseudo-realists) continue to beat the drum for Nature and nationalism. Fine. But the Kelsenian political realist will keep pushing, and will say simply this in the intellectual and political arena: as long as You and Me do not live to see a centralised international legal order with coercive power, there will be blood – the blood of brutes – and no one shall dare say that he or she could not have seen war coming.

25 Concluding Remarks on a Man and a Method

'Professor! You are a republican. I am a monarchist. You are a liberal. I am a conservative. You are a Jew. I am a Catholic. Why are you helping me?' The young man in the Vienna of the 1920s was serious. Agonising over this question for quite some time, he had one day had enough, and wanted to hear it directly from his by then distinguished thesis supervisor. He headed for Wickenburggasse 23, located in the Eighth District opposite Josefstadt prison, and simply asked the question of Hans Kelsen at his apartment. And of course, there and then, the able doctoral student had his answer: Kelsen hugged him and explained: 'My dear friend, exactly because you are everything that I am *not*, I value and support you.'[5]

Let me fast-forward to the evening of 27 May 1952. The weather was fair. Not too warm, not too cold, about normal for Berkeley at such time of the year. The same day, in the Old World of Paris, the Inner Six signed the European Defence Community Treaty, one of the most ambitious attempts to pacify Europe by creating a sort of European Army. What could have been a milestone for European security, though, was never put into effect. In August 1954, the French Assemblée Nationale failed to ratify the treaty, and today the EU-wide rise of nationalistic Eurosceptics and Schmittian populists makes it hard to believe that there will be a real push for further European integration any time soon. To see all this unfolding would sadden Kelsen, but not surprise him. Politics can go many ways.

He had spoken for slightly over an hour. And the host of what was the tenth Bernard Moses Memorial Lecture, the annual occasion dedicated to the memory of this iconic head of the Department of History, Economics and Jurisprudence (Watson 1961), had found all the right introductory words for Kelsen, progressing through the many chapters of his life and career. The atmosphere was warm, as was the reception by those present in the audience. And then there was a final round of affectionate applause for what was to be his farewell lecture.[6]

Nothing in his lecture, simply titled 'What is Justice?', was new (Kelsen 1952a). And how could it have been otherwise? From first to last – from his roots in Vienna to his new home in America; from his early days in the *k. u. k.* War Ministry during the Great War to his professorship at Berkeley's Political Science Department in the early days of the Cold War – Hans Kelsen was as consistent as he was sharp. If we take the ideal of freedom seriously, we cannot delegate the question of what is right and wrong, good and bad, fair and unfair, to any higher authority than You and Me, or Us. We must beware of the false promise of absolute justice. And we must beware also of the Schmittians and strongmen, and their myths.

At the beginning of the book I described how I was about to set out a progressive vision of political realism, developed within the intellectual context of open society ideals. Readers will judge the merits of my Kelsen: exploring his biography and focusing on his politics, I have used the previous chapters and sections to show you Kelsen the clear-eyed political thinker, political realist and foreign-policy realist.

From where I stand in political and IR theory, I must say that his so-called 'idealism' is far more realistic than the assumptions and arguments of many 'realists', let alone Schmittians and pseudo-realists. After I had peeled off layer after layer of Kelsen's life and philosophy, there were many times when I was myself surprised as he revealed himself as a calm yet passionate, measured yet focused, man of realism. Human nature is not perfect or perfectible. The state is no happy-go-lucky association of Kantian angels, but a coercive order that we can never allow to wither away. And war is not an ever-present possibility because we do not know the tragedies it brings, but because there is nothing with real teeth in an anarchical world order that would prevent You and Me from fighting it all out on the battlefield.

And thus I must leave you to your Kelsen rather as he left us to our justice. In his Berkeley farewell lecture, soft in tone as ever, he said what he had said so many times before in his life and penned in his many books, articles, essays and letters (Kelsen 1957a: 24):

> I cannot say what justice is, the absolute justice for which mankind is longing. I must acquiesce in a relative justice and I can only say what justice is

to me. Since science is my profession, and hence the most important thing in my life, justice, to me, is that social order under whose protection the search for truth can prosper. 'My' justice, then, is the justice of freedom, the justice of peace, the justice of democracy – the justice of tolerance.

To this beautiful, and beautifully realistic, statement I should like to add: I cannot say what political realism is. I can say only what political realism and foreign-policy realism mean to me: looking social reality in the eye – recognising (as hard as that may be) that all the good, bad and ugly we see in political and international life is man-made – and because of this fundamental recognition of the political, they mean working unceasingly towards progress and reform, strengthening the rule of law and global justice, human rights and a cosmopolitan world order.

This book has argued for approaching Hans Kelsen from the perspective of what I have called a Critically inspired or progressive variant of political realism. I have tried to make a dual case: first, for Hans Kelsen the political realist; and second, for the reconciliation of foreign-policy realism with a progressive politics of open society ideals. It was beyond my analytical scope to situate Kelsen in the wider body of contemporary political and IR theory, and to apply Kelsenian themes to the concrete problems of today's world politics. As to the former, I might have overplayed his realistic views on human nature, power and anarchy, at the expense of his thoughts on developmental psychology, norm internalisation, and international society and law, all themes that might interest constructivists, and perhaps English School theorists too. As to the latter, there is so much more to explore in how Kelsen sought to defend the open society ideals of freedom and democracy, human rights and peace, all of which are, of course, core themes of progressives and liberals old and new. And thus my hope is that these topics will be explored by scholars better suited to these tasks than I could have been, or will be. I am standing firmly on this side of the barricades, where I have always stood: call it liberal realism or realist liberalism.

In writing this book I have also learned what a remarkable man among remarkable men and women he had been throughout his life and career. A teacher, friend and example to Morgenthau and Herz, he was gentle and kind to many, many others in the profession of science. As Helen Silving-Ryu (1964: 297), mentored by Kelsen at Vienna in the mid-1920s and later law Professor at the University of Puerto Rico, put it: taking courses with him was 'partaking in a unique life experience – the experience of observing what a truly great scholar stands for in human terms' (see Paz 2014).

Or as Benjamin Akzin, another legendary student of Kelsen's and former President of the Israel Political Science Association, said in light of Kelsen's talk at the thirty-fifth Annual Meeting of the American Society of International

Law, held at the Carleton Hotel in Washington, D.C., on 25 April 1941 (quoted in Kelsen and Herz 1941: 89):

> I see quite a number of people here in the audience who, like myself, have been at different times and in different places students of Professor Kelsen, and I think all of us have felt again the great intellectual happiness that comes from listening to one of his stimulating lectures and speeches. We, his former pupils, are very grateful to him for having given us once more food for thought that will last for a long time.

With stories like these I could go on and on: not only because this book has been, from the very start, an appreciative and sympathetic assessment of Hans Kelsen, but because, in terms of intellectual history, there are just so many of his former pupils or early Kelsenians (see, for example, Lipsky 1953; Engel 1964).

And yet the future confronts us. And of course, the future confronts us in the present: that is, the future of an open society is made and re-made by us in the here and now – by You and Me. This may be trivial, and perhaps it is even all too trivial. But then: beware of bystanders.

And thus today's Kelsenians must not lose themselves in a kind of backward-looking 'Kelsenology', as former Austrian Vice-Chancellor and Justice Minister Clemens Jabloner (2019) recently cautioned. What is more important is that we do what Kelsen, the scholar, would have wanted us to do: use Pure positivism, orthodox or refined, as a scientific method to unearth the metaphysical and anti-democratic blah hidden in philosophy, law and politics. Recall: choices made, roads taken or not.

NOTES

INTRODUCTION

1. Books are written alone – but of course, not entirely so. While the Bibliography gives the reader the full picture of what I have been using to make the case for Hans Kelsen the progressive political realist (as I develop it in this book), at this stage, here as well as in subsequent notes, I would like to single out a few works in order to give my line of argument some more intellectual and methodological context. In terms of Kelsenian ideas in the analytical and normative study of politics and IR, I found the following useful: Suganami (2007); Jütersonke (2010); Hjorth (2011); Scheuerman (2012, 2014, 2018); Ingram (2014); Stirk (2014, 2015a); Hathaway and Shapiro (2018); Rosenboim (2017); Invernizzi-Accetti (2018). For recent law readings of Kelsen, see Vinx (2007); Turner (2010); Marmor (2011); Duarte d'Almeida, Gardner and Green (2013); Gragl (2018); Kletzer (2018); Paulson (2018); Langford, Bryan and McGarry (2019); Orakhelashvili (2019). I would say that the must-read works with a special focus on Kelsenian questions of international law, written over the last two decades, are Kennedy (1994); Zolo (1998); Koskenniemi (2001, 2005); Treviño (2009 [1949]); von Bernstorff (2010); Busch, von Schmädel and Staudigl-Ciechowicz (2011); Cohen (2012); García-Salmones Rovira (2013, 2020); Kammerhofer and D'Aspremont (2014); Ranney (2018). And last not least, the body of literature that seeks to situate Kelsen as being one of the finest Western philosophers or theorists of democracy is both rich and timely; definitely see Dreier (1990); Jestaedt and Lepsius (2006); Kalyvas (2006); Ehs (2009a); De Angelis (2009); Baume (2012, 2018); Herrera (2014); Rice (2016); Özmen (2017); Ragazzoni (2017); Thomä (2018); Wolkenstein (2019).

2. Most of the events surrounding Kelsen's life and work on two continents – first in Europe until June of 1940, thereafter in America – are described in two autobiographical accounts. As of now, they are unfortunately available only in the original German. One is a handwritten twelve-page 'Selbstdarstellung' of February 1927 (Kelsen 1927a), and the other is a typewritten forty-six-page 'Autobiographie' of October 1947 (Kelsen 1947a); as to their specifics, historical origins and broader context, see Jestaedt's commentary (Kelsen 1927a, 1947a: 586–96). To date, the standard bearer for Kelsen's life is Rudolf Aladár Métall (1969), a lifelong companion (former student, assistant and friend), although Thomas Olechowski (2020), law Professor at Vienna and Co-director of the Viennese Hans Kelsen-Institut with a special interest in history, has recently published what is set to become the standard biography of Hans Kelsen for many years to come; the book arrived too late

to be included here as a whole. Unless noted otherwise, throughout this book, for information about Kelsen's life and biographical details I have relied first and foremost on Kelsen (1927a, 1947a); Métall (1969); Jabloner (1998); Jestaedt (2007a); Walter, Ogris and Olechowski (2009); Olechowski (2011, 2013a); Jabloner, Olechowski and Zeleny (2016).

3. *k. u. k.* stands for *kaiserlich und königlich*: that is, 'imperial and royal'.

4. And thus, for sure, when I look at Kelsen I see the Pure theorist of law, state and international legal order – and, as I argue in this book, a progressive political realist – but at one and the same time I see Kelsen the man, young and ageing, a father and husband, and so on: Bohemian by birth; Viennese Jew turned Catholic and later Protestant; always agnostic; a gifted but not outstanding schoolboy; a man who loved literature; volunteer soldier; bored law student, soon the best of his generation; top professor; star jurist; pure positivist; modern mandarin; good with the generals; liberal socialist; intelligence consultant; passionate internationalist; progressive Old World intellectual; a bold man, with a calm and clear mind, who lived for science and truth; intellectual streetfighter; and fascinating open society idealist/realist.

5. The 'revisionist genre' (Scheuermann 2019: 3) is quite an impressive body of work in today's political and IR theory, and even though I fear that some of my fellow colleagues in this camp have lately been somewhat downplaying what I would say are the basics of any political realism – human nature, the political, power – I would none the less argue that the following items at the least should be on every broadly revisionist-inspired political realism reading list in the fields of politics, philosophy and international law: Fox (1985); Booth (1991, 2005); Craig (2003); Lebow (2003); Williams (2005, 2007); Molloy (2006); Schou Tjalve (2008); Scheuerman (2009, 2011, 2012, 2018); Bell (2010); Jütersonke (2010); Levine (2012); Sleat (2013, 2018); Rossi and Sleat (2014); Rösch (2015); Brostrom (2016); Hall and Sleat (2017); Finlayson (2017); Kostagiannis (2017); Nardin (2017); Prinz and Rossi (2017); McQueen (2018a, 2018b); Peoples (2018); Schuett and Hollingworth (2018); Adair-Toteff (2019); Brinn (2019); Hjorth (2020). There is so much more, to be sure. All of which is to say: political realism and realpolitik are not the same (see also Bew 2016, 2018).

6. It is impossible – for me, at least as a political and IR theorist, not a trained jurist – even remotely to summarise the incredibly rich and impressive body of law literature on Kelsen. As I have noted above, the Bibliography contains this book's entire source material, but regarding Kelsen's law aspect I found the following particularly helpful: Stewart (1990); Dyzenhaus (1997); Paulson and Litschewski-Paulson (1999); Green (2003); Paulson (2003); Paulson and Stolleis (2005); Somek (2007); Aliprantis and Olechowski (2014); Vinx (2015); Bryan, Langford and McGarry (2015, 2016); Telman (2016a); Langford, Bryan and McGarry (2017); van Ooyen (2017, 2019); Jabloner, Kuklik and Olechowski (2018).

7. Since I cannot possibly know – given my present non-academic life and career – how many more books in political and IR theory I will manage to write (ideas are plentiful, though), it is perhaps fitting here that I say something briefly about my own intellectual roots or upbringing, and more importantly, the people to whom I am so very grateful. Professor John C. Williams and Dr Peter M. R. Stirk were my

postgraduate supervisors at Durham University from 2004 to 2009, and I cannot thank them enough for guiding me so thoroughly and good-heartedly through both my MA and my PhD in Politics. Chris J. Brown, Emeritus Professor of International Relations at the London School of Economics and Political Science, examined my MA by Research on the theme of contractarian approaches to legitimacy in normative IR theory, with special reference to Thomas Hobbes, Jean-Jacques Rousseau, Immanuel Kant and John Rawls; given that I had actually been a trained economist with a fairly different career path in mind, my work in political and IR theory would probably have ended all too prematurely if it had not been for his generous encouragement to keep going for the doctorate. Richard Little, Emeritus Professor of International Relations at the University of Bristol, chaired my PhD examination in the summer of 2009; I will forever treasure the memory of how graciously and kindly he let me defend my thesis on political realism's use or rejection of Freudian ideas of human nature, and how later in the afternoon of what was a sunny day (in many ways), I walked him to Durham train station. Each one of these fine scholars has shaped my thinking about the struggle for power and peace, or the role of force and ethics, in international society; and should I ever come to the realisation that I may actually be not so much a foreign-policy realist but an English School-style political and IR theorist after all, I am more than happy and proud to credit them as towering contemporary influences.

Chapter 1. Kelsen's Enemies

1. We know about this FBI file on Kelsen thanks to the Freedom of Information Request (FOIA 0946294-00) made by Oliver Rathkolb, Professor of Contemporary History at the University of Vienna. A full copy of the file, a redacted version, is available at the Hans Kelsen-Institut (see Rathkolb 2009). Unless indicated otherwise, for the biographical details of the Kelsen/FBI story, and of his life in the years 1944–55 more generally, I am much indebted to Rathkolb (2009); Olechowski and Wedrac (2015); Olechowski (2016a, 2016b).

2. Leo Gross was Kelsen's assistant at Cologne. In 1933 both had to flee Germany: Kelsen to Geneva, Gross to London. A decade later, in 1942, they saw each other again in America. Gross was teaching at Tufts and Kelsen at Harvard. Until Kelsen moved to Berkeley in 1942, they were 'virtually neighbors' and 'Gross cordially accorded the Kelsens the role of "auntie" and "uncle"'. With Hans writing letters of recommendation for Leo, the Kelsens were 'a source of support for the Grosses' (Kirchhoff 2017: 247).

3. Walter Lippmann also thanked Kelsen for his political theory of Bolshevism, in a letter dated 2 November 1948: 'I am just leaving for Europe and I am taking it along in my brief case to read on the way.'

4. Unless otherwise indicated, all biographical details on Hans J. Morgenthau and on the Kelsen–Morgenthau relationship are taken from the autobiographical accounts of Morgenthau (1984a [1977]), as well as from Frei (2001); Koskenniemi (2001); Mazur (2004); Scheuerman (2009, 2016); Mazur (2006); Jütersonke (2010); Schuett (2011); von Bernstorff (2016); Navari (2018). Likewise, all biographical details on John H. Herz and on the Kelsen–Herz relationship are taken from Herz

(1984), as well as from Stirk (2005b, 2014, 2018); Karis (2006); Hacke and Pug-lierin (2007); Donhauser (2008); Sylvest (2010); Puglierin (2011).

5. See the *Schriftenreihe des Hans Kelsen-Instituts*. The first volume, *Hans Kelsen zum Gedenken*, dates back to 1974. For the latest, 2019 volume, see Jabloner, Olechowski and Zeleny (2019).

6. Together with Leo Gross, Virginia McClam (1971a) prepared 'an album of letters of congratulations in honor of Prof. Kelsen's 90th birthday'.

7. According to Mazur (2006: 5), 'the most direct influences upon Morgenthau' were Reinhold Niebuhr and Hans Kelsen. The literature on how Morgenthau was – or was not – intellectually influenced has become very large. For Morgenthau and Reinhold Niebuhr, see Rice (2008); for Hans Kelsen, see note 4 in this chapter; for Max Weber, see Turner and Mazur (2009); for Sigmund Freud, see Schuett (2007); for Aristotle, see Lang, Jr (2007); for the Sophists, see Johnson (1996); for Hugo Sinzheimer, see Scheuerman (2008); for Friedrich Nietzsche, see Frei (2001); for Carl Schmitt, see Scheuerman (2007). In this context, on the relationship between Morgenthau's foreign-policy realism and the English School of international rela-tions, see Little (2003); Troy (2018).

8. For the scholarly literature on the realist critique of the alleged 'idealist' Kelsen – most notably voiced by his so-called realist students Morgenthau and Herz, and also by E. H. Carr and Hedley Bull (as well as by Georg Schwarzenberger) – see Koskenniemi (2001: 413–509); Stirk (2005b, 2014, 2018); Scheuerman (2009, 2012, 2013, 2014); Jütersonke (2010); Sylvest (2010); Telman (2010); von Bernstorff (2010: 220–4, 255–8); Armstrong, Farrell and Lambert (2012); Lebow (2014); Söllner (2014).

9. The titanic task of editing the complete works of Kelsen, carried out by Matthias Jestaedt in Freiburg, in collaboration with the Viennese Hans Kelsen-Institut, is pro-gressing. As of now, the eighth out of the projected thirty-two volumes (2007–42) has been published (see Jestaedt 2020).

CHAPTER 2. KELSEN'S MILIEU

1. For biographical details related to Kelsen and World War I, see Busch (2009).

2. See the cable from Washington to Vienna, dated 18 October 1919, in 'Correspon-dence Between the United States and Austria-Hungary Regarding an Armistice', 78.

3. For all of this section's biographical details I rely on Rathkolb (2000); Busch (2009: 61–2); Feichtinger (2009, 2010: Ch. 4); Ehs (2010); García-Salmones Rovira (2013: Ch. 7); Ehs and Gassner (2014); Olechowski and Wedrac (2015: 291); Haas Edersheim (n.d.).

4. On what in Chapter 3 I call the 'Freudian moment' in Kelsen's personal and politi-cal philosophy, see Losano (1989 [1977]); Adamovich (1997); Jabloner (1998); Rathkolb (2000); Rolnik (2003); Avscharova and Huttar (2009); Feichtinger (2010: Ch. 4); Lupton (2010); Schuett (2011, 2015, 2018); Busch (2016); Feicht-inger (2016); Rentsch (2016).

5. The story of Kelsen's work for the 'Liberated Areas Branch' of the FEA and the relevant biographical details are in Rathkolb (2009: 341); Olechowski and Wedrac (2015: 283–5).

6. On Kelsen and the Austrian Constitution, including all biographical details, see Olechowski (2009); Jabloner (2015).

7. Not published, though partly recycled in some of his subsequent works, these eight memoranda (Olechowski 2016b: 106) are as follows: (1) 'On the Agreement for the Prosecution of European Axis War Criminals'; (2) 'On the Rule of Ex Post Facto Law'; (3) 'On the Definition of Aggression'; (4) 'On the Draft Executive Agreement relating to the Prosecution of European Axis War Criminals'; (5) 'On the Instrument of Surrender signed by the Japanese Government'; (6) 'On Codification of the Law of War'; (7) 'On the Punishment of War Criminals and the Charter of the United Nations'; (8) 'On War Crimes as Related to the Preparation, Launching, and Opening of Hostilities Without Warning'. I would like to thank one of the anonymous reviewers for emphasising the importance of these memos in their own right (historical, juristic, political), and in the context of my argument in this book – Kelsen the practical political realist – in particular.

8. In fact, Kelsen also asked Tucker to prepare a second edition of his *Principles of International Law* (1952b); and Tucker asked Nicholas Onuf, Professor Emeritus of International Relations at Florida International and one of today's leading constructivist IR theorists, to help him revise this edition (see Onuf 2008: preface).

Chapter 3. Kelsen's Freudian Moment

1. For the following biographical details, see also Lepsius (2009).

2. Kelsen did comment, though, on the Allies' plans for reconstructing post-war Germany. In a letter to *The New York Times*, he advocated that there should be 'no legal continuity' between Nazi Germany and the new democratic Germany (Kelsen 1947b; see also Kelsen 1947c; Olechowski 2013b). Walter Lippmann (1947) thanked him in a letter for his 'immensely clarifying' piece.

3. As someone with a longstanding interest in Freud and Freudianism in political and IR theory (Schuett 2007, 2010a, 2010b), I cannot resist the temptation to fire off a few shots in the Freud Wars myself here. First, it is hardly Freud's fault that over the years, and especially, though certainly not only, in the United States, Freudianism has become big business (as noted long ago by Kazin 1957). Second, it is pretty much self-evident that the Freud critics themselves make a decent academic living out of their project of dismantling or taking down Freud (see, for example, Crews 2017). And, third, to repeat like a mantra that Freud is all tosh, fraud and hokum is somewhat short-sighted or crude anyway. As Eric Kandel (1999: 505), winner of the 2000 Nobel Prize in Physiology or Medicine and Co-director of the Mortimer B. Zuckerman Institute Mind.Brain.Behavior at Columbia, keeps reminding us: 'psychoanalysis still represents the most coherent and intellectually satisfying view of the mind'.

Chapter 4. Kelsen's Foreign-Policy Realism

1. See Article II of the treaty, quoted in Hathaway and Shapiro (2018: 128); see also Miller (1928: 10).

2. To Morgenthau, this is 'the first of the rules that diplomacy can neglect only at the risk of war' (Morgenthau 1967 [1948a]: 540–1).

3. As Waltz (1959a: 188) tells us: 'Then what explains war among states? Rousseau's answer is really that war occurs because there is nothing to prevent it.'

CHAPTER 5. KELSEN'S STYLE OF POLITICAL THINKING

1. The following biographical details are taken from 'Karl Raimund Popper: 1902–1994' (1997); Hacohen (2000); Niemann (2014); Stadler (2015).
2. Popper in the original German: 'In der freien Luft Englands konnte ich aufatmen. Es war, wie wenn die Fenster geöffnet worden wären. Der Name „Offene Gesellschaft" stammt von diesem Erlebnis' (quoted in Zimmer and Morgenstern 2015: 70).
3. From Popper we learn that Kraft even met 'a brilliant student of Kelsen's [Margit Fuchs] who, some years later, became Kraft's wife [Margit Kraft-Fuchs]' (see Popper 1962: 16).
4. See also Noberto Bobbio on Kelsen, Hobbes and peace: 'It is no coincidence, probably, that after having studied Kelsen I spent a lot of time studying Hobbes' political thought. For both, peace is the fundamental good that only the law can guarantee' (Bobbio and Zolo 1998).
5. The student is August Maria Knoll, who was a known Sociology Professor at Vienna and, in 1963, a co-founder of the Documentation Centre of Austrian Resistance (DÖW), located in Vienna, a public trust fostering the critical study of Austria's National Socialist past. The Kelsen/Knoll tale is told by Norbert Leser (2011: 116), one of Austria's foremost intellectuals on social democracy and Austro-Marxism and, in turn, Knoll's student.
6. For the occasion of Kelsen's final retirement from teaching at the University of California, Berkeley, in 1952, then-Assistant Political Science Professor George Lipsky – who incidentally left Berkeley in 1953 to spend the 1953–4 academic year at the Council on Foreign Relations (CFR) as a Carnegie Fellow, where he was the driving force behind the CFR study group on IR theory (McCourt 2020) – pieced together a *Festschrift*. The resulting *Law and Politics in the World Community: Essays on Hans Kelsen's Pure Theory and Related Problems in International Law* (1953) has proven to be a fine collection of seventeen papers, with Hans Morgenthau, Leo Gross, Erich Hula, Robert Tucker and Quincy Wright among the many contributors (see Myers 1954). It is fitting here to end these book notes on a Kelsenian thought: as Quincy Wright once noted, ostensibly during World War II: 'It only takes a minority to create a war, but it takes all the people to create peace-mindedness' (quoted in *The New York Times* 1970). That is to say: it takes You and Me.

BIBLIOGRAPHY

Abrahamsen, David (1946), *The Mind and Death of a Genius*, New York: Columbia University Press.

Achen, Christopher H. and Larry M. Bartels (2016), *Democracy for Realists: Why Elections Do Not Produce Responsive Government*, Princeton: Princeton University Press.

Adair-Toteff, Christopher (2019), *Raymond Aron's Philosophy of Political Responsibility: Freedom, Democracy and National Identity*, Edinburgh: Edinburgh University Press.

Adamovich, Ludwig (1997), 'Kelsen und die Tiefenpsychologie. Stattgefundene und nicht stattgefundene Begegnungen', in Robert Walter and Clemens Jabloner (eds), *Hans Kelsens Wege sozialphilosophischer Forschung (Schriftenreihe des Hans Kelsen-Instituts, vol. 20)*, Vienna: Manz, pp. 129–41.

Aliprantis, Nikitas and Thomas Olechowski (eds) (2014), *Hans Kelsen: Die Aktualität eines großen Rechtswissenschafters und Soziologen des 20. Jahrhunderts (Schriftenreihe des Hans Kelsen-Instituts, vol. 38)*, Vienna: Manz.

Antiseri, Dario (2002), *Popper's Vienna: World 3 of Vienna 1870–1930*, Aurora: Davies Group Publishers.

Armstrong, David, Theo Farrell and Helene Lambert (2012), *International Law and International Relations* (2nd edn), Cambridge: Cambridge University Press.

Ashley, Richard K. (1984), 'The Poverty of Neorealism', *International Organization*, vol. 38, no. 2, pp. 225–86.

Auerbach, Erich (2007 [1929]), *Dante: Poet of the Secular World*, trans. Ralph Manheim, New York: New York Review of Books.

Auerbach, Erich (2003 [1946]), *Mimesis: The Representation of Reality in Western Literature*, trans. Willard R. Trask, Princeton: Princeton University Press.

Avscharova, Alina and Martina Huttar (2009), 'Ohne Seele, ohne Staat: Hans Kelsen und Sigmund Freud', in Tamara Ehs (ed.), *Hans Kelsen: Eine politikwissenschaftliche Einführung*, Vienna: Facultas, pp.171–91.

Balibar, Étienne (2017), *Citizen Subject: Foundations for Philosophical Anthropology*, trans. Steven Miller, New York: Fordham University Press.

Baume, Sandrine (2012), *Hans Kelsen and the Case for Democracy*, Colchester: ECPR Press.

Baume, Sandrine (2018), 'Rehabilitating Political Parties: An Examination of the Writings of Hans Kelsen', *Intellectual History Review*, vol. 28, no. 3, pp. 425–49.

Bell, Duncan (ed.) (2010), *Political Thought and International Relations*, Oxford: Oxford University Press.

Benedict XVI (2011), 'Address to the German Parliament: The Listening Heart: Reflections on the Foundations of Law', Berlin, 22 September 2011.

Benersky, Joseph J. (1983), *Carl Schmitt: Theorist for the Reich*, Princeton: Princeton University Press.

Benner, Erica (2017), *Be Like the Fox: Machiavelli's Lifelong Quest for Freedom*, London: Penguin.

Benner, Erica (2018), 'Political Realism and Human Nature', in Robert Schuett and Miles Hollingworth (eds), *The Edinburgh Companion to Political Realism*, Edinburgh: Edinburgh University Press, pp. 11–22.

Bessner, Daniel and Nicolas Guilhot (2015), 'How Realism Waltzed Off: Liberalism and Decisionmaking in Kenneth Waltz's Neorealism', *International Security*, vol. 40, no. 2, pp. 87–118.

Bew, John (2016), *Realpolitik: A History*, Oxford: Oxford University Press.

Bew, John (2018), 'Political Realism and Realpolitik: German Realpolitik and the Contingent Nature of Anglo-American Political Realism', in Robert Schuett and Miles Hollingworth (eds), *The Edinburgh Companion to Political Realism*, Edinburgh: Edinburgh University Press, pp. 49–60.

Blair, Tony (2020), 'Labour's Task is Not to Make Itself Feel Better – It's to Win Power', *The Guardian*, 11 January.

Bobbio, Noberto and Danilo Zolo (1998), 'Hans Kelsen, the Theory of Law and the International Legal System: A Talk', *European Journal of International Law*, vol. 9, no. 2, pp. 355–67.

Bonicelli, Paul (2012), 'Obama the Realist?', *Foreign Policy*, 10 December.

Booth, Ken (1991), 'Security in Anarchy: Utopian Realism in Theory and Practice', *International Affairs*, vol. 67, no. 3, pp. 527–45.

Booth, Ken (2005), 'Offensive Realists, Tolerant Realists and Real Realists', in 'Roundtable: The Battle Rages On; John Mearsheimer versus Paul Rogers, Richard Little, Christopher Hill, Chris Brown and Ken Booth', *International Relations*, vol. 19, no. 3, pp. 337–60, at 350–4.

Booth, Ken (2008), *Theory of World Security*, Cambridge: Cambridge University Press.

Boyer, John W. (2008), '"We Are All Islanders to Begin With": The University of Chicago and the World in the Late Nineteenth and Twentieth Centuries', *The University of Chicago Record*, vol. 42, no. 2, pp. 2–21.

Breyfogle, Todd (2018), 'Political Realism and the Open Society: The Enemy Within', in Robert Schuett and Miles Hollingworth (eds), *The Edinburgh Companion to Political Realism*, Edinburgh: Edinburgh University Press, pp. 554–66.

Brinn, Gearóid (2019), 'Smashing the State Gently: Radical Realism and Realist Anarchism', *European Journal of Political Theory*, epub ahead of print, 7 August.

Brooks, David (2007), 'Obama, Gospel and Verse', *The New York Times*, 26 April.

Brostrom, Jannika (2016), 'Morality and the National Interest: Towards a "Moral Realist" Research Agenda', *Cambridge Review of International Affairs*, vol. 29, no. 4, pp. 1624–39.

Brown, Andrew (2011), 'Pope Benedict's Challenge to Positivism in the Bundestag', *The Guardian*, 28 September.

Brown, Chris (1992), *International Relations Theory: New Normative Approaches*, Hemel Hempstead: Harvester Wheatsheaf.

Brown, Chris (2002), *Sovereignty, Rights and Justice: International Political Theory Today*, Cambridge: Polity Press.

Brown, Chris (2005), '"No Jazz on the Radio" . . . John Mearsheimer and British IR', in 'Roundtable: The Battle Rages On; John Mearsheimer versus Paul Rogers, Richard Little, Christopher Hill, Chris Brown and Ken Booth', *International Relations*, vol. 19, no. 3, 348–50.

Brown, Michael E., Sean M. Lynn-Jones and Steven E. Miller (1996), *Debating the Democratic Peace*, Cambridge, MA: MIT Press.

Bryan, Ian, Peter Langford and John McGarry (eds) (2015), *The Foundation of the Juridico-Political: Concept Formation in Hans Kelsen and Max Weber*, Oxon: Routledge.

Bryan, Ian, Peter Langford and John McGarry (eds) (2016), *The Reconstruction of the Juridico-Political: Affinity and Divergence in Kelsen and Weber*, Oxon: Routledge.

Bull, Hedley (1977), *The Anarchical Society: A Study of Order in World Politics*, London: Macmillan.

Bull, Hedley (1986), 'Hans Kelsen and International Law', in Richard Tur and William Twining (eds), *Essays on Kelsen*, Oxford: Clarendon Press, pp. 321–36.

Burke, Edmund (1986 [1790]), *Reflections on the Revolution in France . . .* , ed. Conor C. O'Brien, London: Penguin.

Busch, Hans-Joachim (2016), 'The Individual and the Democratic State: Remarks on Kelsen's Reception of Freud and its Importance for a Critical

Political Psychology and the Development of Democracy', in Peter Langford, Ian Bryan and John McGarry (eds), *The Foundation of the Juridico-Political: Concept Formation in Hans Kelsen and Max Weber*, Oxon: Routledge, pp. 140–62.

Busch, Jürgen (2009), 'Hans Kelsen im Ersten Weltkrieg: Achsenzeit einer Weltkarriere', in Robert Walter, Werner Ogris and Thomas Olechowski (eds), *Hans Kelsen: Leben, Werk, Wirksamkeit*, Vienna: Manz, pp. 57–80.

Busch, Jürgen, Judith von Schmädel and Kamila Staudigl-Ciechowicz (2011), 'Peace through Law: Kelsen's (and His School's) Struggle for Universal Peace', in Péter Cserne and Miklós Könczöl (eds), *Legal and Political Theory in the Post-National Age*, Frankfurt: Central and Eastern European Forum for Legal, Political and Social Theory Yearbook, pp. 161–80.

Buzan, Barry (1996), 'The Timeless Wisdom of Realism?', in Steve Smith, Ken Booth and Marysia Zalewski (eds), *International Theory: Positivism and Beyond*, Cambridge: Cambridge University Press, pp. 47–65.

Carr, E. H. (1936), 'Public Opinion as a Safeguard of Peace', *International Affairs*, vol. 15, no. 6, pp. 846–62.

Carr, E. H. (1939), *The Twenty Years' Crisis, 1919–1939: An Introduction to the Study of International Relations*, London: Macmillan.

Carr, E. H. (1942), *Conditions of Peace*, London: Macmillan.

Carr, E. H. (1961), *What Is History?*, London: Macmillan.

Cohen, Jean L. (2012), *Globalization and Sovereignty: Rethinking Legality, Legitimacy and Constitutionalism*, Cambridge: Cambridge University Press.

Coleman, Francis X. J. (1986), *Neither Angel nor Beast: The Life and Work of Blaise Pascal*, Oxon: Routledge.

'Correspondence Between the United States and Austria-Hungary Regarding an Armistice' (1919), *The American Journal of International Law*, vol. 13, no. 2, Supplement: Official Documents, pp. 73–9.

Craig, Campbell (1992), 'The New Meaning of Modern War in the Thought of Reinhold Niebuhr', *Journal of the History of Ideas*, vol. 53, no. 4, pp. 687–701.

Craig, Campbell (2003), *Glimmer of a New Leviathan: Total War in the Realism of Niebuhr, Morgenthau, and Waltz*, New York: Columbia University Press.

Crews, Frederick (2017), *Freud: Making of an Illusion*, New York: Metropolitan Books.

De Angelis, Gabriele (2009), 'Ideals and Institutions: Hans Kelsen's Political Theory', *History of Political Thought*, vol. 30, no. 3, pp. 524–46.

Desch, Michael C. (2019), *Cult of the Irrelevant: The Waning Influence of Social Science on National Security*, Princeton: Princeton University Press.

Diamond, Larry (2019), *Ill Winds: Saving Democracy from Russian Rage, Chinese Ambition, and American Complacency*, New York: Penguin.

Dickinson, G. Lowes (1916), *The European Anarchy*, New York: Macmillan.

Dionne, Jr, E. J. and Joy-Ann Reid (2017), *We Are the Change We Seek: The Speeches of Barack Obama*, New York: Bloomsbury.

Dirda, Michael (2007), 'Dante: The Supreme Realist', *New York Review of Books*, vol. 54, no. 1, pp. 54–8.

Disraeli, Benjamin (1859), 'Speech in the House of Commons on February 28, 1859' [quoted in William Safire (2008), *Safire's Political Dictionary*, New York: Oxford University Press, p. ix].

Donhauser, Gerhard (2008), 'John Herz', in Robert Walter, Clemens Jabloner and Klaus Zeleny (eds), *Der Kreis um Hans Kelsen: Die Anfangsjahre der Reinen Rechtslehre (Schriftenreihe des Hans Kelsen-Instituts, vol. 30)*, Vienna: Manz, pp. 145–52.

Dreier, Horst (1990), *Rechtslehre, Staatssoziologie und Demokratietheorie bei Hans Kelsen* (2nd edn), Baden-Baden: Nomos.

Dreier, Horst (2009), 'Wertrelativismus und Demokratietheorie', in Robert Walter and Klaus Zeleny (eds), *Reflexionen über Demokratie und Recht: Festakt aus Anlass des 60. Geburtstages von Clemens Jabloner*, Vienna: Manz, pp. 13–31.

Drezner, Daniel W. (2013), 'International Lawyers Give It the Old College Try', *Foreign Policy*, 4 September.

Drezner, Daniel W. (2016), 'You Know It's Hard Out There for a Foreign Policy Realist', *The Washington Post*, 13 April.

Drolet, Jean-François and Michael C. Williams (2018), 'Radical Conservatism and Global Order: International Theory and the New Right', *International Theory*, vol. 10, no. 3, pp. 285–313.

Drucker Society (n.d.), 'Drucker's Childhood and Youth in Vienna', <http://druckersociety.at/index.php/peterdruckerhome/biography> (last accessed 27 April 2020).

Duarte d'Almeida, Luís, John Gardner and Leslie Green (eds) (2013), *Kelsen Revisited: New Essays on the Pure Theory of Law*, London: Bloomsbury.

Duxbury, Neil (2008), 'Kelsen's Endgame', *Cambridge Law Journal*, vol. 67, no. 1, pp. 51–61.

Dyzenhaus, David (1997), *Legality and Legitimacy: Carl Schmitt, Hans Kelsen, and Hermann Heller in Weimar*, Oxford: Clarendon Press.

Dyzenhaus, David (2000), 'The Gorgon Head of Power: Heller and Kelsen on the Rule of Law', in Peter C. Caldwell and William E. Scheuerman (eds), *From Liberal Democracy to Fascism: Legal and Political Thought in the Weimar Republic*, Boston: Humanities Press, pp. 20–46.

Ebenstein, William (1952), *Introduction to Political Philosophy*, New York: Rinehart.

Egashira, Susumu and Shigeki Tomo (n.d.), 'Spann's Influence on Hayek: Dissertation and After', unpublished manuscript [quoted in Friedrich A. Hayek (2015), *The Collected Works of F.A. Hayek, Volume 11*, ed. Lawrence H. White, Chicago: University of Chicago Press, p. x].

Ehrenburg, Ilya Grigoryevich (1972 [1962]), *Selections from People, Years, Life*, Oxford: Pergamon Press.

Ehs, Tamara (ed.) (2009a), *Hans Kelsen: Eine politikwissenschaftliche Einführung*, Vienna: Nomos.

Ehs, Tamara (2009b), 'Erziehung zur Demokratie: Hans Kelsen als Volksbildner', in Robert Walter, Werner Ogris and Thomas Olechowski (eds), *Hans Kelsen: Leben, Werk, Wirksamkeit*, Vienna: Manz, pp. 81–96.

Ehs, Tamara (2010), 'Vertreibung in drei Schritten. Kelsens Netzwerk und die Anfänge österreichischer Politikwissenschaft', *Österreichische Zeitschrift für Geschichtswissenschaften*, vol. 21, no. 3, pp. 147–74.

Ehs, Tamara and Miriam Gassner (2014), 'Hans Kelsen (1881–1973): Legal Scholar Between Europe and the Americas', *Transatlantic Perspectives*, 7 June.

Elshtain, Jean Bethke (1989), 'Freud's Discourse of War/Politics', in James Der Derian and Michael J. Shapiro (eds), *International/Intertextual Relations: Postmodern Readings of World Politics*, New York: Lexington, pp. 49–67.

Elshtain, Jean Bethke (2008), 'On Never Reaching the Coast of Utopia', *International Relations*, vol. 22, no. 2, pp. 147–72.

Elshtain, Jean Bethke (2009), 'Woman, the State, and War', *International Relations*, vol. 23, no. 2, pp. 289–303.

Emerson, Ralph Waldo (1979 [1841]), 'Self-Reliance', in Alfred R. Ferguson and Jean Ferguson Carr (eds), *The Collected Works of Ralph Waldo Emerson*, vol. 2, Cambridge, MA: Harvard University Press, pp. 25–52.

Emerson, Ralph Waldo (1843), 'When you strike at a king, you must kill him' [quoted in Sheldon M. Novick, 'What Emerson Said', *The New York Times*, 15 October 1989].

Engel, Salo (ed.) (1964), *Law, State, and International Legal Order: Essays in Honor of Hans Kelsen*, with the cooperation of Rudolf A. Métall, Knoxville: University of Tennessee Press.

Escudé, Carlos (1997), *Foreign Policy Theory in Menem's Argentina*, Gainesville: University Press of Florida.

Etzioni, Amitai (2008), 'Freud, International Relations Are Calling', politicalmavens.com, 5 November, <http://politicalmavens.com/index.php/2008/11/05/freud-international-relations-are-calling> (last accessed 27 April 2020).

Feichtinger, Johannes (2009), 'Transatlantische Vernetzungen: Der Weg Hans Kelsens und seines Kreises in die Emigration', in Robert Walter, Werner Ogris and Thomas Olechowski (eds), *Hans Kelsen: Leben, Werk, Wirksamkeit*, Vienna: Manz, pp. 321–38.

Feichtinger, Johannes (2010), *Wissenschaft als reflexives Projekt. Von Bolzano über Freud zu Kelsen: Österreichische Wissenschaftsgeschichte 1848–1938*, Bielefeld: transcript.

Feichtinger, Johannes (2016), 'Intellectual Affinities: Ernst Mach, Sigmund Freud, Hans Kelsen and the Austrian Anti-Essentialist Approach to Science and Scholarship', in Peter Langford, Ian Bryan and John McGarry (eds), *The Foundation of the Juridico-Political: Concept Formation in Hans Kelsen and Max Weber*, Oxon: Routledge, pp. 117–39.

Finlayson, Lorna (2017), 'With Radicals Like These, Who Needs Conservatives? Doom, Gloom, and Realism in Political Theory', *European Journal of Political Theory*, vol. 16, no. 3, pp. 264–82.

Fox, William T. R. (1985), 'E. H. Carr and Political Realism: Vision and Revision', *Review of International Studies*, vol. 11, no. 1, pp. 1–16.

Frankel, Benjamin (1996), 'Restating the Realist Case: An Introduction', in Benjamin Frankel (ed.), *Realism: Restatements and Renewal*, London: Frank Cass, pp. ix–xx.

Frei, Christoph (2001), *Hans J. Morgenthau: An Intellectual Biography*, Baton Rouge: Louisiana State University Press.

Freud, Sigmund (1900), *The Interpretation of Dreams*, in James Strachey, Anna Freud, Alix Strachey and Alan Tyson (eds), *The Standard Edition of the Complete Psychological Works of Sigmund Freud*, London: Hogarth, 1953–74, vols 4 and 5.

Freud, Sigmund (1913), *Totem and Taboo*, in James Strachey, Anna Freud, Alix Strachey and Alan Tyson (eds), *The Standard Edition of the Complete Psychological Works of Sigmund Freud*, London: Hogarth, 1953–74, vol. 13.

Freud, Sigmund (1915), 'Thoughts for the Times on War and Death', in James Strachey, Anna Freud, Alix Strachey and Alan Tyson (eds), *The Standard Edition of the Complete Psychological Works of Sigmund Freud*, London: Hogarth, 1953–74, vol. 14.

Freud, Sigmund (1917), 'A Difficulty in the Path of Psycho-Analysis', in James Strachey, Anna Freud, Alix Strachey and Alan Tyson (eds), *The Standard Edition of the Complete Psychological Works of Sigmund Freud*, London: Hogarth, 1953–74, vol. 17.

Freud, Sigmund (1921), *Group Psychology and the Analysis of the Ego*, in James Strachey, Anna Freud, Alix Strachey and Alan Tyson (eds), *The Standard Edition of the Complete Psychological Works of Sigmund Freud*, London: Hogarth, 1953–74, vol. 18.

Freud, Sigmund (1923), *The Ego and the Id*, in James Strachey, Anna Freud, Alix Strachey and Alan Tyson (eds), *The Standard Edition of the Complete Psychological Works of Sigmund Freud*, London: Hogarth, 1953–74, vol. 19.

Freud, Sigmund (1930), *Civilization and Its Discontents*, in James Strachey, Anna Freud, Alix Strachey and Alan Tyson (eds), *The Standard Edition of the Complete Psychological Works of Sigmund Freud*, London: Hogarth, 1953–74, vol. 21.

Freud, Sigmund (1933), 'Why War?', in James Strachey, Anna Freud, Alix Strachey and Alan Tyson (eds), *The Standard Edition of the Complete Psychological Works of Sigmund Freud*, London: Hogarth, 1953–74, vol. 22.

Friedman, George (2015), *Flashpoints: The Emerging Crisis in Europe*, New York: Doubleday.

Friedman, Milton (1953), *Essays in Positive Economics*, Chicago: University of Chicago Press.

Fukuyama, Francis (2006 [1992]), *The End of History and the Last Man*, with a new afterword, New York: Free Press.

García-Salmones Rovira, Mónica (2013), *The Project of Positivism in International Law*, Oxford: Oxford University Press.

García-Salmones Rovira, Mónica (2020), 'Not Just Pure Theory: Hans Kelsen (1881–1973) and International Criminal Law', in Frédéric Mégret and Immi Tallgren (eds), *The Dawn of a Discipline: International Criminal Justice and Its Early Exponents*, Cambridge: Cambridge University Press.

Gardner, David P. (1967), *The University of California Loyalty Oath Controversy, 1949–1952*, Berkeley: University of California Press.

Gay, John Allen (2014), 'Is Realism's Home on the Right?', *The National Interest*, 1 October.

Gewen, Barry (2017), 'Kissinger's Moral Example', *The National Interest*, 17 April.

Gibbs, Walter (2009), 'Norwegian Nobel Laureate, Once Shunned, Is Now Celebrated', *The New York Times*, 27 February.

Gilpin, Robert (1986), 'The Richness of the Tradition of Political Realism', in Robert O. Keohane (ed.), *Neorealism and Its Critics*, New York: Columbia University, pp. 301–21.

Gilpin, Robert (1996), 'No One Loves a Political Realist', *Security Studies*, vol. 5, no. 3, pp. 3–26.

Goldberg, Jeffrey (2016), 'The Obama Doctrine', *The Atlantic*, April.

Gombrich, Ernst H. (1999), 'Personal Recollections of the Publication of the Open Society', in I. C. Jarvie and Sandra Pralong (eds), *Popper's Open Society After Fifty Years: The Continuing Relevance of Karl Popper*, London: Routledge, ch. 2.

Gragl, Paul (2018), *Legal Monism: Law, Philosophy, and Politics*, Oxford: Oxford University Press.

Green, Michael S. (2003), 'Hans Kelsen and the Logic of Legal Systems', *Alabama Law Review*, vol. 54, no. 2, pp. 365–413.

Gross, Leo (1945), 'Review: Peace through Law by Hans Kelsen', *Social Research*, vol. 12, no. 2, pp. 260–2.

Gurian, Waldemar (1940), 'Letter to Jerome Kerwin, dated August 23, 1940' [Hutchins Administration, Box 287, folder 5; quoted in John W. Boyer (2008), '"We Are All Islanders to Begin With": The University of Chicago and the World in the Late Nineteenth and Twentieth Centuries', *The University of Chicago Record*, vol. 42, no. 2, p. 14].

Guzzini, Stefano (1998), *Realism in International Relations and International Political Economy*, London: Routledge.

Haas Edersheim, Elizabeth (n.d.), 'A Tribute to Peter F. Drucker', <www.druckersociety.at/index.php/peterdruckerhome/commentaries/elizabeth-haas-edersheim> (last accessed 27 April 2020).

Hacke, Christian and Jana Puglierin (2007), 'John H. Herz: Balancing Utopia and Reality', *International Relations*, vol. 21, no. 3, pp. 367–82.

Hacohen, Malachi Haim (2000), *Karl Popper: The Formative Years, 1902–1945, Politics and Philosophy in Interwar Vienna*, Cambridge: Cambridge University Press.

Hall, Edward (2017), 'Ethics, Morality and the Case for Realist Political Theory', *Critical Review of International Social and Political Philosophy*, vol. 20, no. 3, pp. 278–95.

Hall, Edward and Matt Sleat (2017), 'Ethics, Morality and the Case for Realist Political Theory', *Critical Review of International Social and Political Philosophy*, vol. 20, no. 3, pp. 278–95.

Hall, Ian (2014), 'The Second Image Traversed: Waltz's Theory of Foreign Policy', *Australian Journal of Political Science*, vol. 49, no. 3, pp. 353–40.

Hamsun, Knut (2011 [1892]), *Mysteries*, trans. Gerry Bothmer, New York: Allen & Unwin.

Hanrieder, Wolfram F. (1971), 'Book Review: Hans J. Morgenthau: Truth and Power: Essays of a Decade, 1960–70', *American Political Science Review*, vol. 65, no. 3, pp. 879–80.

Hans Kelsen-Institut (ed.) (1974), *Hans Kelsen zum Gedenken*, Vienna: Europaverlag.

Hart, H. L. A. (1999 [1962–3]), 'Kelsen Visited (1962–3)', in Stanley L. Paulson and Bonnie Litschewski-Paulson (eds), *Normativity and Norms: Critical Perspectives on Kelsenian Themes*, Oxford: Oxford University Press, pp. 69–88.

Harvard Magazine (2012), 'Kissinger Returns', 12 April.

Hathaway, Oona A. and Scott J. Shapiro (2018), *The Internationalists: How a Radical Plan to Outlaw War Remade the World*, New York: Simon & Schuster.

Hayek, Friedrich A. (2014 [1970]), 'The Errors of Constructivism', in Bruce Caldwell (ed.), *The Collected Works of F. A. Hayek, Volume XV*, Chicago: University of Chicago Press, pp. 338–57.

Hayek, Friedrich A. (1978), 'Coping with Ignorance', *Imprimis*, vol. 7, no. 7.

Hayek, Friedrich A. (2015), *The Collected Works of F.A. Hayek, Volume 11*, ed. Lawrence H. White, Chicago: University of Chicago Press.

Hegel, Georg F. W. (1942 [1821]), *Philosophy of Right*, trans. T. M. Knox, Oxford: Clarendon Press.

Heilbrunn, Jacob (2015), 'The Interview: Henry Kissinger', *The National Interest*, 19 August.

Heilbrunn, Jacob (2018), 'A Foreign Policy Realist Challenges America's Zeal for Intervention', *The New York Times*, 20 November.

Herrera, Carlos Miguel (2014), 'Kelsen als Demokrat und Freiheitsdenker', in Nikitas Aliprantis and Thomas Olechowski (eds), *Hans Kelsen: Die Aktualität eines großen Rechtswissenschafters und Soziologen des 20. Jahrhunderts (Schriftenreihe des Hans Kelsen-Instituts, vol. 38)*, Vienna: Manz, pp. 95–108.

Herz, Hans (1931), *Die Identität des Staates*, Düsseldorf: Ohligschläger.

Herz, John H. (1951), *Political Realism and Political Idealism: A Study in Theories and Realities*, Chicago: University of Chicago Press.

Herz, John H. (1964), 'The Pure Theory of Law Revisited: Hans Kelsen's Doctrine of International Law in the Nuclear Age', in Salo Engel (ed.), *Law, State, and International Legal Order: Essays in Honor of Hans Kelsen*, Knoxville: University of Tennessee Press, pp. 107–18.

Herz, John H. (1971), 'Letter to Hans Kelsen, dated October 4, 1971' [Herz Papers, Box 2, General Correspondence 1971–1973; quoted in Jana Puglierin (2011), *John H. Herz: Leben und Denken zwischen Idealismus und Realismus, Deutschland und Amerika*, Berlin: Duncker & Humblot, p. 35 (my translation)].

Herz, John H. (1981), 'Political Realism Revisited', *International Studies Quarterly*, vol. 25, no. 2, pp. 182–97.

Herz, John H. (1984), *Vom Überleben*, Düsseldorf: Droste.

Herz, John H. (2005), 'Letter to the Morgenthau Conference', in Christian Hacke, Gottfried-Karl Kindermann and Kai M. Schellhorn (eds), *The Heritage, Challenge, and Future of Realism. In Memoriam Hans J. Morgenthau (1904–1980)*, Göttingen: V+R, pp. 23–8.

Hjorth, Ronnie (2011), 'Equality in the Theory of International Society: Kelsen, Rawls and the English School', *Review of International Studies*, vol. 37, no. 5, pp. 2585–602.

Hjorth, Ronnie (2020), 'The Romance of Realism: Pessimism as Tragedy', in Tim Stevens and Nicholas Michelsen (eds), *Pessimism in International Relations: Provocations, Possibilities, Politics*, London: Palgrave, pp. 37–52.

Hobbes, Thomas (1996 [1651]), *Leviathan*, revised student edition, ed. Richard Tuck, Cambridge: Cambridge University Press.

Hobsbawm, Eric (1988a [1962]), *The Age of Revolution: Europe 1789–1848*, London: Abacus.

Hobsbawm, Eric (1988b [1975]), *The Age of Capital: 1848–1875*, London: Abacus.

Hobsbawm, Eric (1989 [1987]), *The Age of Empire: 1875–1914*, London: Abacus.

Hobsbawm, Eric (1995 [1994]), *The Age of Extremes: The Short Twentieth Century 1914–1991*, London: Abacus.

Hoffmann, Stanley and David P. Fidler (eds) (1991), *Rousseau on International Relations*, Oxford: Clarendon Press.

Hollingworth, Miles (2013), *Saint Augustine of Hippo: An Intellectual Biography*, Oxford: Oxford University Press.

Hollingworth, Miles (2018a), *Ludwig Wittgenstein*, Oxford: Oxford University Press.

Hollingworth, Miles (2018b), 'Augustine of Hippo', in Robert Schuett and Miles Hollingworth (eds), *The Edinburgh Companion to Political Realism*, Edinburgh: Edinburgh University Press, pp. 151–63.

Hollingworth, Miles and Robert Schuett (2018), 'Introduction: Political Realism, Liberal Democracy, and World Politics', in Robert Schuett and Miles Hollingworth (eds), *The Edinburgh Companion to Political Realism*, Edinburgh: Edinburgh University Press, pp. 1–8.

Holmes, Jr, Oliver Wendell (2017 [1911]), '"The Class of '61": Fiftieth Anniversary Reunion', in Max Lerner (ed.), *The Mind and Faith of Justice Holmes: His Speeches, Essays, Letters, and Judicial Opinions*, Oxon: Routledge, pp. 25–7.

Hülsmann, Jörg Guido (2007), *Mises: The Last Knight of Liberalism*, Auburn, AL: Ludwig von Mises Institute.

Hurd, Ian (2019), *How to Do Things with International Law*, Princeton: Princeton University Press.

Hutchison, Percy (1934), 'E. M. Forster on Lowes Dickinson', *The New York Times Book Review*, 10 June.

Ingram, David (2014), 'Reconciling Positivism and Realism: Kelsen and Habermas on Democracy and Human Rights', *Philosophy and Social Criticism*, vol. 40, no. 3, pp. 237–67.

Invernizzi-Accetti, Carlo (2015), *Relativism and Religion: Why Democratic Societies Do Not Need Moral Absolutes*, New York: Columbia University Press.

Invernizzi-Accetti, Carlo (2018), 'Reconciling Legal Positivism and Human Rights: Hans Kelsen's Argument from Relativism', *Journal of Human Rights*, vol. 17, no. 2, pp. 215–28.

Ish-Shalom, Piki (2006), 'The Triptych of Realism, Elitism, and Conservatism', *International Studies Quarterly*, vol. 8, no. 3, pp. 441–68.

Jabloner, Clemens (2014 [1997]), 'Menschenbild und Friedenssicherung', in Nikitas Aliprantis and Thomas Olechowski (eds), *Hans Kelsen: Die*

Aktualität eines großen Rechtswissenschafters und Soziologen des 20. Jahrhunderts (Schriftenreihe des Hans Kelsen-Instituts, vol. 38), Vienna: Manz, pp. 133–50.

Jabloner, Clemens (1998), 'Kelsen and his Circle: The Viennese Years', *European Journal of International Law*, vol. 9, no. 2, pp. 368–85.

Jabloner, Clemens (2015), 'Kelsens Prägung der österreichischen Bundesverfassung', in Lucile Dreidemy, Elisabeth Röhrlich, Richard Hufschmied, Agnes Meisinger, Florian Wenninger, Eugen Pfister, Katharina Prager, Maria Wirth and Berhold Molden (eds), *Bananen, Cola, Zeitgeschichte: Oliver Rathkolb und das lange 20. Jahrhundert*, Vienna: Böhlau, pp. 165–76.

Jabloner, Clemens (2016), 'In Defense of Modern Times: A Keynote Address', in D. A. Jeremy Telman (ed.), *Hans Kelsen in America: Selective Affinities and the Mysteries of Academic Influence*, New York: Springer, pp. 331–42.

Jabloner, Clemens (2019), 'Eröffnungsworte', Presentation of the edition of Hans Kelsen's *Allgemeiner Staatslehre*, Vienna (20 November 2019).

Jabloner, Clemens, Jan Kuklik and Thomas Olechowski (eds) (2018), *Hans Kelsen in der tschechischen und internationalen Rechtslehre (Schriftenreihe des Hans Kelsen-Instituts, vol. 39)*, Vienna: Manz.

Jabloner, Clemens, Thomas Olechowski and Klaus Zeleny (eds) (2016), *Das internationale Wirken Hans Kelsens (Schriftenreihe des Hans Kelsen-Instituts, vol. 38)*, Vienna: Manz.

Jabloner, Clemens, Thomas Olechowski and Klaus Zeleny (eds) (2019), *Hans Kelsen in seiner Zeit (Schriftenreihe des Hans Kelsen-Instituts, vol. 40)*, Vienna: Manz.

Jellinek, Georg (1929), *Allgemeine Staatslehre*, Berlin: Springer.

Jestaedt, Matthias (ed.) (2007–42), in collaboration with the Viennese Hans Kelsen-Institut, *Hans Kelsen Werke (HKW) (Hans Kelsen's Collected Works)*, Tübingen: Mohr Siebeck.

Jestaedt, Matthias (2007a), 'Chronik und Stammbaum', in Matthias Jestaedt (ed.), *Hans Kelsen Werke, Bd. 1: Veröffentlichte Schriften 1905–1910 und Selbstzeugnisse [HKW 1]*, Tübingen: Mohr Siebeck, pp. 93–105.

Jestaedt, Matthias (2007b), 'Vorwort des Herausgebers', in Matthias Jestaedt (ed.), *Hans Kelsen Werke, Bd. 1: Veröffentlichte Schriften 1905–1910 und Selbstzeugnisse [HKW 1]*, Tübingen: Mohr Siebeck, pp. vii–x.

Jestaedt, Matthias (2014), 'Das Postulat einer streng wissenschaftlichen Erkenntnis des Rechts', in Nikitas Aliprantis and Thomas Olechowski (eds), *Hans Kelsen: Die Aktualität eines großen Rechtswissenschafters und Soziologen des 20. Jahrhunderts (Schriftenreihe des Hans Kelsen-Instituts, vol. 38)*, Vienna: Manz, pp. 3–12.

Jestaedt, Matthias (ed.) (2020), in collaboration with the Hans Kelsen-Institut, *Hans Kelsen Werke, Bd. 8: Veröffentlichte Schriften 1922 [HKW 8]*, Tübingen: Mohr Siebeck.

Jestaedt, Matthias and Oliver Lepsius (2006), 'Der Rechts- und der Demokratietheoretiker Hans Kelsen: Eine Einführung', in Matthias Jestaedt and Oliver Lepsius (eds), *Hans Kelsen: Verteidigung der Demokratie: Abhandlungen zur Demokratietheorie*, Tübingen: Mohr Siebeck, pp. vii–xxix.

Jewish Daily Bulletin (1933), 'Nazis Boo Appointment of Kelsen to Prague Post', 2 June.

Johnson, Thomas J. (1996), 'The Idea of Power Politics: The Sophistic Foundations of Realism', in Benjamin Frankel (ed.), *Roots of Realism*, London: Cass, pp. 194–247.

Jones, Ernest (1955), *Sigmund Freud: Life and Work, Volume Two, Years of Maturity, 1901–1919*, London: Hogarth Press.

Jones, Ernest (1957), *Sigmund Freud: Life and Work, Volume Three, The Last Phase, 1919–1939*, London: Hogarth Press.

Jung, Carl G. (1963), *Memories, Dreams, Reflections*, New York: Pantheon.

Jütersonke, Oliver (2010), *Morgenthau, Law, and Realism*, Cambridge: Cambridge University Press.

Kagan, Robert (2008), *The Return of History and the End of Dreams*, London: Atlantic Books.

Kalyvas, Andreas (2006), 'The Basic Norm and Democracy in Hans Kelsen's Legal and Political Theory', *Philosophy and Social Criticism* vol. 32, no. 5.

Kammerhofer, Jörg and Jean D'Aspremont (eds) (2014), *International Legal Positivism in a Post-Modern World*, Cambridge: Cambridge University Press.

Kandel, Eric (1999), 'Biology and the Future of Psychoanalysis: A New Intellectual Framework for Psychiatry Revisited', *American Journal of Psychiatry*, vol. 156, no. 4, pp. 505–24.

Kant, Immanuel (1991a [1784]), 'Idea for a Universal History with a Cosmopolitan Purpose', in Hans Reiss (ed.), *Kant's Political Writings*, Cambridge: Cambridge University Press, pp. 41–53.

Kant, Immanuel (1991b [1793]), 'On the Common Saying: "This May be True in Theory, But It Does Not Apply in Practice"', in Hans Reiss (ed.), *Kant's Political Writings*, Cambridge: Cambridge University Press, pp. 61–92.

Kant, Immanuel (1991c [1795]), 'Perpetual Peace: A Philosophical Sketch', in Hans Reiss (ed.), *Kant's Political Writings*, Cambridge: Cambridge University Press, pp. 93–130.

Kaplan, Abraham (1957), 'Freud and Modern Philosophy', in Benjamin Nelson (ed.), *Freud and the 20th Century*, London: Allen & Unwin, pp. 205–25.

Kaplan, Fred (2014), 'Obama's World I: The Realist', *Politico Magazine*, March/April.

Karis, Thomas G. (2006), 'John Herz', *PS: Political Science & Politics*, vol. 39, no. 4, pp. 939–40.

'Karl Raimund Popper: 1902–1994' (1997), *Proceedings of the British Academy*, vol. 94, pp. 645–84.

Katz, Barry M. (1989), *Foreign Intelligence: Research and Analysis in the Office of Strategic Services, 1942–1945*, Cambridge, MA: Harvard University Press.

Kazin, Alfred (1957), 'The Freudian Revolution Analyzed', in Benjamin Nelson (ed.), *Freud and the 20th Century*, London: Allen & Unwin, pp. 13–21.

Kelsen, Hans (2007 [1905]), *Die Staatslehre des Dante Alighieri*, in Matthias Jestaedt (ed.), *Hans Kelsen Werke, Bd. 1: Veröffentlichte Schriften 1905–1910 und Selbstzeugnisse [HKW 1]*, Tübingen: Mohr Siebeck, pp. 134–300.

Kelsen, Hans (2008 [1911]), 'Hauptprobleme der Staatsrechtslehre, entwickelt aus der Lehre vom Rechtssatze', in Matthias Jestaedt (ed.), *Hans Kelsen Werke, Bd. 2: Veröffentlichte Schriften 1911 [HKW 2]*, Tübingen: Mohr Siebeck, pp. 21–878.

Kelsen, Hans (1920), *Sozialismus und Staat*, Leipzig: Hirschfeld.

Kelsen, Hans (1922a), 'Der Begriff des Staates und die Sozialpsychologie: Mit besonderer Berücksichtigung von Freuds Theorie der Masse', *Imago*, vol. 8, no. 2, pp. 97–141.

Kelsen, Hans (1922b), *Der Soziologische und der Juristische Staatsbegriff: Kritische Untersuchung des Verhältnisses von Staat und Recht*, Tübingen: Mohr Siebeck.

Kelsen, Hans (1922/3), 'Gott und Staat', *Logos: Internationale Zeitschrift für Philosophie der Kultur*, vol. 11, pp. 261–84.

Kelsen, Hans (1924), 'The Conception of the State and Social Psychology, with a Special Reference to Freud's Group Theory', *International Journal of Psycho-Analysis*, vol. 5, pp. 1–38.

Kelsen, Hans (2007 [1927a]), 'Selbstdarstellung', in Matthias Jestaedt (ed.), *Hans Kelsen Werke, Bd. 1: Veröffentlichte Schriften 1905–1910 und Selbstzeugnisse [HKW 1]*, Tübingen: Mohr Siebeck, pp. 19–27.

Kelsen, Hans (1927b), 'Remarks', in *Veröffentlichungen der Vereinigung der Deutschen Staatsrechtslehrer, vol. 3*, Berlin: Walter de Gruyter, pp. 54–5 [quoted in David Dyzenhaus (2000), 'The Gorgon Head of Power: Heller and Kelsen on the Rule of Law', in Peter C. Caldwell and William E. Scheuerman (eds), *From Liberal Democracy to Fascism: Legal and Political Thought in the Weimar Republic*, Boston: Humanities Press, p. 20].

Kelsen, Hans (2006 [1929a]), *Vom Wesen und Wert der Demokratie (2. Aufl.)*, in Matthias Jestaedt and Oliver Lepsius (eds), *Hans Kelsen: Verteidigung der Demokratie: Abhandlungen zur Demokratietheorie*, Tübingen: Mohr Siebeck, pp. 149–228.

Kelsen, Hans (2013 [1929b]), *The Essence and Value of Democracy*, ed. Nadia Urbinati and Carlo Invernizzi Accetti, trans. Brian Graf, Lanham, MD: Rowman & Littlefield.

Kelsen, Hans (1932), *Théorie générale du droit international public: problèmes choisis*, Paris: Sirey.

Kelsen, Hans (1967 [1934a]), *Pure Theory of Law*, transl. from the 2nd German edn by Max Knight, Berkeley: University of California Press.

Kelsen, Hans (2008 [1934b]), *Reine Rechtslehre*, ed. Mathias Jestaedt, Tübingen: Mohr Siebeck.

Kelsen, Hans (1934c), 'Reference Letter for Hans J. Morgenthau, dated March 15, 1934' [Hutchins Administration, Box 287, folder 5; quoted in John W. Boyer (2008), '"We Are All Islanders to Begin With": The University of Chicago and the World in the Late Nineteenth and Twentieth Centuries', *The University of Chicago Record*, vol. 42, no. 2, p. 14].

Kelsen, Hans (2006 [1937]), 'Wissenschaft und Demokratie', in Matthias Jestaedt and Oliver Lepsius (eds), *Hans Kelsen: Verteidigung der Demokratie: Abhandlungen zur Demokratietheorie*, Tübingen: Mohr Siebeck, pp. 238–47.

Kelsen, Hans (1938), 'Letter to Charles Merriam, dated July 15, 1938' [Merriam Papers, Box 51, folder 7; quoted in quoted in John W. Boyer (2008), '"We Are All Islanders to Begin With": The University of Chicago and the World in the Late Nineteenth and Twentieth Centuries', *The University of Chicago Record*, vol. 42, no. 2, p. 13].

Kelsen, Hans (1941), 'The Law as a Specific Social Technique', *University of Chicago Law Review*, vol. 9, no. 1, pp. 75–97.

Kelsen, Hans (1942), *Law and Peace in International Relations*, Cambridge, MA: Harvard University Press.

Kelsen, Hans (1944a), *Peace through Law*, Chapel Hill: University of North Carolina Press.

Kelsen, Hans (1944b), 'Austria: Her Actual Legal Status and Re-Establishment as an Independent State' [copy on file with the Hans Kelsen-Institute; quoted in Thomas Olechowski and Stefan Wedrac (2015), 'Hans Kelsen und Washington', in Lucile Dreidemy, Elisabeth Röhrlich, Richard Hufschmied, Agnes Meisinger, Florian Wenninger, Eugen Pfister, Katharina Prager, Maria Wirth and Berhold Molden (eds), *Bananen, Cola, Zeitgeschichte: Oliver Rathkolb und das lange 20. Jahrhundert*, Vienna: Böhlau, p. 284].

Kelsen, Hans (2007 [1945]), *General Theory of Law and the State*, trans. Anders Wedberg, Clark: Lawbook Exchange.

Kelsen, Hans (2007 [1947a]), 'Autobiographie', in Matthias Jestaedt (ed.), *Hans Kelsen Werke, Bd. 1: Veröffentlichte Schriften 1905–1910 und Selbstzeugnisse* [HKW 1], Tübingen: Mohr Siebeck, pp. 29–91.

Kelsen, Hans (1947b), 'German Peace Terms', *The New York Times*, 7 September.

Kelsen, Hans (1947c), 'International Affairs: Is a Peace Treaty with Germany Legally Possible and Politically Desirable?', *The American Political Science Review*, vol. 41, no. 6, pp. 1188–93.

Kelsen, Hans (1948a), *The Political Theory of Bolshevism: A Critical Analysis*, Berkeley: University of California Press.

Kelsen, Hans (1948b), 'Collective and Individual Responsibility for Acts of State in International Law', *The Jewish Yearbook of International Law*, pp. 226–39.

Kelsen, Hans (1949), 'The Natural-Law Doctrine Before the Tribunal of Science', *The Western Political Quarterly*, vol. 2, no. 4, pp. 481–513.

Kelsen, Hans (1950a), 'Interview', *Harvard Crimson*, 1 November [quoted in Oliver Rathkolb (2009), 'Hans Kelsen und das FBI während des McCarthysmus in den USA', in Robert Walter, Werner Ogris and Thomas Olechowski (eds), *Hans Kelsen: Leben, Werk, Wirksamkeit*, Vienna: Manz, p. 345].

Kelsen, Hans (1950b), 'Letter to the Editor', *Harvard Crimson*, 4 December [quoted in Oliver Rathkolb (2009), 'Hans Kelsen und das FBI während des McCarthysmus in den USA', in Robert Walter, Werner Ogris and Thomas Olechowski (eds), *Hans Kelsen: Leben, Werk, Wirksamkeit*, Vienna: Manz, p. 345].

Kelsen, Hans (1950c), 'Causality and Imputation', *Ethics*, vol. 61, no. 1, pp. 1–11.

Kelsen, Hans (1952a), 'Bernard Moses Memorial Lecture: "What is Justice?"', *University of California, Berkeley*, 27 May, <https://gradlectures.berkeley.edu/lecture/what-is-justice/> (last accessed 27 April 2020).

Kelsen, Hans (1952b), *Principles of International Law* (2nd edn), rev./ed. Robert W. Tucker, New York: Rinehart.

Kelsen, Hans (1954), 'Letter to Hans J. Morgenthau, dated January 9, 1954' [Morgenthau Papers, Box 33, Folder 6 (General Correspondence; Kelsen, Hans; 1934–1971); and copy on file with the Hans Kelsen-Institut].

Kelsen, Hans (1955a), *The Communist Theory of Law*, New York: Frederick A. Praeger.

Kelsen, Hans (1955b), 'Foundations of Democracy', *Ethics*, vol. 66, no. 1, pp. 1–101.

Kelsen, Hans (1957a), 'What Is Justice?', in Hans Kelsen (ed.), *What is Justice? Justice, Law, and Politics in the Mirror of Science*, Berkeley: University of California Press, pp. 1–24.

Kelsen, Hans (1957b), *Collective Security under International Law*, Newport, RI: Naval War College.

Kelsen, Hans (1957c), 'Why Should the Law be Obeyed?', in Hans Kelsen (ed.), *What is Justice? Justice, Law, and Politics in the Mirror of Science*, Berkeley: University of California Press, pp. 257–65.

Kelsen, Hans (2017 [1960a]), *Reine Rechtslehre (2. Aufl.)*, ed. Matthias Jestaedt, Tübingen: Mohr Siebeck.

Kelsen, Hans (1960b), 'Hans Kelsen und der Entwurf der Bundesverfassung', *ORF*, 9 November 1960, <https://tvthek.orf.at/history/Ereignisse-Persoen-lichkeiten/13557903/Hans-Kelsen-und-der-Entwurf-der-Bundesverfas-sung/13396741> (last accessed 27 April 2020).

Kelsen, Hans (1963), 'Letter to Henk L. Mulder, dated May 5, 1963' [Vienna Circle Archive (Institute Vienna Circle, Vienna); quoted in Clemens Jabloner (1998), 'Kelsen and his Circle: The Viennese Years', *European Journal of International Law*, vol. 9, no. 2, p. 371].

Kelsen, Hans (1986 [1964]), 'The Function of a Constitution', in Richard Tur and William Twining (eds), *Essays on Kelsen*, Oxford: Clarendon Press, pp. 109–19.

Kelsen, Hans (1970), 'Letter to Hans J. Morgenthau, dated May 4, 1970' [Morgenthau Papers, Box 33, Folder 6 (General Correspondence; Kelsen, Hans; 1934–1971); and copy on file with the Hans Kelsen-Institut].

Kelsen, Hans (1973), 'God and the State', in Hans Kelsen (ed.), *Essays in Legal and Moral Philosophy*, Dordrecht: Springer, pp. 61–82.

Kelsen, Hans (1990 [1979]), *General Theory of Norms*, trans. Michael Hartney, Oxford: Oxford University Press.

Kelsen, Hans and John H. Herz (1941), 'Essential Conditions of International Justice', *Proceedings of the American Society of International Law at Its Annual Meeting (1921–1969)*, vol. 35, pp. 70–98.

Kennan, George F. (2002 [1956]), 'The Soviet Will Never Recover (interview by Joseph Alsop, *Saturday Evening Post*, November 24, 1956)', in T. Christopher Jespersen (ed.), *Interviews with George F. Kennan*, Jackson: University Press of Mississippi.

Kennan, George F. (1993), *Around the Cragged Hill: A Personal and Political Philosophy*, New York: Norton.

Kennedy, David (1994), 'The International Style in Postwar Law and Policy', *Utah Law Review*, vol. 1, pp. 7–103.

Keohane, Robert O. (1986), 'Realism, Neorealism, and the Study of World Politics', in Robert O. Keohane (ed.), *Neorealism and its Critics*, New York: Columbia University Press, pp. 1–26.

Kirchhoff, Markus (2017), 'The Westphalian System as a Jewish Concern: Re-Reading Leo Gross' 1948 "Westphalia" Article', in Raphael Gross (ed.), *Simon Dubnow Institute Yearbook YV/2016*, Göttingen: Vandenhoeck & Ruprecht, pp. 239–64.

Kirsch, Adam (2017), 'Why the Freud Wars Will Never End', *The Wall Street Journal*, 29 September.

Kissinger, Henry A. (1980), 'Memorial Remarks for Hans Morgenthau', 23 July, <https://www.henryakissinger.com/remembrances/hans-morgenthau> (last accessed 27 April 2020).

Kissinger, Henry A. (2014), *World Order*, New York: Penguin, pp. 23–41.

Kletzer, Christoph (2015), 'Kelsen on Vaihinger', in Maksymilian Del Mar and William Twining (eds), *Legal Fictions in Theory and Practice*, Berlin: Springer, pp. 23–9.

Kletzer, Christoph (2018), *The Idea of a Pure Theory of Law: An Interpretation and Defence*, London: Bloomsbury.

Köhler, Peter (2005), *Die schönsten Zitate der Politiker*, Baden-Baden: Humboldt.

Kolakowski, Leszek (1960), *Der Mensch ohne Alternative: Von der Möglichkeit und Unmöglichkeit, Marxist zu sein*, Munich: Piper.

Koskenniemi, Martti (2000), 'Carl Schmitt, Hans Morgenthau, and the Image of Law in International Relations', in Michael Byers (ed.), *The Role of Law in International Politics: Essays in International Relations and International Law*, Oxford: Oxford University Press, pp. 17–35.

Koskenniemi, Martti (2001), *The Gentle Civilizer of Nations: The Rise and Fall of International Law 1870–1960*, Cambridge: Cambridge University Press.

Koskenniemi, Martti (2005), *From Apology to Utopia: The Structure of International Legal Argument*, Cambridge: Cambridge University Press.

Kostagiannis, Konstantinos (2017), *Realist Thought and the Nation-State: Power Politics in the Age of Nationalism*, New York: Palgrave.

Krastev, Ivan and Stephen Holmes (2019), *The Light that Failed: A Reckoning*, London: Penguin.

Kropsky, Jason (2019), 'Between Politics and Morality: Hans Kelsen's Contributions to the Changing Notion of International Criminal Responsibility'. CUNY Academic Works, <https://academicworks.cuny.edu/gc_etds/3249/> (last accessed 30 April 2020).

Kurzweil, Edith (2008), 'Sigmund Freud: Conquistador of the Unconscious', in Joseph P. Merlino, Marilyn Jacobs, Judy Ann Kaplan and K. Lynn Moritz (eds), *Freud at 150: 21st-century Essays on a Man of Genius*, Lanham, MD: Rowman & Littlefield, pp. 3–16.

Kusnet, David (2016), 'Obama is the Nation's Orator-in-chief, and He Deserves the Title and the Accolades', *The Guardian*, 12 January.

La Torre, Massimo (2010), *Law as Institution*, Cham: Springer.

Ladavac, Nicoletta Bersier (2009), 'Hans Kelsen in Genf: Die Friedensproblematik zwischen Wissenschaft und Politik', in Robert Walter, Werner Ogris and Thomas Olechowski (eds), *Hans Kelsen: Leben, Werk, Wirksamkeit*, Vienna: Manz, pp. 289–303.

Lang, Jr, Anthony F. (2007), 'Morgenthau, Agency, and Aristotle', in Michael C. Williams (ed.), *Realism Reconsidered: The Legacy of Hans Morgenthau in International Relations*, Oxford: Oxford University Press, pp. 18–41.

Langford, Peter, Ian Bryan and John McGarry (eds) (2017), *Kelsenian Legal Science and the Nature of Law*, Berlin: Springer.

Langford, Peter, Ian Bryan and John McGarry (eds) (2019), *Hans Kelsen and the Natural Law Tradition*, Leiden: Brill.

Lasar, Matthew (1999), *Pacifica Radio: The Rise of an Alternative Network*, Philadelphia: Temple University Press.

Laski, Harold (1938), *A Grammar of Politics* (4th edn), London: Allen & Unwin.

Layne, Christopher (1994), 'Kant or Cant: The Myth of the Democratic Peace', *International* Security, vol. 19, no. 2, pp. 5–49.

Leben, Charles (2010), *The Advancement of International Law*, Oxford: Hart Publishing.

Lebow, Richard Ned (2003), *The Tragic Vision of Politics: Ethics, Interests and Orders*, Cambridge: Cambridge University Press.

Lebow, Richard Ned (2010), *Why Nations Fight: Past and Future Motives for War*, Cambridge: Cambridge University Press.

Lebow, Richard Ned (2014), 'German Jews and American Realism', in Felix Rösch (ed.), *Émigré Scholars and the Genesis of International Relations*, Basingstoke: Palgrave, pp. 212–43.

Lee, Ann Feder (2011), *The Hawaii State Constitution*, Oxford: Oxford University Press.

Lepsius, Oliver (2009), 'Hans Kelsen und der Nationalsozialismus', in Robert Walter, Werner Ogris and Thomas Olechowski (eds), *Hans Kelsen: Leben, Werk, Wirksamkeit*, Vienna: Manz, pp. 271–88.

Lepsius, Oliver (2017), 'Hans Kelsen on Dante Alighieri's Political Philosophy', *The European Journal of International Law*, vol. 27, no. 4, pp. 1153–67.

Lerner, Adam B. (2020), 'What's It Like to Be a State? An Argument for State Consciousness', *International Theory*, epub ahead of print, 14 January.

Leser, Norbert (1966), 'Austro-Marxism: A Reappraisal', *Journal of Contemporary History*, vol. 1, no. 2, pp: 117–33.

Leser, Norbert (2011), *Skurrile Begegnungen: Mosaike zur österreichischen Geistesgeschichte*, Vienna: Böhlau.

Levi, Primo (2017 [1986]), *The Drowned and the Saved*, trans. Raymond Rosenthal, New York: Simon & Schuster.

Levine, Daniel (2012), *Recovering International Relations: The Promise of Sustainable Critique*, Oxford: Oxford University Press.

Lieber, Keir A. (2009), 'Introduction', in Keir A. Lieber (ed.), *War, Peace, and International Political Realism*, Notre Dame, IN: University of Notre Dame Press.

Lind, Michael (2015), 'Carl Schmitt's War on Liberalism', *The National Interest*, 23 April.

Lippmann, Walter (2008 [1915a]), *The Stakes of Diplomacy*, New Brunswick, NJ: Transaction.

Lippmann, Walter (1915b), 'Freud and the Layman', *The New Republic*, 17 April, pp. 9–10.

Lippmann, Walter (1993 [1925]), *The Phantom Public*, New Brunswick, NJ: Transaction.

Lippmann, Walter (1947), 'Letter to Hans Kelsen, dated September 8, 1947' [copy on file with the Hans Kelsen-Institut].

Lippmann, Walter (1948), 'Letter from Walter Lippmann to Hans Kelsen, dated November 2, 1948' [copy on file with the Hans Kelsen-Institut].

Lipsky, George A. (ed.) (1953), *Law and Politics in World Community: Essays on Hans Kelsen's Pure Theory and Related Problems in International Law*, Berkeley: University of California Press.

Little, Richard (2003), 'The English School vs. American Realism: A Meeting of Minds or Divided by a Common Language?', *Review of International Studies*, vol. 29, no. 3, pp. 443–60.

Little, Richard (2007), *The Balance of Power in International Relations: Metaphors, Myths and Models*, Cambridge: Cambridge University Press.

Llewellyn, Karl N. (1962), *Jurisprudence: Realism in Theory and Practice*, Chicago: University of Chicago Press.

Losano, Mario G. (1989 [1977]), 'Kelsen and Freud', in Víctor Alarcón and Oscar Correas (eds), *El otro Kelsen*, Mexico: Universidad Nacional Autónoma de México, Instituto de Investigaciones Jurídicas, pp. 99–110.

Lovin, Robin W. (1995), *Reinhold Niebuhr and Christian Realism*, Cambridge: Cambridge University Press.

Lowenstein, James G. (1994), 'Interview for the Foreign Affairs Oral History Project', interviewed by Dennis Kux (Association for Diplomatic Studies and Training), 8 February.

Lupton, Julia Reinhard (2010), 'Invitation to a Totem Meal: Kelsen, Schmitt, Freud', in Paul Cefalu and Bryan Reynolds (eds), *Early Modern English Literature and Theory*, New York: Palgrave, pp. 121–42.

McClam, Virginia (1971a), 'Letter to Robert Tucker, dated August 12, 1971' [copy on file with the Hans Kelsen-Institut].

McClam, Virginia (1971b), 'Letter to Robert Tucker, dated October 19, 1971' [copy on file with the Hans Kelsen-Institut].

McCourt, David M. (2020), 'Introduction', in David M. McCourt (ed.), *American Power and International Theory at the Council on Foreign Relations, 1953–54*, Ann Arbor: University of Michigan Press, pp. 1–52.

McQueen, Alison (2018a), *Political Realism in Apocalyptic Times*, Cambridge: Cambridge University Press.

McQueen, Alison (2018b), 'The Case for Kinship: Political Realism and Classical Realism', in Matt Sleat (ed.), *Politics Recovered: Essays on Realist Political Thought*, New York: Columbia University Press, ch. 10.

Marmor, Andrei (2011), *Philosophy of Law*, Princeton: Princeton University Press.

Mazur, George O. (ed.) (2004), *One Hundred Year Commemoration to the Life of Hans Morgenthau: 1904–2004*, New York: Semenenko.

Mazur, George O. (ed.) (2006), *Twenty-Five Year Memorial Commemoration to the Life of Hans Morgenthau*, New York: Semenenko.

Mearsheimer, John J. (1990), 'Back to the Future: Instability in Europe After the Cold War', *International Security*, vol. 15, no. 1, pp. 5–56.

Mearsheimer, John J. (1994–5), 'The False Promise of International Institutions', *International* Security, vol. 19, no. 3, pp. 5–49.

Mearsheimer, John J. (2001), *The Tragedy of Great Power Politics*, New York: W. W. Norton.

Mearsheimer, John J. (2002), 'Through the Realist Lens: Conversation with John Mearsheimer', *Conversations with History*, interviewed by Harry Kreisler, Institute of International Studies, University of California at Berkeley, 8 April.

Mearsheimer, John J. (2005), 'Better to Be Godzilla Than Bambi', *Foreign Policy*, vol. 146, pp. 47–8.

Mearsheimer, John J. (2006), 'Conversations in International Relations: Interview with John J. Mearsheimer (Part II)', *International Relations*, vol. 20, no. 2, pp. 231–43.

Mearsheimer, John J. (2012), 'Nuclear-Armed Iran Would Bring "Stability" but Risks', *PBS NewsHour*, 9 July.

Mearsheimer, John J. (2018), *Great Delusion: Liberal Dreams and International Realities*, New Haven, CT: Yale University Press.

Mearsheimer, John J. and Stephen M. Walt (2007), *The Israel Lobby and U.S. Foreign Policy*, New York: Farrar, Straus and Giroux.

Menand, Louis (2017), 'What Happens When War is Outlawed', *The New Yorker*, 11 September.

Métall, Rudolf A. (1969), *Hans Kelsen: Leben und Werk*, Vienna: Franz Deuticke.

Milkov, Nikolay (2012), 'Karl Popper's Debt to Leonard Nelson', in *Grazer Philosophische Studien*, vol. 86, pp. 137–56.

Miller, Hunter (1928), *The Peace Pact of Paris: A Study of the Briand–Kellogg Treaty*, New York: G. P. Putnam's Sons.

Mintz, Samuel I. (1962), *The Hunting of Leviathan*, Cambridge: Cambridge University Press.

Miriam Gassner (2016), 'Hans Kelsen und die sowjetische Rechtslehre', in Clemens Jabloner, Thomas Olechowski and Klaus Zeleny (eds), *Das internationale Wirken Hans Kelsens (Schriftenreihe des Hans Kelsen-Instituts, vol. 38)*, Vienna: Manz, pp. 141–67.

Mollov, M. Benjamin (2002), *Power and Transcendence: Hans J. Morgenthau and the Jewish Experience*, Lanham, MD: Lexington Books.

Molloy, Sean (2006), *The Hidden History of Realism: A Genealogy of Power Politics*, New York: Palgrave.

Morgenthau, Hans J. (1930a), 'Über die Herkunft des Politischen aus dem Wesen des Menschen'. Unpublished manuscript [Morgenthau Papers, Box 151; copy on file with the author].

Morgenthau, Hans J. (2012 [1930b]), *The Concept of the Political*, ed. Hartmut Behr and Felix Rösch, Basingstoke: Palgrave.

Morgenthau, Hans J. (1934), *La Réalité des normes, en particulier des normes du droit international*, Paris: F. Alcan.

Morgenthau, Hans J. (1940), 'Positivism, Functionalism, and International Law', *American Journal of International Law*, vol. 34, pp. 260–84.

Morgenthau, Hans J. (1945), 'The Machiavellian Utopia', *Ethics*, vol. 55, no. 2, pp. 145–7.

Morgenthau, Hans J. (1946), *Scientific Man vs. Power Politics*, London: Latimer House.

Morgenthau, Hans J. (1967 [1948a]), *Politics among Nations: The Struggle for Power and Peace* (4th edn), New York: Alfred A. Knopf.

Morgenthau, Hans J. (1948b), 'Letter to Hans Kelsen, dated March 18, 1948' [Morgenthau Papers, Box 33, Folder 6 (General Correspondence; Kelsen, Hans; 1934–1971); copy on file with the author].

Morgenthau, Hans J. (1948c), 'Letter to Hans Kelsen, dated November 8, 1948' [Morgenthau Papers, Box 33, Folder 6 (General Correspondence; Kelsen, Hans; 1934–1971); copy on file with the author].

Morgenthau, Hans J. (1951), *In Defense of the National Interest: A Critical Examination of American Foreign Policy*, New York: Alfred A. Knopf.

Morgenthau, Hans J. (1952), 'Letter to Hans Kelsen, dated December 23, 1952' [Morgenthau Papers, Box 33, Folder 6 (General Correspondence; Kelsen, Hans; 1934–1971); copy on file with the author].

Morgenthau, Hans J. (1962a), *Politics in the Twentieth Century, vol. I, The Decline of Democratic Politics*, Chicago: University of Chicago Press.

Morgenthau, Hans J. (1962b), 'About Cynicism, Perfectionism, and Realism and International Affairs', in Morgenthau, *The Decline of Democratic Politics*, Chicago: University of Chicago Press, pp. 127–30.

Morgenthau, Hans J. (1964), 'The Impartiality of the International Police', in Salo Engel (ed.), *Law, State, and International Legal Order: Essays in Honor of Hans Kelsen*, Knoxville: University of Tennessee Press, pp. 209–23.

Morgenthau, Hans J. (1967), 'The Intellectual in Government', 13 April 1967 [Morgenthau Papers, Box 172; quoted in M. Benjamin Mollov (2002),

Power and Transcendence: Hans J. Morgenthau and the Jewish Experience, Lanham, MD: Lexington Books, p. 65].

Morgenthau, Hans J. (1969), 'Letter to Hannah Arendt, dated June 5, 1969' [Arendt Papers, no. 8721, Arendt-Center, Oldenburg/Germany; quoted in Alexander Reichwein (2016), 'The Responsibility of the Intellectuals in Times of Political Crisis', *Med Andre Ord. Studieblad, Institute for Statskundskab, Kobenhavn Universitet* 9 (November)].

Morgenthau, Hans J. (1970a), *Truth and Power: Essays of a Decade, 1960–70*, New York: Praeger.

Morgenthau, Hans J. (1970b), 'Letter to Hans Kelsen, dated April 28, 1970' [Morgenthau Papers, Box 33, Folder 6 (General Correspondence; Kelsen, Hans; 1934–1971); copy on file with the author]).

Morgenthau, Hans J. (1971), 'Letter to Hans Kelsen, dated October 4, 1971' [Morgenthau Papers, Box 33, Folder 6 (General Correspondence; Kelsen, Hans; 1934–1971); quoted in Oliver Jütersonke (2010), *Morgenthau, Law, and Realism*, Cambridge: Cambridge University Press, p. 101].

Morgenthau, Hans J. (1984a [1977]), 'Fragment of an Intellectual Autobiography: 1904–1932', in Kenneth W. Thompson and Robert J. Myers (eds), *Truth and Tragedy: A Tribute to Hans J. Morgenthau*, New Brunswick, NJ: Transaction, pp. 1–17.

Morgenthau, Hans J. (1984b), 'Interview with Bernhard Johnson', in Kenneth W. Thompson and R. J. Meyers (eds), *Truth and Tragedy: A Tribute to Hans J. Morgenthau*, New Brunswick, NJ: Transaction, pp. 333–86.

Myers, Denys P. (1954), 'Book Review: Law and Politics in the World Community. Essays on Hans Kelsen's Pure Theory and Related Problems in International Law', *American Journal of International Law*, vol. 48, no. 3, pp. 514–15.

Nardin, Terry (2017), 'The New Realism and the Old', *Critical Review of International Social and Political Philosophy*, vol. 20, no. 3, pp. 314–30.

Navari, Cornelia (ed.) (2018), *Hans J. Morgenthau and the American Experience*, New York: Palgrave.

Neschwara, Christian (2009), 'Hans Kelsen und das Problem der Dispensehen', in Robert Walter, Werner Ogris and Thomas Olechowski (eds), *Hans Kelsen: Leben, Werk, Wirksamkeit*, Vienna: Manz, pp. 249–68.

Neumann, Franz (1944), *Behemoth: The Structure and Practice of National Socialism*, Oxford: Oxford University Press.

Niebuhr, Reinhold (2001 [1932]), *Moral Man and Immoral Society: A Study in Ethics and Politics*, London: Westminster John Knox.

Niebuhr, Reinhold (1940), *Christianity and Power Politics*, New York: Scribner's Sons.

Niebuhr, Reinhold (1944), *The Children of Light and the Children of Darkness: A Vindication of Democracy and a Critique of its Traditional Defense*, New York: Charles Scribner's Sons.

Niebuhr, Reinhold (2008 [1952]), *The Irony of American History*, Chicago: Chicago University Press.

Niemann, Hans-Joachim (2014), *Karl Popper and the Two New Secrets of Life*, Tübingen: Mohr Siebeck.

Olechowski, Thomas (2009), 'Der Beitrag Hans Kelsens zur österreichischen Bundesverfassung', in Robert Walter, Werner Ogris and Thomas Olechowski (eds), *Hans Kelsen: Leben, Werk, Wirksamkeit*, Vienna: Manz, pp. 211–30.

Olechowski, Thomas (2011), 'Biographische Untersuchungen zu Hans Kelsen', *Rechtsgeschichtliche Vorträge*, vol. 64 (Budapest: ELTE), pp. 3–22.

Olechowski, Thomas (2013a), 'Biographical Researches on Hans Kelsen in the Years 1881–1920', *Právněhistorické studie*, vol. 43, pp. 279–93.

Olechowski, Thomas (2013b), 'Kelsen Debellatio-These', in Clemens Jabloner, Dieter Kolonovits, Gabriele Kucsko-Stadlmayer, René Laurer, Heinz Mayer and Rudolf Thienel (eds), *Gedenkschrift für Robert Walter*, Vienna: Manz, pp. 531–52.

Olechowski, Thomas (2016a), 'Hans Kelsen in Berkeley: Des Wandermüden letzte Ruhestätte', *Beiträge zur Rechtsgeschichte Österreichs*, pp. 58–73.

Olechowski, Thomas (2016b), 'Hans Kelsen, the Second World War and the US Government', in D. A. Jeremy Telman (ed.), *Hans Kelsen in America: Selective Affinities and the Mysteries of Academic Influence*, New York: Springer, pp. 101–12.

Olechowski, Thomas (2020), *Hans Kelsen: Biographie eines Rechtswissenschaftlers*, Tübingen: Mohr Siebeck.

Olechowski, Thomas and Jürgen Busch (2009), 'Hans Kelsen als Professor an der Deutschen Universität Prag: Biographische Aspekte der Kelsen-Sander-Kontroverse', in Karel Malý and Ladislav Soukup (eds), *Československé právo a právní věda v meziválečném období 1918–1938 a jejich místo v Evropě*, Prague: Karolinum, pp. 1106–34.

Olechowski, Thomas and Stefan Wedrac (2015), 'Hans Kelsen und Washington', in Lucile Dreidemy, Elisabeth Röhrlich, Richard Hufschmied, Agnes Meisinger, Florian Wenninger, Eugen Pfister, Katharina Prager, Maria Wirth and Berhold Molden (eds), *Bananen, Cola, Zeitgeschichte: Oliver Rathkolb und das lange 20. Jahrhundert*, Vienna: Böhlau, pp. 280–95.

Onuf, Nicholas (2008), *International Legal Theory: Essays and Engagements, 1966–2006*, Oxon: Routledge.

Orakhelashvili, Alexander (2019), *Domesticating Kelsen: Towards the Pure Theory of English Law*, Cheltenham: Edward Elgar.

Oren, Ido (2009), 'The Unrealism of Contemporary Realism: The Tension between Realist Theory and Realists' Practice', *Perspectives on Politics*, vol. 7, no. 2, pp. 283–301.

Osterkamp, Jana (2009), 'Hans Kelsen in der Tschechoslowakei', in Robert Walter, Werner Ogris and Thomas Olechowski (eds), *Hans Kelsen: Leben, Werk, Wirksamkeit*, Vienna: Manz, pp. 309–18.

Ottenheimer, Jr, Edward J. (1950), 'Non-Signer of U of Cal Oath To Come Here', *The Harvard Crimson*, 11 December.

Özmen, Elif (ed.) (2017), *Hans Kelsens Politische Philosophie*, Tübingen: Mohr Siebeck.

Palmerston, Henry John Temple (1848), 'Remarks in the House of Commons', 1 March [quoted in Edward Heath (1969), 'Realism in British Foreign Policy', *Foreign Affairs*, vol. 48, no. 1, pp. 39–50].

Paulson, Stanley L. (2003), 'Hans Kelsen and Normative Legal Positivism', in Thomas Baldwin (ed.), *The Cambridge History of Philosophy 1870– 1945*, Cambridge: Cambridge University Press, pp. 737–43.

Paulson, Stanley L. (2018), 'The Purity Thesis', *Ratio Juris*, vol. 31, no. 3, pp. 276–306.

Paulson, Stanley L. and Bonnie Litschewski-Paulson (eds) (1999), *Normativity and Norms: Critical Perspectives on Kelsenian Themes*, Oxford: Oxford University Press.

Paulson, Stanley L. and Michael Stolleis (eds) (2005), *Hans Kelsen: Staatsrechtslehrer und Rechtstheoretiker des 20. Jahrhunderts*, Tübingen: Mohr Siebeck.

Parashar, Swati, J. Ann Tickner and Jacqui True (2018), *Revisiting Gendered States: Feminist Imaginings of the State in International Relations*, Oxford: Oxford University Press.

Paz, Reut Yael (2014), 'A Forgotten Kelsenian? The Story of Helen Silving-Ryu (1906–1993)', *The European Journal of International Law*, vol. 25, no. 4, pp. 1123–46.

Peoples, Columba (2018), 'Life in the Nuclear Age: Classical Realism, Critical Theory and the Technopolitics of the Nuclear Condition', *Journal of International Political Theory*, vol. 15, no. 3, pp. 279–96.

Perlmutter, Amos (1997), *Making the World Safe for Democracy: A Century of Wilsonianism and its Totalitarian Challengers*, Chapel Hill: University of North Carolina Press.

Pils, Ramon (2016), *Terminologiewörterbuch Hans Kelsen: Deutsch-Englisches Glossar für die Übersetzungspraxis (Schriftenreihe des Hans Kelsen-Instituts, vol. 37)*, Vienna: Manz.

Pinker, Stephen (2016 [2002]), *The Blank Slate*, New York: Viking.

Plattner, Marc F. (2020), 'Democracy Embattled', *Journal of Democracy*, vol. 31, no. 1.

Popper, Karl R. (1943), 'Letter to Ernst Gombrich, dated December 9, 1943' [quoted in Ernst H. Gombrich (1999), 'Personal Recollections of the Publication of the Open Society', in I. C. Jarvie and Sandra Pralong (eds), *Popper's Open Society After Fifty Years: The Continuing Relevance of Karl Popper*, London: Routledge, p. 21].

Popper, Karl R. (1945), *The Open Society and Its Enemies*, London: Routledge.

Popper, Karl R. (2011 [1962]), 'Julius Kraft, 1898–1960', in Jeremy Shearmur and Piers Norris Turner (eds), *After the Open Society: Selected Social and Political Writings*, Oxon: Routledge, pp. 13–24.

Popper, Karl R. (1984), 'Letter to Friedrich Hayek, dated April 30, 1984' [Popper Archives, 305, 17; quoted in Malachi Haim Hacohen (2000), *Karl Popper: The Formative Years, 1902–1945, Politics and Philosophy in Interwar Vienna*, Cambridge: Cambridge University Press, p. 502].

Popper, Karl R. (2015 [1991]), 'Popper and the Vienna Circle – Excerpt from an Interview with Sir Karl Popper', in Friedrich Stadler (ed.), *The Vienna Circle: Studies in the Origins, Development, and Influence of Logical Empiricism*, Berlin: Springer.

Popper, Karl R. (1997 [1992]), 'Tribute to the Life and Work of Friedrich Hayek', in Stephen F. Frowen (ed.), *Hayek: Economist and Social Philosopher*, Basingstoke: Palgrave, pp. 311–12.

Popper, Karl R. (2006), *Frühe Schriften*, ed. Troels Eggers Hansen. Tübingen: Mohr Siebeck.

Posner, Richard A. (2001), 'Kelsen, Hayek, and the Economic Analysis of Law', Lecture Paper for the Eighteenth Annual Meeting of the European Association for Law and Economics in Vienna, 4 September.

Posner, Richard A. (2005), *Law, Pragmatism, and Democracy*, Cambridge, MA: Harvard University Press.

Potacs, Michael (2009), 'Hans Kelsen und der Marxismus', in Robert Walter, Werner Ogris and Thomas Olechowski (eds), *Hans Kelsen: Leben, Werk, Wirksamkeit*, Vienna: Manz, pp. 183–94.

Potacs, Michael (2014), 'Marxismus und Kelsen', in Nikitas Aliprantis and Thomas Olechowski (eds), *Hans Kelsen: Die Aktualität eines großen Rechtswissenschafters und Soziologen des 20. Jahrhunderts (Schriftenreihe des Hans Kelsen-Instituts, vol. 38)*, Vienna: Manz, pp. 183–94.

Pound, Roscoe (1934), 'Law and the Science of Law in Recent Theories', *Yale Law Journal*, vol. 43, p. 525.

Pound, Roscoe (1942), 'Letter to Eric C. Bellquist, dated January 9, 1942' [Roscoe Pound Papers, Harvard University Law School; quoted in John

W. Boyer (2008), '"We Are All Islanders to Begin With": The University of Chicago and the World in the Late Nineteenth and Twentieth Centuries', *The University of Chicago Record*, vol. 42, no. 2, p. 13].

Powell, Thomas Reed (1942), 'Letter to Raymond Garfield Gettell, dated January 9, 1942' [quoted in Oliver Lepsius (2009), 'Hans Kelsen und der Nationalsozialismus', in Robert Walter, Werner Ogris and Thomas Olechowski (eds), *Hans Kelsen: Leben, Werk, Wirksamkeit*, Vienna: Manz, p. 283].

Power, Samantha (2002), *A Problem from Hell: America and the Age of Genocide*, New York: Basic Books.

Preble, Christopher A. and John Mueller (2014), *A Dangerous World? Threat Perception and U.S. National Security*, Washington D.C.: Cato Institute Press.

Prinz, Janosch and Enzo Rossi (2017), 'Political Realism as Ideology Critique', *Critical Review of International Social and Political Philosophy*, vol. 20, no. 3, pp. 348–65.

Puglierin, Jana (2011), *John H. Herz: Leben und Denken zwischen Idealismus und Realismus, Deutschland und Amerika*, Berlin: Duncker & Humblot.

Ragazzoni, David (2017), 'Political Compromise in Party Democracy: An Overlooked Puzzle in Kelsen's Democratic Theory', in Christian Rostboll and Theresa Scavenius (eds), *Compromise and Disagreement in Contemporary Political Theory*, New York: Routledge, pp. 95–111.

Ranney, James Taylor (2018), *World Peace Through Law: Replacing War with the Global Rule of Law*, Oxon: Routledge.

Rathkolb, Oliver (2000), 'Hans Kelsens Perzeptionen Freudscher Psychoanalyse (unter Berücksichtigung rechtstheoretischer Auseinandersetzungen)', in Eveline List (ed.), *Psychoanalyse und Recht (Schriftenreihe der Verwaltungsakademie des Bundes, vol. 5)*, Vienna: Orac, pp. 85–91.

Rathkolb, Oliver (2009), 'Hans Kelsen und das FBI während des McCarthysmus in den USA', in Robert Walter, Werner Ogris and Thomas Olechowski (eds), *Hans Kelsen: Leben, Werk, Wirksamkeit*, Vienna: Manz, pp. 339–48.

Rawls, John (1971), *Theory of Justice*, Cambridge: Belknap.

Rawls, John (1999), *The Law of Peoples; with, The Idea of Public Reason Revisited*, Cambridge, MA: Harvard University Press.

Rentsch, Bettina K. (2016), 'Hans Kelsen's Psychoanalytic Heritage: An Ehrenzweigian Reconstruction', in D. A. Jeremy Telman (ed.), *Hans Kelsen in America: Selective Affinities and the Mysteries of Academic Influence*, New York: Springer, pp. 161–74.

Rice, Daniel F. (2008), 'Reinhold Niebuhr and Hans Morgenthau: A Friendship with Contrasting Shades of Realism', *Journal of American Studies*, vol. 42, pp. 255–9.

Rice, Daniel F. (2016), 'Kelsen and Niebuhr on Democracy', in D. A. Jeremy Telman (ed.), *Hans Kelsen in America: Selective Affinities and the Mysteries of Academic Influence*, New York: Springer, pp. 35–60.

Roazen, Paul (1969), *Freud: Political and Social Thought*, London: Hogarth Press.

Robbins, Lionel (1939), *The Economic Causes of War*, London: J. Cape.

Robertson, Ritchie (2002), *The 'Jewish Question' in German Literature, 1749–1939: Emancipation and its Discontents*, Oxford: Oxford University Press.

Rolnik, Eran (2003), 'A Brush with the Law: Freud and Hans Kelsen', *International Conference 'Trauma and Memory: Subjective and Collective Experiences: Legal, Medical and Cultural Perspectives'*, 18 December.

Roosevelt, Franklin D. (1943), 'Executive Order 9380 Establishing the Foreign Economic Administration', 25 September 1943 (online by Gerhard Peters and John T. Woolley (eds), *The American Presidency Project*, <http://www.presidency.ucsb.edu/ws/?pid=16317> (last accessed 27 April 2020).

Rorty, Richard (1996), 'Sigmund on the Couch', *The New York Times*, 22 September.

Rösch, Felix (2015), *Power, Knowledge, and Dissent in Morgenthau's Worldview*, New York: Palgrave.

Rosenboim, Or (2017), *The Emergence of Globalism: Visions of World Order in Britain and the United States, 1939–1950*, Princeton: Princeton University Press.

Rosenthal, Joel H. (2004), 'From Andrew Carnegie to Hans Morgenthau: A Lesson in Ethics and International Affairs', *Carnegie Council for Ethics in International Affairs*, 4 March.

Rossi, Enzo and Matt Sleat (2014), 'Realism in Normative Political Theory', *Philosophy Compass*, vol. 9, no. 10, pp. 689–701.

Rousseau, Jean-Jacques (1997a [1755]), 'Discourse on the Origin and Foundation of Inequality among Men', in Victor Gourevitch (ed.), *The Discourses and Other Early Political Writings*, Cambridge: Cambridge University Press, pp. 111–222.

Rousseau, Jean-Jacques (1997b [1762]), 'Of the Social Contract or Principles of Political Right', in Victor Gourevitch (ed.), *The Social Contract and Other Later Political Writings*, Cambridge: Cambridge University Press, pp. 39–152.

Rudoren, Jodi (2015), 'Rebukes from White House Risk Buoying Netanyahu', *The New York Times*, 24 March.

Safire, William (2008), *Safire's Political Dictionary*, New York: Oxford University Press.

Saunders, Paul J. (2014), 'Barack Obama Is Not a Realist', *The National Interest*, 26 August.

Schambeck, Herbert (2015), 'Leben und Wirken von Hans Kelsen: Rechtsberater des Kaisers und der Republik', *Kontakt*, pp. 1–9.

Schauer, Frederick (2015), 'Legal Fictions Revisited', in Maksymilian Del Mar and William Twining (eds), *Legal Fictions in Theory and Practice*, Berlin: Springer, pp. 113–29.

Scheuerman, William E. (2007), 'Carl Schmitt and Hans Morgenthau: Realism and Beyond', in Michael C. Williams (ed.), *Realism Reconsidered: The Legacy of Hans Morgenthau in International Relations*, Oxford: Oxford University Press, pp. 62–92.

Scheuerman, William E. (2008), 'Realism and the Left: The Case of Hans J. Morgenthau', *Review of International Studies*, vol. 34, pp. 29–51.

Scheuerman, William E. (2009), *Morgenthau: Realism and Beyond*, Cambridge: Polity.

Scheuerman, William E. (2011), *The Realist Case for Global Reform*, Cambridge: Polity.

Scheuerman, William E. (2012), 'Realism and the Kantian Tradition: A Revisionist Account', *International Relations*, vol. 26, no. 4, pp. 453–77.

Scheuerman, William E. (2013), 'The Realist Revival in Political Philosophy, or: Why New Is Not Always Improved', *International Politics*, vol. 50, pp. 798–814.

Scheuerman, William E. (2014), 'Professor Kelsen's Amazing Disappearing Act', in Felix Rösch (ed.), *Émigré Scholars and the Genesis of International Relations*, Basingstoke: Palgrave, pp. 81–102.

Scheuerman, William E. (2016), 'More Fragments of an Intellectual Biography: Hans J. Morgenthau (1904–1980)', in Richard Ned Lebow, Peer Schouten and Hidemi Suganami (eds), *The Return of the Theorists: Dialogues with Great Thinkers in International Relations*, London: Palgrave, pp. 227–35.

Scheuerman, William E. (2018), 'Political Realism and Global Reform: How Realists Learned to Hate "the Bomb" – and Desire World Government', in Robert Schuett and Miles Hollingworth (eds), *The Edinburgh Companion to Political Realism*, Edinburgh: Edinburgh University Press, pp. 97–108.

Scheuerman, William E. (2019), 'Donald Trump meets Carl Schmitt', *Philosophy and Social Criticism*, epub ahead of print.

Schlink, Bernhard (1999), 'Best Lawyer; Pure Law', *The New York Times*, 18 April.

Schmitt, Carl (1940), 'Der Führer schützt das Recht: zur Reichstagsrede Adolf Hitlers vom 13. Juli 1934', in Carl Schmitt (ed.), *Positionen und Begriffe im Kampf mit Weimar – Genf – Versailles 1923–1939*, Berlin: Duncker und Humblot.

Schorske, Carl E. (1979), *Fin de Siècle Vienna: Politics and Culture*, New York: Alfred A. Knopf.

Schouten, P. (2011), 'Theory Talk #40: Kenneth Neal Waltz – The Physiocrat of International Politics', *Theory Talks*, 3 June.

Schou Tjalve, V. (2008), *Realist Strategies of Republican Peace: Niebuhr, Morgenthau, and the Politics of Patriotic Defense*, New York: Palgrave.

Schuett, Robert (2007), 'Freudian Roots of Political Realism: The Importance of Sigmund Freud to Hans J. Morgenthau's Theory of International Power Politics', *History of the Human Sciences*, vol. 20, no. 4, pp. 53–78.

Schuett, Robert (2010a), 'Classical Realism, Freud and Human Nature in International Relations', *History of the Human Sciences*, vol. 23, no. 2, pp. 21–46.

Schuett, Robert (2010b), *Political Realism, Freud, and Human Nature in International Relations: The Resurrection of the Realist Man*, New York: Palgrave.

Schuett, Robert (2011), 'Peace Through Transformation: Political Realism and the Progressivism of National Security', *International Relations*, vol. 25, no. 2, pp. 185–203.

Schuett, Robert (2015), 'Open Societies, Cosmopolitanism and the Kelsenian State as a Safeguard against Nationalism', in Robert Schuett and Peter M. R. Stirk (eds), *The Concept of the State in International Relations: Philosophy, Sovereignty and Cosmopolitanism*, Edinburgh: Edinburgh University Press, pp. 221–43.

Schuett, Robert (2018), 'Hans Kelsen: A Political Realist?', in Robert Schuett and Miles Hollingworth (eds), *The Edinburgh Companion to Political Realism*, Edinburgh: Edinburgh University Press, pp. 303–16.

Schuett, Robert and Miles Hollingworth (eds) (2018), *The Edinburgh Companion to Political Realism*, Edinburgh: Edinburgh University Press.

Sebenius, James K., R. Nicholas Burns and Robert H. Mnookin (2018), *Kissinger the Negotiator: Lessons from Dealmaking at the Highest Level*, New York: HarperCollins.

Silverman, Paul (1984), 'Law and Economics in Interwar Vienna: Kelsen, Mises, and the Regeneration of Austrian Liberalism', PhD dissertation, University of Chicago.

Silving-Ryu, Helen (1964), 'The Lasting Value of Kelsenism', in Salo Engel (ed.), *Law, State, and International Legal Order: Essays in Honor of Hans Kelsen*, Knoxville: University of Tennessee Press, pp. 297–306.

Simmons, Beth A. (2009), *Mobilizing for Human Rights: International Law in Domestic Politics*, Cambridge: Cambridge University Press.

Sleat, Matt (2013), *Liberal Realism: A Realist Theory of Liberal Politics*, Manchester: Manchester University Press.

Sleat, Matt (ed.) (2018), *Politics Recovered: Essays on Realist Political Thought*, New York: Columbia University Press.

Slocombe, Richard (2010), *British Posters of the Second World War*, London: Imperial War Museum.

Smith, Jordan Michael (2012), 'Can Democrats Get Realist?', *The American Conservative*, 9 May.

Söllner, Alfons (2014), 'From International Law to International Relations: Émigré Scholars in American Political Science and International Relations', in

Felix Rösch (ed.), *Émigré Scholars and the Genesis of International Relations*, Basingstoke: Palgrave, pp. 197–211.

Solomon, Ty (2012), 'Human Nature and the Limits of the Self: Hans Morgenthau on Love and Power', *International Studies Review*, vol. 14, no. 2, pp. 201–24.

Somek, Alexander (2006), 'Stateless Law: Kelsen's Conception and its Limits', *Oxford Journal of Legal Studies*, vol. 26, no. 4, pp. 753–74.

Somek, Alexander (2007), 'Kelsen Lives', *European Journal of International Law*, vol. 18, no. 3, pp. 409–51.

Soros, George (2019), *In Defense of Open Society*, New York: Public Affairs Books.

Stadler, Friedrich (2015), *The Vienna Circle: Studies in the Origins, Development, and Influence of Logical Empiricism*, Berlin: Springer.

Steel, Ronald L. (1980), *Walter Lippmann and the American Century*, Boston: Little, Brown.

Stewart, Iain (1990), 'The Critical Legal Science of Hans Kelsen', *Journal of Law and Society*, vol. 17, no. 3, pp. 273–308.

Stirk, Peter M. R. (2005a), *Carl Schmitt, Crown Jurist of the Third Reich On Preemptive War, Military Occupation and World Empire*, Lewiston: Edwin Mellen Press.

Stirk, Peter M. R. (2005b), 'John H. Herz: Realism and the Fragility of the International Order', *Review of International Studies*, vol. 31, no. 2, pp. 285–306.

Stirk, Peter M. R. (2006), *Twentieth-Century German Political Thought*, Edinburgh: Edinburgh University Press.

Stirk, Peter M. R. (2014), 'International Law, Émigrés, and the Foundation of International Relations', in Felix Rösch (ed.), *Émigré Scholars and the Genesis of International Relations*, Basingstoke: Palgrave, pp. 61–80.

Stirk, Peter M. R. (2015a), 'The Concept of the State as a Community of Liability', in Robert Schuett and Peter M. R. Stirk (eds), *The Concept of the State in International Relations: Philosophy, Sovereignty and Cosmopolitanism*, Edinburgh: Edinburgh University Press, pp. 163–86.

Stirk, Peter M. R. (2015b), 'Introduction: The Concept of the State in International Relations', in Robert Schuett and Peter M. R. Stirk (eds), *The Concept of the State in International Relations: Philosophy, Sovereignty and Cosmopolitanism*, Edinburgh: Edinburgh University Press, pp. 1–22.

Stirk, Peter M. R. (2018), 'John H. Herz', in Robert Schuett and Miles Hollingworth (eds), *The Edinburgh Companion to Political Realism*, Edinburgh: Edinburgh University Press, pp. 368–79.

Strange, Susan (1999), 'The Westfailure System', *Review of International Studies*, vol. 25, no. 3, pp. 345–54.

Strauss, Leo (1953), *Natural Right and History*, Chicago: University of Chicago Press.

Suganami, Hidemi (2007), 'Understanding Sovereignty through Kelsen/Schmitt', *Review of International Studies*, vol. 33, pp. 511–30.

Sumner, William Graham (1934), 'War', in *Essays of William Graham Sumner*, New Haven, CT: Yale University Press.

Suri, Jeremi (2018), 'Learning from Henry Kissinger', *The New York Times*, 2 August.

Sylvest, Casper (2010), 'Realism and International Law: The Challenge of John H. Herz', *International Theory*, vol. 2, no. 3, pp. 410–45.

Taliaferro, Jeffrey W. (2019), *Defending Frenemies: Alliances, Politics, and Nuclear Nonproliferation in U.S. Foreign Policy*, Oxford: Oxford University Press.

Tellis, Ashley (1996), 'Reconstructing Political Realism: The Long March to Scientific Theory', in Benjamin Frankel (ed.), *Roots of Realism*, London: Cass, pp. 3–94.

Telman, D. A. Jeremy (2010), 'A Path Not Taken: Hans Kelsen's Pure Theory of Law in the Land of the Legal Realists', in Robert Walter, Clemens Jabloner and Klaus Zeleny (eds), *Hans Kelsen Anderswo – Hans Kelsen Abroad: Der Einfluss der Reinen Rechtslehre auf die Rechtstheorie in verschiedenen Ländern*, Vienna: Manz, pp. 353–76.

Telman, D. A. Jeremy (2016a), 'Hans Kelsen for Americans', in D. A. Jeremy Telman (ed.), *Hans Kelsen in America: Selective Affinities and the Mysteries of Academic Influence*, New York: Springer, pp. 1–16.

Telman, D. A. Jeremy (ed.) (2016b), *Hans Kelsen in America: Selective Affinities and the Mysteries of Academic Influence*, New York: Springer.

The National Interest (2019), 'Standing Up For Realism', 3 May.

The New York Times (1936), 'Jews in Prague Beaten. German Nationalist Students Rally Against Exiled Professor', 23 October.

The New York Times (1970), 'Dr. Quincy Wright, 79', 18 October.

The New York Times (1973), 'Dr. Hans Kelsen, Legal Scholar, 91', 20 April.

The New York Times (2019), *Military Spending*, New York: Rosen Publishing Group.

Thomä, Dieter (2018), *Puer robustus: Eine Philosophie des Störenfrieds, Mit einem neuen Nachwort über Donald Trump und den Populismus*, Berlin: Suhrkamp.

Tingyang, Zhao (2018), 'Political Realism and the Western Mind', in Robert Schuett and Miles Hollingworth (eds), *The Edinburgh Companion to Political Realism*, Edinburgh: Edinburgh University Press, pp. 23–36.

Treviño, A. Javier (2009 [1949]), 'Transaction Introduction', in Hans Kelsen, *General Theory of Law and State*, New Brunswick, NJ: Transaction, pp. xxi–xxxiv.

Troy, Jodok (2018), 'Political Realism and the English School', in Robert Schuett and Miles Hollingworth (eds), *The Edinburgh Companion to Political Realism*, Edinburgh: Edinburgh University Press, pp. 85–96.

Tucker, Robert (1971), 'Letter to Hans Kelsen, dated September 1971' [copy on file with the Hans Kelsen-Institut].

Tunkin, G. I. (1974), *Theory of International Law*, trans. William E. Butler, Cambridge, MA: Harvard University Press.

Turner, Stephen P. (2010), *Explaining the Normative*, Cambridge: Polity.

Turner, Stephen P. (2016), 'The Rule of Law Deflated: Weber and Kelsen', *Lo Stato*, vol. 6.

Turner, Stephen P. and George O. Mazur (2009), 'Morgenthau as a Weberian Methodologist', *European Journal of International Relations*, vol. 15, no. 3, pp. 477–504.

van Ooyen, Robert Chr. (2017), *Hans Kelsen und die offene Gesellschaft* (2nd edn), Berlin: Springer.

van Ooyen, Robert Chr. (2019), *Hans Kelsen: Neuere Forschungen und Literatur*, Berlin: Verlag für Verwaltungswissenschaft.

Vinx, Lars (2007), *Hans Kelsen's Pure Theory of Law: Legality and Legitimacy*, Oxford: Oxford University Press.

Vinx, Lars (2015), *The Guardian of the Constitution: Hans Kelsen and Carl Schmitt on the Limits of Constitutional Law*, Cambridge: Cambridge University Press.

Vinx, Lars (2016), 'The Kelsen–Hart Debate: Hart's Critique of Kelsen's Legal Monism Reconsidered', in D. A. Jeremy Telman (ed.), *Hans Kelsen in America: Selective Affinities and the Mysteries of Academic Influence*, New York: Springer, pp. 85–99.

Voegelin, Eric (1945), 'Review of Kelsen, General Theory of Law and State, and Ebenstein, Pure Theory of Law', *Louisiana Law Review*, vol. 6, no. 3, pp. 489–92.

von Bernstorff, Jochen (2010), *The Public International Law Theory of Hans Kelsen: Believing in Universal Law*, Cambridge: Cambridge University Press.

von Bernstorff, Jochen (2016), 'Peace and Global Justice through Prosecuting the Crime of Aggression? Kelsen and Morgenthau on the Nuremberg Trials and the International Judicial Function', in D. A. Jeremy Telman (ed.), *Hans Kelsen in America: Selective Affinities and the Mysteries of Academic Influence*, New York: Springer, pp. 85–99.

von Schmädel, Judith (2011), 'Kelsen's Peace through Law and its Reception by his Contemporaries', *Hitotsubashi Journal of Law and Politics*, vol. 39, no. 2, pp. 71–83.

Wacks, Raymond (2017), *Understanding Jurisprudence and Legal Theory* (5th edn), Oxford: Oxford University Press.

Walker, Christopher, Shanti Kalathil and Jessica Ludwig (2020), 'The Cutting Edge of Sharp Power', *Journal of Democracy*, vol. 31, no. 1.

Walt, Stephen M. (2016), 'Obama Was Not a Realist President', *Foreign Policy*, 7 April.

Walt, Stephen M. (2017), 'There's Still No Reason to Think the Kellogg–Briand Pact Accomplished Anything', *Foreign Policy*, 29 September.

Walt, Stephen M. (2018), *The Hell of Good Intentions: America's Foreign Policy Elite and the Decline of U.S. Primacy*, New York: Farrar, Straus and Giroux.

Walter, Robert, Werner Ogris and Thomas Olechowski (eds) (2009), *Hans Kelsen: Leben, Werk, Wirksamkeit*, Vienna: Manz.

Waltz, Kenneth N. (1959a), *Man, the State, and War: A Theoretical Analysis*, New York: Columbia University Press.

Waltz, Kenneth N. (2018 [1959b]), *Man, the State, and War: A Theoretical Analysis, Anniversary Edition*, New York: Columbia University Press.

Waltz, Kenneth N. (1979), *Theory of International Politics*, Reading: Addison-Wesley.

Waltz, Kenneth N. (1981), 'The Spread of Nuclear Weapons: More May Be Better', *Adelphi Papers*, no. 171, London: International Institute for Strategic Studies.

Waltz, Kenneth N. (1990a), 'Nuclear Myths and Political Realities', *The American Political Science Review*, vol. 84, no. 3, pp. 731–45.

Waltz, Kenneth N. (1990b), 'Realist Thought and Neorealist Theory', *Journal of International Affairs*, vol. 44, no. 1, pp. 21–37.

Watson, James Earl (1961), *A History of Political Science at the University of California, 1875–1960*, Berkeley: University of California Press.

Weber, Marianne (1926), *Max Weber*, Tübingen: Mohr.

Weil, Martin (1980), 'Hans Morgenthau, Vietnam War Critic', *The Washington Post*, 21 July.

Weinert, Friedel (2009), *Copernicus, Darwin, Freud: Revolutions in the History and Philosophy of Science*, Chichester: Wiley-Blackwell.

Weininger, Otto (1903), *Geschlecht und Charakter: Eine prinzipielle Untersuchung*, Vienna: Wilhelm Braumüller.

Weintraub, Karen (2018), 'Steven Pinker Thinks the Future Is Looking Bright', *The New York Times*, 19 November.

Wells, Herbert G. (1914), *The War that Will End War*, London: Frank & Cecil Palmer.

Welsh, Jennifer (2017), *The Return of History: Conflict, Migration, and Geopolitics in the Twenty-First Century*, Toronto: House of Anansi Press.

Wendt, Alexander (1999), *Social Theory of International Politics*, Cambridge: Cambridge University Press.

Wendt, Alexander (2003), 'Why a World State is Inevitable', *European Journal of International Relations*, vol. 9, no. 4, pp. 491–542.

White, Donald W. (1996), *The American Century: The Rise and Decline of the United States as a World Power*, New Haven, CT: Yale University Press.

Wight, Martin (1966), 'Why Is There No International Theory?', in Herbert Butterfield and Martin Wight (eds), *Diplomatic Investigations: Essays in the Theory of International Politics*, London: Allen & Unwin, pp. 17–34.

Williams, John C. (2015), *Ethics, Diversity, and World Politics: Saving Pluralism from Itself?*, Oxford: Oxford University Press.

Williams, Michael (2005), *The Realist Tradition and the Limits of International Relations*, Cambridge: Cambridge University Press.

Williams, Michael (ed.) (2007), *Realism Reconsidered: The Legacy of Hans Morgenthau in International Relations*, Oxford: Oxford University Press.

Wilson, Woodrow (1917), 'Address Delivered at Joint Session of the Two Houses of Congress, April 2, 1917' (US 65th Congress, 1st Session, Senate Document 5).

Wilson, Woodrow (2006 [1918]), 'The Fourteen Points', in Mario R. DiNunzio (ed.), *Woodrow Wilson: Essential Writings and Speeches of the Scholar President*, New York: New York University Press, pp. 403–7.

Winkler, Harold (1947), 'Letter to Hans Kelsen, dated October 17, 1947' [copy on file with the Hans Kelsen-Institut].

Wolkenstein, Fabio (2019), 'Agents of Popular Sovereignty', *Political Theory*, vol. 47, no. 3, pp. 338–62.

Woolbert, Robert G. (1940), 'The Economic Causes of War', in 'Recent Books on International Relations', *Foreign Affairs*, vol. 18, no. 3, pp. 563–78.

Wright, Quincy (1942), *A Study of War*, Chicago: University of Chicago Press.

Zakaria, Fareed (2008), 'Obama: Foreign Policy Realist', *Newsweek*, 21 August.

Zakaria, Fareed (2011), 'Remembering Samuel Huntington', *Foreign Policy*, 6 January.

Zaretsky, Eli (2017), *Political Freud: A History*, New York: Columbia University Press.

Zimmer, Louis B. (2011), *The Vietnam War Debate: Hans J. Morgenthau and the Attempt to Halt the Drift into Disaster*, Plymouth: Lexington Books.

Zimmer, Robert and Martin Morgenstern (2015), *Karl R. Popper: Eine Einführung in Leben und Werk*, Tübingen: Mohr Siebeck.

Zolo, Danilo (1998), 'Hans Kelsen: International Peace Through International Law', *European Journal of International Law*, vol. 9, pp. 306–24.

INDEX